GAY REBEL OF THE HARLEM RENAISSANCE

Richard Bruce Nugent about 1930.

GAY REBEL OF THE

HARLEM RENAISSANCE

SELECTIONS FROM THE WORK

OF RICHARD BRUCE NUGENT

Richard Bruce Nugent

Edited and with an Introduction by Thomas H. Wirth

Foreword by Henry Louis Gates Jr.

Duke University Press   Durham and London 2002

The credits and copyright acknowledgments at the end of
this volume constitute a continuation of the copyright page.
Printed in the United States of America on acid-free paper ⊛
Typeset in Scala by Tseng Information Systems, Inc.
Library of Congress Cataloguing-in-Publication Data
appear on the last printed page of this book.

In Memory of
Raymond Jenkins
and
Bernard Kay

THE DISTRIBUTION OF THIS BOOK IS SUPPORTED

BY A GENEROUS GRANT FROM THE GILL FOUNDATION.

CONTENTS

FOREWORD   Henry Louis Gates Jr.

The homosexuality of several of the Harlem Renaissance writers is now generally known and is even occasionally mentioned in scholarly studies, but rarely has it been examined in depth. In fact, it is astonishing that so many prominent participants in the Renaissance were reportedly gay, lesbian, or bisexual. The movement that enabled outsider Negro artists to emerge as a group for the first time was also the movement that enabled gay and lesbian artists to express their sexuality with a greater degree of freedom than at any other period in American history. For those both black and homosexual, who knows what it meant to emerge from behind more than one veil for the very first time?

The list of gay and lesbian African Americans is impressive and long, but it is surely headed by Bruce Nugent. Nugent was boldly and proudly gay. He was the most openly homosexual of the Harlem Renaissance writers, and he was one of the best known, along with Alain Locke, Harvard Ph.D., Howard University professor of philosophy, Rhodes Scholar, and the "dean" of the Renaissance itself.

Harlem in the 1920s was something of an uptown Greenwich Village, providing a black gay sanctuary apparently even more open than the Village itself. George Chauncey, in *Gay New York*, tells us that "The Village's most flamboyant homosexuals wore long hair; Harlem's wore long dresses." Long after the event, Langston Hughes wrote Arna Bontemps that he was still laughing at the black newspaper headline "Groom Sails with Best Man." This was an account of Countee Cullen's honeymoon voyage with the handsome Harold Jackman following Cullen's socially successful but sexually disastrous marriage to W. E. B. Du Bois's daughter Yolanda. Nugent and his fellow writers were hardly alone within the black community; they were simply the most visible, the names that have been remembered. Despite predictable denials, homosexuality within the African American community is as old as that community—and homophobia—itself.

Harlem was home to Gladys Bentley, who wore a tuxedo and sang at Hansberry's Clam House, where she knew enough off-color song lyrics to last the night. Well-attended drag balls, particularly at Hamilton Lodge, were so popular and publicly accepted that they were regularly reported by the *Amsterdam*

News with homophobic headlines such as "Pansies Cavort in Most Delovely Manner," while buffet flats with rooms devoted to gay and lesbian action were plentiful. Gay white men cruised Harlem or had more permanent relationships, such as Alexander Gumby's friend who funded Gumby's famous studio and languorous life. Harlem, in other words, could be, in its way, remarkably tolerant of a variety of sexual identities, even though homophobia remained a fundamental aspect of black culture.

Bruce Nugent linked the black world of the Harlem Renaissance with the gay world of bohemian New York. As Thomas Wirth points out, Nugent was "the first African American to write from a self-declared homosexual perspective." Moreover, he was the first writer who directly raised the issue of what being black and being gay might have to do with each other, three full decades before James Baldwin's novel *Giovanni's Room* appeared in 1956.

Wirth, who knew Bruce Nugent well, does us an immeasurable favor by bringing together this collection of Nugent's poems, stories, essays, and visual art, along with a biographical sketch and a thoughtful interpretation. One of the key figures in both the creative world of the Harlem Renaissance and the complex underground world of gay culture, Bruce Nugent at last speaks here for himself.

ACKNOWLEDGMENTS

I shall be forever indebted to Arnold Rampersad for introducing me to Richard Bruce Nugent and supporting my decision to undertake this project. Richard Newman has been unwavering in his enthusiasm and encouragement, even in the most trying circumstances, and has rendered invaluable assistance and advice, as has Abba Elethea (James W. Thompson), a close friend whom I met through Bruce and who has shared many recollections of Bruce with me. My colleague Barbara Hoerner not only contributed to the preservation of the "Salome Series" but also listened patiently to my daily description of the vicissitudes involved in publishing this book. Barbara Smith pointed out to me the important Locke and Nugent correspondence in the Glenn Carrington papers in the Moreland-Spingarn Collection. George Chauncey, Margaret Vendryes, David Levering Lewis, Michael Henry Adams, James Hatch, Shawn Stuart Ruff, Camille Billops, Kevin McGruder, A. B. Christa Schwartz, and many others have contributed useful information and moral support. The amazing talents of paper conservationists Mary Whitten and Winnie Bendiner have rescued a significant portion of Nugent's legacy from the ravages of time and neglect. Finally, I would like to thank the editorial staff of Duke University Press, especially Katie Courtland, for their unwavering enthusiasm and invaluable assistance.

NOTE TO READER

For the most part, Nugent's writings—even many of his published writings—were never rigorously edited. The unpublished work included here was taken directly from manuscript. Therefore, in preparing this book for publication, I found it necessary to make limited modifications in Nugent's punctuation and sentence structure and occasionally to correct his spelling. I have undertaken this task with great caution, mindful always of the need to remain faithful both to his intent and to his particular style.

GAY REBEL OF THE HARLEM RENAISSANCE

INTRODUCTION

Despite the modest size of his published oeuvre, Richard Bruce Nugent is a significant figure of the Harlem Renaissance. He was a key member of the group of younger African American writers and artists who created the legendary publication *FIRE!!* in November 1926—a group that included Langston Hughes, Zora Neale Hurston, Aaron Douglas, and Wallace Thurman. Nugent was the first African American to write from a self-declared homosexual perspective; his work therefore occupies an honored place in the now-burgeoning literature of the gay black male. An openly gay black youth who moved in circles—white and black—where same-sex erotic interest was pervasive but rarely acknowledged publicly, Nugent illuminated, through his life and work, conundrums of race, sex, and class that are of considerable current interest.

Although Nugent's work draws heavily on autobiographical specifics, facts concerning his life are not widely known. Therefore, the first part of this introduction consists of an extended biographical sketch. Since Nugent was obviously influenced by both the crosscurrents of the Harlem Renaissance and the evolving gay male literary tradition, the second part of the introduction discusses the literary and artistic context in which he lived and worked.

My perspective is not that of an academic professional but of a close friend who knew Nugent well. Based on his manuscripts and papers, taped interviews, and archival research, my narrative is also informed by countless hours of conversation with Nugent during the last five-and-a-half years of his life. I offer this book not as a definitive analysis but as an invitation to wider appreciation and further study of his life and work.

I

When nineteen-year-old Richard Bruce Nugent returned with Langston Hughes to New York City from his native Washington, D.C., in August 1925, the Harlem Renaissance was in full swing. Three years earlier, after a decade in which major commercial publishers had issued almost no books by African Americans, Harcourt Brace had published both James Weldon Johnson's seminal anthology, *The Book of American Negro Poetry,* and Claude McKay's *Harlem*

Shadows. In 1923 Jean Toomer's avant-garde *Cane* had astounded readers both black and white. NAACP staff members Walter White and Jessie Fauset had each published a first novel shortly thereafter. Howard University professor Alain Locke had edited the groundbreaking March 1925 issue of *Survey Graphic* entitled "Harlem: Mecca of the New Negro"—an issue so spectacularly successful that it was being expanded into a book-length anthology, *The New Negro.* Countee Cullen's first book of poems, *Color,* was in press. Four of Hughes's own poems appeared in the September issue of America's most stylish magazine—*Vanity Fair*—which had just hit the newsstands.

The house organs of two major civil-rights organizations—the NAACP's *Crisis* and the Urban League's *Opportunity*—regularly featured the work of African American writers and artists as part of a strategy to advance the cause of social and political equality by trying to gain the attention and respect of the white elite and the empathy of white readers. Both organizations sponsored contests and awards banquets as a means of stimulating new talent and bringing it to the attention of those eminent white literati who could be persuaded to serve as judges. Hughes and Nugent were going to New York to attend one of these events—the NAACP-sponsored Krigwa Awards ceremony.

Nugent was not the only talent drawn to Harlem in the second half of 1925. Aaron Douglas, a young artist, left his job teaching school in Kansas and came to Harlem hoping to end his intellectual isolation. Wallace Thurman, having edited a small literary publication in Los Angeles, moved to New York to try his hand at bigger things. Both would soon be involved with Nugent and Hughes in the creation of the premiere issue of a "Negro art quarterly"—*FIRE!!*

Nugent had spent the previous year in Washington living with his grandmother. In the early 1920s, he had lived in New York but had not encountered the Harlem Renaissance luminaries. In Washington, however, he had begun to attend the cultural gatherings hosted by Georgia Douglas Johnson. A mildly eccentric African American poet, she was married to Henry Lincoln Johnson, the distinguished Washington lawyer and politician who had been appointed Recorder of Deeds under President Taft. Mrs. Johnson's salons attracted African American Washingtonians with intellectual and literary interests, as well as visiting luminaries. Mixing with such personages as Jean Toomer, Waldo Frank, and Alain Locke, Nugent found his element. Encountering Alain Locke here was especially important to Nugent's future. As he recalled in a later interview,

> I have kind of known Locke all my life. . . . My grandmother and his mother were friends, but kids don't pay any attention to the son or daughter of a

friend of your grandmother's. So I didn't pay any attention to Locke. He didn't become important until I became an adult.

During [my] "exile" [in Washington] Locke asked me if I would contribute to his book [*The New Negro*]. I did. . . . I contributed a picture—a wash drawing of an African girl standing in a hut, the doorway of a hut, apparently jangling her bracelets—which Locke liked very much. . . . He thought it was beautiful and said, "It looks like it has a story. Can you write something about it?" And I wrote something called "Sahdji." And, it appeared in the book with an illustration by Aaron Douglas.

I didn't draw again for a year. Because I couldn't draw, if Locke did that. He'd wanted the drawing, but then, when I wrote the story, the story was good, but the drawing wasn't, so he got Aaron to do the drawing. It was just very traumatic.[1]

"Sahdji" was Nugent's first published story (this volume, 63). He later reworked it into a ballet, which was published in Alain Locke and Montgomery Gregory's *Plays of Negro Life* (1927). With music by William Grant Still, "Sahdji" was mounted at the Eastman School of Music in 1931 to considerable acclaim.

To Georgia Douglas Johnson, Nugent was more than just another habitué of her salon. She saw in him a kindred spirit—a young, eccentric genius struggling for recognition—and took him under her wing. They collaborated on a short play, *Paupaulekejo*, which was apparently performed in Washington in late 1926, after Nugent's relocation to New York. Nugent remained close to "Georgia Douglas," as he called her, even after leaving Washington. In later years, she continued to encourage him in their intermittent correspondence.

It was at Georgia Douglas Johnson's home that Nugent met Langston Hughes, who had returned to Washington to live with his mother after a voyage to Africa and a sojourn in Paris. As Nugent later wrote: "I *met* Langston Hughes. . . . He was a made-to-order Hero for me. At twenty three he was only a scant four years older than I, and he had done everything—all the things young men dream of but never quite get done—worked on ships, gone to exotic places, known known people, written poetry that had appeared in print—everything. I suppose his looks contributed to the glamorous ideal . . . as did his voice and gentle manner."[2] Hughes and Nugent saw a lot of each other—attending plays, films, vaudeville—sometimes pretending to be foreigners to get into the segregated theaters. Perhaps Nugent's cavalier attitude toward money rubbed off a little on Hughes, for Hughes quit his job, and his mother threatened to throw him out because he (most uncharacteristically) was not helping to pay the rent.

Langston Hughes in 1934.

In New York at the Krigwa event, where he received two prizes, Hughes introduced Nugent to Harlem Renaissance luminaries W. E. B. Du Bois, Eric Walrond, Rudolph Fisher, and Countee Cullen, as well as to the remarkable Carl Van Vechten. A cosmopolitan white novelist and music critic, Van Vechten made it his business to know and promote talented African Americans. The previous year, Van Vechten had met Walter White—a fellow novelist and an official of the NAACP—through Knopf, their common publisher. White, in turn, had introduced him to Harlem's elite. Within a few months Van Vechten had turned his own life upside down, spending enormous amounts of time with his new Harlem friends; inviting them to his midtown apartment for cocktails, dinners, and parties; introducing them to the elegant and powerful members of his circle. It was Van Vechten who arranged for the publication of Hughes's poems in *Vanity Fair*, for which he wrote an introduction. He also convinced Alfred Knopf to publish Hughes's first book, *The Weary Blues*.

On the very day of the Krigwa awards, Van Vechten hit upon *Nigger Heaven* as the title for the novel he was writing about Harlem—a title that would assure huge sales and explosive controversy when it appeared a year later. Joined by most of the African American press, W. E. B. Du Bois, then editor of the NAACP magazine, *Crisis*, excoriated Van Vechten; Countee Cullen was deeply pained. However, James Weldon Johnson, secretary of the NAACP and, with the possible exception of Du Bois, the most distinguished African American of his generation, defended Van Vechten. So did Langston Hughes. When the furor sub-

LANGSTON HUGHES: A MEMORY

At the time I first knew Langston, Alain Locke was generally considered to be the person who had his hand on the Black artistic pulse. A small group of us irreverents called him "the mother hen" of the Negro Movement. Even back then, one or two of us—Wallie Thurman, Gwendolyn Bennett and I, to name a few—thought of him only as a convenient titular head. To us, Locke was a pompous, dictatorial (though learned and knowledgeable) little man directing *how* things should go and *who* should be publicized as *important* members of this (his) select group. Some seven of us indicated our respect by calling ourselves "The Nigger*atti*." *We* thought that it was Langston who had his "hand on the pulse," and I thought it was a much kinder, more unselfish and more inclusive hand.

I had met Langston one Friday night in the summer of 1925 after one of the usual evening soirees at the home of Georgia Douglas Johnson—that unusual and beautiful poet living in Washington D.C. at the time. To me Langston was a beautiful revelation. He was about my own age; yet he had had adventures all over the world. That evening there was an instant rapport between us, and when we decided to leave at about the same time, he walked me down S Street to Thirteenth (where I was living with my grandmother), where we turned around, and I walked him back up S Street to near Seventeenth (where he was staying at his mother's), only to realize that we were in the middle of a thought and exchange which was still not finished, so we walked back to my house, then to his, and so on through the night. It was a preview of how our relationship was to be.—Richard Bruce Nugent, undated manuscript sided, Van Vechten continued to visit Harlem, and his many African American friends continued to enjoy his hospitality. Nevertheless, his association with the Harlem Renaissance remained controversial.

In the thirties Van Vechten turned to photography, documenting through his portraits virtually all the leading modernist cultural figures of his time. He pointedly included African Americans; between 1930 and 1960, he photographed every African American of any note in the worlds of literature, music, theater, and entertainment. His friendships with Langston Hughes, James Weldon Johnson, and many others lasted for the rest of their lives (for Nugent on Van Vechten, see 226).

The day after the Krigwa award ceremony, Hughes dined at Van Vechten's apartment, with Nugent joining them after dinner. When he returned to New York a few months later, Nugent quickly followed up on Hughes's introductions. Within a year he met and moved in with Wallace Thurman, joined Jean Toomer's Harlem Gurdjieff group, saw one of his drawings published on the cover of *Opportunity*, and joined Thurman, Hughes, Aaron Douglas, Zora Neale Hurston, Gwendolyn Bennett, and John P. Davis to work on the premiere issue of *FIRE!!*, which they hoped would become the first African American art quarterly.

A crucial element in Bruce Nugent's social success was his striking persona. He was a brilliant conversationalist, specializing in charm and shock. A true bohemian, he often had no place to sleep. Although his demeanor was not at all effeminate, in conversation he expressed a flagrantly ambiguous sexuality and made no secret of his erotic interest in men. Wallace Thurman described him vividly in *Infants of the Spring,* a roman à clef published in 1932. Nugent appears in the person of Paul Arbian (note that the surname is derived from Nugent's initials, R.B.N.):

> Paul was very tall. His face was the color of a bleached saffron leaf. His hair was wiry and untrained. It was his habit not to wear a necktie because he knew that his neck was too well modeled to be hidden from public gaze. He wore no sox either, nor underwear, and those few clothes he did deign to affect were musty and disheveled. . . .
>
> [Paul was] sitting tailor fashion on the floor, his six foot body, graceful and magnetic, his dirty yellow face aglow with some inner incandescence, his short hair defiantly disarrayed, his open shirt collar forming a dirty and inadequate frame for his classically curved neck. He was telling about his latest vagabond adventure. His voice was soft toned and melodious. His slender hands and long fingers described graceful curves in the air.

As usual when he spoke, everyone remained silent and listened intently as if hypnotized.[3]

One character in *Infants* describes Arbian's artwork as "nothing but highly colored phalli." Nugent's own drawings, if somewhat more varied in their subject matter, were equally unconventional.

Who was this exotic young man?

Richard Bruce Nugent was born in Washington, D.C., on 2 July 1906. His mother, Pauline Minerva Bruce Nugent, was one of the light-skinned Washington Bruces. The family was descended from Daniel Bruce (1779–1853), son of Robert Bruce, a loyalist Scottish entrepreneur, and Frances, a Native American. The Bruces had been free since the early eighteenth century. Pauline Bruce's marriage to the handsome Richard Henry Nugent Jr. had caused her family some distress because of his slightly darker complexion and lack of an equivalent pedigree.

As children in the South, Bruce Nugent's paternal grandparents, Narcissus George and Richard Henry Nugent, had been separated by slave sales from their own parents. They were adopted and educated by Germantown and Philadelphia Quakers. The senior Mr. Nugent was employed as a doorman at the Supreme Court; he was a protégé of Chief Justice Edward Douglass White. Bruce's father worked as a Pullman porter until Justice White arranged for his employment as an elevator man in the Capitol.

In violation of the prim and proper mores of Washington's "blue-veined" elite, Bruce's parents welcomed accomplished people from the arts into their home. Composer Will Marion Cook and his wife, the renowned singer and actress Abbie Mitchell, were visitors. The Nugents also took their sons regularly to performances of the Lafayette Players, an African American theater group resident in Washington that performed for audiences excluded from the white theaters.

Books, too, were part of young Bruce's early life.

My father had a very esoteric library. There was *everything* in his library, and I read everything. From the time I was five, I was reading everything. . . .

One of those books . . . told you all of the cures for things . . . and about babies and being born . . . and there were beautiful, wonderful pictures in it [that] told you all about diseases with wonderful names like "syphilis" and "gonorrhea. . . ."

Nugent in 1929. Photograph from his English Certificate of Registration, required of aliens. He was in England touring with *Porgy*.

Nugent's father, Richard Henry Nugent Jr. (far right), sang in Washington, D. C.'s Clef Club Quartet.

I remember once, when I was in high school, about eleven years old, and I wrote a story, because Miss Grimké—that's Angelina Grimké—had asked us each to write a story. And so I wrote this love story. . . . The girl was named "Hymen" and, you know, all of the . . . technical names that struck my fancy. I gave these names to people and to places and to flowers, and Angelina Grimké asked me to read it in front of the class. I did, so proud of my story. *And she never turned a hair.* I became great friends with Angelina Grimké later, and we had many a laugh about that story.[4]

Nugent discovered in his father's copy of Krafft-Ebing numerous case studies that left him in no doubt as to the nature of his own budding sexuality.

He attended Dunbar High School, the pride of Washington's African American community, staffed with the best and the brightest college graduates of their generation. As a matter of course, they included African American history in their lessons and worked to instill race pride in their students.

When Bruce was thirteen, his father died of galloping consumption—a combination of tuberculosis and asthma. Bruce's mother, perhaps because of the tensions resulting from her marriage, refused to throw herself onto the charity

of her family. She moved to New York, where she could pass for white, to work as a domestic and waitress for wages much higher than she could earn in Washington. She left Bruce and his younger brother, Gary Lambert (Pete) Nugent, in the care of her sister, Mabel English. Bruce and Pete later joined their mother in New York.

Pete became a renowned tap dancer. He learned to dance on the street, winning a dance contest at age eleven. At sixteen he left home to perform in the chorus on the Theatrical Owners Booking Association (TOBA) circuit, doing tap shows for thirty dollars a week. A year later he landed on Broadway in *Honeymoon Lane*, which starred Kate Smith. In the thirties his troupe, "Pete, Peaches, and Duke," was a leading "class act." During World War II Pete Nugent spent his military service touring in Irving Berlin's production, *This Is the Army*, entertaining American troops around the world. He stopped dancing in 1952, as the market for tap declined. A dance school he co-founded with Honi Coles failed, but by the 1960s he was road manager for the Temptations. When Pete Nugent died in 1973, he was only sixty-three.

Bruce Nugent loved New York. When he first arrived, his mother lived on West Eighteenth Street near Eighth Avenue. Soon, however, the presence of

Bruce's brother, Gary Lambert "Pete" Nugent (right), was a highly regarded "tapper." He is shown here with Irving "Peaches" Beaman (left) and Duke Miller in their very successful "class act," "Pete, Peaches, and Duke," in the 1932–33 season.

the two Negro boys in her room became difficult to explain. Moreover, Bruce had decided he wanted to move to Harlem because of the trees that lined the streets. So, Mrs. Nugent boarded her sons there.

Meanwhile Bruce had discovered Greenwich Village. Young, bright, exotic, and sexually available, he had no difficulty insinuating himself into the most outré circles of the avant-garde.

As his mother's earnings were insufficient to support two boys and herself, Bruce went to work in a series of mundane jobs. Even in such jobs, however, Bruce manifested a talent for meeting the famous and fabulous. As a delivery boy for Youmans Hats on Fifth Avenue, he delivered hats to the abodes of many stylish customers, including Buster Keaton. As errand boy and art apprentice at the catalog house of Stone, Van Dresser and Company, he had occasion to deliver photographic proofs to and become acquainted with Rudolph Valentino. At the then-fashionable Martha Washington Hotel, he became the favorite bellhop of the silent film star, Jedda Goudal.

It was while working at the Martha Washington that Bruce fell in love with kitchen employee Juan José Viana, the model for Nugent's character Beauty in "Smoke, Lilies and Jade." Viana was the scion of a prominent Panamanian family. He had been sent to New York to learn "American ways." Later in life, Bruce told stories of following Juan José back to Panama, of impregnating a singer who was also enamored of Viana, of being shot in the elbow by Viana's brother, who was disgusted by Juan José's relationship with Bruce, of living with Viana in Panama City after Viana's family forced them to leave their house in Colon, of running away from Viana several times, of being rescued from a pimp by Viana, of running away again and working his way to Cuba, and of being found there by Viana and sent back to New York. He repeated these stories in at least one formal interview, and there is reference to a trip to Panama in the short autobiographical sketch published in Cullen's anthology, *Caroling Dusk,* in 1927. Improbable as these stories are, it is also true that Nugent has been acknowledged as a reliable source of information by the many historians of the Harlem Renaissance who interviewed him. Time after time, his version of events has been corroborated by documentation discovered later.

In any event, Nugent began taking art classes, first at the New York Evening School of Industrial Arts, then at Traphagen School of Fashion. Late in 1924 he informed his mother that he was now an artist and would no longer work for a living. In response, Mrs. Nugent informed her son that she could not and would not support him. She sent him back to Washington to live with his paternal grandmother.

When he returned to Washington, Bruce decided to experiment with "passing":

> I passed . . . in Washington because it was convenient to do it. Why bother to bear the stigma [of being a Negro] when I could say . . . or, since I was a little cleverer than having to say it, adopt a name, adopt an address, have cards printed, and use it and be Ricardo Nugenti de Dosceta instead of Richard Bruce Nugent, with an address . . . that was the address of the Spanish legation, instead of 1231 T Street. . . . Why not? Why not go to Wardman Park . . . into the hotel where nobody would ask what you were *if* you got in. And I *did* that. And it was fun . . . I went into the Wardman Park Hotel when I got off the train in Washington when my mother had sent me home . . . to discipline me. . . .
>
> With my cardboard suitcase tied up with a rope, I knew that I shouldn't walk to the Wardman Park and Hotel . . . that's the only name of a hotel

I knew that was [a] quote "classy" hotel—a white folks' hotel. So I took a cab. I walked for blocks and blocks and blocks until I was about . . . maybe a mile away from the hotel and then I got a cab and then to the Wardman Park and Hotel. It had a flight of stairs that went way up. I got out, and these colored bellboys came down, took one look at me, and one look at my rope-wrapped thing, and I thought, "Oh, Lord, here it comes." So I went upstairs quick and just left them to pick up the bag or leave it there, whichever . . . but I was fairly certain that they'd pick it up, and it happened, when I got to the head of the stairs, I ran into a woman whom I'd met in New York . . . Princess Matchabelli, whom I'd met at Joe Lauren's in the Village. And she greeted me. The bellhops saw Princess Matchabelli greeting me. They hastened up the steps with my bag, and Matchabelli was with a gentleman—I might say a very haaaandsome gentleman—who was attached to the Spanish legation. And Matchabelli asked me the usual questions: "Where are you staying . . . ?"

I said I was going to stay here, and she said, "Oh, don't!" And I said, "Well, I have to. I don't have any place else right now." And so this gentleman who was with her said, "Well, you can stay out at the legation until you get a place to stay. I'll help you find a place." And why wouldn't he? After all, I was Matchabelli's *friend*! She kissed me. . . .

So that's how I got to be Ricardo Nugenti de Dosceta, with the address of the Spanish legation on my card at the time I passed in Washington. . . . I stayed at the legation four days, and then I went to my grandmother's. . . . Why did I go there . . . ? Because it was stupid to pass. It was a nuisance to pass. Besides, I couldn't get a job, and I had to have a job. So I went to my grandmother's. And I got a job at a men's club.[5]

Langston Hughes describes "Ricardo" in a June 1925 letter to Carl Van Vechten:

I've met a couple of interesting fellows about my own age,—one a pianist and the other an artist, and we have been amusing ourselves going downtown to the white theatres "passing" for South Americans, and walking up Fourteenth Street barefooted on warm evenings for the express purpose of shocking the natives. The artist boy has had some of his sketches taken by Harper's Bazaar. They are not at all Negro but very good for one who has had so little training. I'd like you to meet him. He has some amusing ideas for a Negro ballet and some clever ideas for short stories if he weren't too lazy to write them. . . .

Aaron Douglas's cover drawing
for *FIRE!!* (1926).

I hope to see you again by August anyway. Perhaps Ricardo will come up then, too.[6]

"Ricardo" Nugent did indeed make the trip.

The high point in Nugent's Harlem Renaissance experience was his participation in the creation of *FIRE!!* During their late-night walks in Washington, he and Hughes had developed the idea of an "art quarterly" devoted to younger African American artists. The editor was Wallace Thurman, with whom Nugent shared accommodations for nearly two years. Aaron Douglas and Zora Neale Hurston were enlisted as contributors. Gwendolyn Bennett, a young writer and artist with several *Opportunity* covers to her credit, joined the group, as did John P. Davis, a graduate of Bates College who had already published several short stories and who would soon enter Harvard Law School. They called themselves "the Niggeratti"—an irreverent take-off on the pretentiously literate white audience for whose enlightenment the older impresarios (Du Bois, James Weldon Johnson, Charles S. Johnson, and Alain Locke) were showcasing African American talent.[7]

The Niggeratti figured among the more independent and rebellious of the younger talents, who by 1926 had begun to chafe at the subtle and not-so-subtle censorship involved in always putting their best feet forward for the sake of racial uplift. Like their white contemporaries of "the lost generation," they were convinced that great art must be based on "truth," however disagreeable that truth might be to some. In an article in the 23 June 1926 issue of *The Nation*, Langston Hughes proclaimed their manifesto: "We younger Negro artists who create now intend to express our individual dark-skinned selves without fear or shame. If white people are pleased we are glad. If they are not, it doesn't matter. We know we are beautiful. And ugly, too. The tom-tom cries and the tom-tom laughs. If colored people are pleased we are glad. If they are not, their displeasure doesn't matter either. We build our temples for tomorrow, strong as we know how, and we stand on top of the mountain, free within ourselves."[8]

During the summer of 1926 the Niggeratti labored to bring their vision to fruition. *FIRE!!* burst into print in November. Little that appeared in *FIRE!!* would have been permitted on the pages of *Crisis. Opportunity* gave creative writers a freer forum, but it, too, was the house organ of a civil-rights organization. The readers of these magazines were decidedly middle-class, and, because they were members of the sponsoring organizations, they could communicate any displeasure quite forcefully to the editors. There were ample opportunities for such readers to take offense in the pages of *FIRE!!*

Thurman's story, "Cordelia the Crude," deals with promiscuity and prostitution. The "Elevator Boy" of Hughes's poem quits his job, displaying none of the heroic initiative associated with racial uplift. Gwendolyn Bennett's "Wedding Day" depicts an interracial relationship filled with deception and pain. Hurston's short play, "Color Struck," explores the "dirty secret of black America"—skin-color prejudice within the African American community. Threatening the prevailing patriarchal norm, her masterful story "Sweat" relentlessly dissects an abusive relationship. All these works can be interpreted as reinforcing racial stereotypes.

Most transgressive of all was Nugent's stream-of-consciousness prose composition, "Smoke, Lilies and Jade" (75). Written from an explicitly homoerotic perspective, complete with bedroom scenes, it attracted more criticism than any other piece in *FIRE!!* Not quite enough criticism, however, to get the publication banned in Boston (which might have generated enough publicity to rescue the fledgling quarterly from the financial difficulties that ended its run with the first issue).

Shortly after the publication of *FIRE!!*, Nugent and Thurman moved to 267 West 136th Street—an address that soon became known as "Niggeratti Manor."

The building had been purchased by Iolanthe Sydney, a Harlem business-woman who had previously turned another building, quite profitably, into a rooming house for Pullman porters. At 267 West 136th Street she created a miniature artist's colony; here, the rent was minimal and seldom collected. Thurman and Nugent, whose mother was a client of Sydney's employment agency, found this arrangement irresistible. Other residents "of the artistic persuasion" included actor/singer Service Bell and aspiring artist Rex Gorleigh. Before long, Thurman's blonde lover, Harold Stefansson, nephew of the explorer Vilhjalmur Stefansson, moved in, too.

"Niggeratti Manor" soon gained renown as a continuous party scene. Thurman faithfully recorded the happenings in *Infants of the Spring*. Often characterized as satirical, *Infants* might more usefully be thought of as a collection of campy brunch conversations about the escapades of Niggeratti Manor's residents, with Thurman and Nugent as the reigning divas. In later interviews, Nugent would vouch for the accuracy of Thurman's narrative in *Infants*, with the important exception of Paul Arbian's (Nugent's) death, which, Nugent explained, was "the only way Wallie could think of to end the book." Nugent himself wrote a parallel novel, *Gentleman Jigger*, excerpts of which are included in this volume (163–210).

Nugent's Harlem Renaissance didn't end here. In the fall of 1927 a "cattle call" went out for African American actors to try out for parts in DuBose and Dorothy Heyward's play, *Porgy*. On a lark, some of the Niggeratti and their friends answered the call. Nugent, Thurman, and young Dorothy West were hired. Although Thurman left the company in December 1927, Nugent continued not only in the extended Broadway run but with the subsequent tour of dozens of cities, culminating in a trip to England in the spring of 1929. *Porgy* closed late in January 1930, after a run of more than two years.

Based on DuBose Heyward's novel of the same name, *Porgy* was a departure for its producer, The Theatre Guild, which had never done anything even remotely "Negro" before. The director was Rouben Mamoulian, a young Armenian who went on to direct *Oklahoma!*, *Carousel*, and such noteworthy films as *Queen Christina* with Greta Garbo and *Dr. Jekyll and Mr. Hyde* with Fredric March. A resounding success, *Porgy* became the basis for George Gershwin's now-classic opera, *Porgy and Bess*, the first production of which was also directed by Mamoulian.

Langston Hughes characterized the *Porgy* cast as "composed of the finest Negro actors ever assembled in one production up to that time."[9] Nugent's colleagues included Frank Wilson (Porgy), Evelyn Ellis (Bess), Jack Carter

Nugent and Philander Thomas (back row) sailing to England in April 1929 with the
Porgy principals (left to right): Rouben Mamoulian, director; Rose McClendon; John
Yorke, company manager (?); and Frank Wilson, who played the title role.

(Crown), Percy Verwayne (Sportin' Life), Edna Thomas, Richard Huey, Jules
Bledsoe, Georgette Harvey (who had spent several years in imperial Russia and
barely escaped from the revolution through Siberia; this volume, 211), and the
superb character actor Leigh Whipper, whose career spanned much of the century. Paul Robeson played Crown for six weeks in the spring of 1928.

Rose McClendon was Serena. With the possible exception of Robeson, she
was the most distinguished performer of them all. McClendon's Broadway
career began with *Deep River*. Then she starred in *In Abraham's Bosom*. After

Porgy, she led the cast of *Never No More*, a harrowing drama about a lynching. Illness forced her to leave the cast of the Broadway production of Langston Hughes's *Mulatto* in 1935, and she died in 1936, tragically young but widely respected by theatergoers and critics of all races as an artist of the first rank (214).

Another important theatrical figure associated with *Porgy* was Cheryl Crawford, the assistant stage manager. Ms. Crawford went on to found the Group Theatre, the first production of which was Paul Green's *The House of Connelly*, which opened in 1931 with Rose McClendon in the cast.

Listed on the *Porgy* program among the "Fishermen, Stevedores, etc.," Nugent did not have a speaking role. In his plaid shirt, he decorated the stage when the curtain rose on the dice game in Catfish Row. As Alain Locke wrote to a friend, "*Porgy* will be with you soon, and you will have a delightful experience ahead of you, both with the play and some of the players. Richard Bruce, one of the minor players, but not a minor personality is a great friend of mine. He is ex-Bruce Nugent, if you remember."[10]

During *Porgy*'s road-tour Nugent and Rose McClendon became close friends. Since McClendon's husband, a chiropractor, did not tour with the company, Nugent often served as her escort at the social events to which the stars of the show were invited by those few members of the local elites who were prepared to entertain black people. Nugent, as a gay man, was a "safe" companion. Their friendship continued after *Porgy* closed; Nugent attended McClendon in her final illness.

On tour Nugent added to his retinue of admirers. Richmond Barthé, soon to achieve renown as a sculptor, fell in love with him the moment the curtain rose in Chicago. In St. Louis Nugent met E. Simms Campbell, a talented artist who created many covers for *Crisis*, illustrated Sterling Brown's volume of poetry, *Southern Road*, and later became the lead cartoonist for *Esquire*. (Few readers of that stylish magazine had the slightest idea that Campbell was black.) Barthé and Campbell were soon on their way to New York. In Buffalo, Nugent became involved with the local mafia don. While in England, Nugent spent a weekend at the country home of E. M. Forster and flew in private airplanes to parties in the south of France.

Nugent's openly expressed sexual interest in men, which he resolutely refused to hide, surely affected the group dynamics of the artists and writers around him and contributed significantly to the freewheeling exuberance so characteristic of the Niggeratti. Some were comfortable in this bohemian environment; others were not. Arna Bontemps, an important African American writer and close friend of Langston Hughes, for example, was never part of the group, despite the fact that he had known Thurman in Los Angeles and helped him find lodging when he first came to New York. Resolutely heterosexual, Bontemps was a married Seventh Day Adventist. However, Aaron Douglas—also married, serious minded, and not at all a "party person"—definitely *was* one of the Niggeratti: Nugent often slept on the Douglases' floor when he had no place else to stay.

Like Bontemps, Countee Cullen was not one of the Niggeratti. He lived with his foster father in the parsonage of Salem Methodist Episcopal Church, his homoerotic interests hidden from the public. Reverend Cullen strongly objected to Nugent's presence when Countee invited him to visit: Nugent was beyond the pale. Countee occasionally invited Nugent over anyway.

As a gay man in '20s Harlem, Nugent had plenty of company.[11] Many of the major Harlem Renaissance figures were also sexually attracted to and, to varying degrees, sexually involved with, other men—Wallace Thurman, Countee Cullen, Claude McKay, Richmond Barthé, Carl Van Vechten, Alain Locke, and, probably, Langston Hughes among them. So were many of their less-eminent friends, who included Harold Jackman, Cullen's best friend; L. S. Alexander Gumby, who was supported by a stockbroker and who collected books, which he exhibited in his "studio" on upper Fifth Avenue; Edward Perry, an artist and actor in *Porgy* who also wrote for the *Inter-State Tattler*; and Philander Thomas, another "Porgyite." Nugent also associated with the circle of svelte gay men who surrounded A'lelia Walker, heiress to the cosmetics fortune built by her mother, Madame C. J. Walker—a circle which included Edward Perry; Caska Bonds, a voice coach who, with his mother's permission, had been adopted at the age of seven by a wealthy Englishman and educated in England; Eddie Manchester, who became notorious as an intermediary who could procure the sexual services of young African American males for wealthy whites; and Clinton Moore, the proprietor of a succession of "buffet flats" where liquor and sex were freely available if one could afford the price.

Edouard Roditi, a gay writer who visited Harlem in the 1930s, recalled in a 1983 interview that "there was a whole small crowd of rather nice gay blacks around Countee Cullen. They used to meet practically every evening at Caska Bonds's and sit by the hour playing cards."[12] Born in Paris of American parents and educated in France and England, Roditi belonged to the European avant-garde; in 1929 he published the first surrealist manifesto in English. He met Cullen and Jackman in Paris.[13] He was sexually involved with Jackman and, on visiting the United States, also became sexually involved with Nugent.[14]

RICHARD BRUCE NUGENT

Richard Bruce Nugent—who comes from one of Washington's "first" families; because he has been to South America and can tell many tales of thrilling experiences there; because he came to New York when the New Negro Renaissance was beginning; because he was the most colorful and sensational member of the younger group of Negro artists; because he was an associate of Wallace Thurman's, inhabiting with him the notorious 267 house; because he used to write letters to great men, telling them how wonderful he was and how well they could get along together spiritually; because he can tell the most vivid and imaginative tales about famous people and places, and you will believe they are true; because he has written in a beautiful style a novel of homosexual love called, "Smoke, Lilies and Jade"; because he has written a fine [story], "Sahdji," which is published in *The New Negro;* because he was a member of the *Porgy* cast; because he was asked to leave a dance in Boston when one of the hosts saw his collar was open and he was not wearing a tie; because he was admiringly daring about going places in his vagabond's garb; because of his escapades and associates in London; because he is a fascinating conversationalist; because he is a brilliantly talented artist; because the figures and lines in his drawings are weirdly fascinating; because he is a good companion; because he enjoys life with no care for tomorrow; because he has just drawn a strikingly beautiful set of illustrations from the Bible; because he is writing a novel about his experiences at 267; because he is collaborating on a book with this columnist; and finally because he won't mind being the thirteenth member of this gallery.—Edward Perry, *The Inter-State Tattler,* 18 July 1930

Self-portrait of Carl Van
Vechten (1934).

During the twenties Harlem became one of the centers of night life in New
York. In addition to alcohol and jazz, relatively easy access to sex partners—
both male and female—drew the more bohemian elements of the white elite
uptown to Harlem. Virgil Thomson, the composer and, later, powerful music
critic for the *New York Herald Tribune;* Chick Austin, Director of the Hartford
Atheneum; and Philip Johnson, the renowned modern architect, were among
those who took advantage of these opportunities.[15]

Carl Van Vechten led the way.[16] One memorable evening is described in Carl
Van Vechten's handwritten diary entry for 15 February 1929:

> Home for dinner—Ettie Stettheimer & Virgil Thompson who after dinner
> played his remarkable opera to words of Gertrude Stein! "Four Saints in
> Three Acts." Alma and Ma[urice] Wertheim were here, Carrie Stettheimer,
> Max Ewing, Mabel Luhan who brought Martie Ma . . . , Dorothy Harvey,
> Hal [Witter] Bynner, Arthur F . . . , Harry Block, Muriel Draper, Emily
> Clark & Zena Naylor—I went to a drag in Harlem with Harry, Hal, Emily,
> Virgil, & Martie. We picked up Eddie Manchester & went to the Lenox Ave
> Club where I danced with Louis Cole in drag & then to Pod's & Jerry's.
> Home at 7:30 A.M.[17]

Despite a high concentration of men who were sexually interested in other men, this was not a "gay community" as we currently understand the term. In a later interview, Nugent explained, "Harlem was very much like the Village. People did what they wanted to do with whom they wanted to do it. You didn't get on the rooftops and shout, 'I fucked my wife last night.' So why would you get on the roof and say 'I loved prick.' You didn't. You just did what you wanted to do. Nobody was in the closet. There wasn't any closet."[18]

In another interview, Nugent elaborated: "Homosexuality has always been a dirty word. I cannot remember, in my seventy-some years, the time when it wasn't a dirty word. But, on the other hand, homosexuality, the practice of it, was not a dirty thing. The dirtiness about any of it was the flaunting of it. And I use 'flaunting' advisedly. Because there's a difference between flaunting it and just not trying to keep it hidden. So, if one met with the amenities of polite society, who's going to question what your impolitenesses were?"[19]

In comparison with his contemporaries, Nugent often did go over the line and "flaunt it," although he apparently maintained a studied ambiguity as to whether he was attracted to women as well as men. Nonetheless, his brilliant conversation, charm, and, in the African American community, the cachet of the Bruce family name sustained his social respectability.

Nugent moved in a social matrix in which the existence of extramarital sexual relationships of all kinds—homosexual and heterosexual—was taken for granted. The matrix was defined by sophisticated, "modern" attitudes and a general rejection of conventional sexual mores, not by sexual orientation. Both extramarital dalliances and same-sex interests were effectively "open secrets"—acceptable in private, gossiped about, but not publicly acknowledged. Embedded *within* the matrix, and inseparable from it, was a network of friendships among men who were sexually drawn to other men.

The activities of Nugent and his friends, along with those of other Harlem notables, were duly reported in the columns of *Amsterdam News* (many of which were written by Edward Perry) and the *Inter-State Tattler*. There were even sly references to sexual preferences: "What is this thing anyhow . . . *Richard Bruce* and *Mary Faire*, both equally well-known in Harlem and the Village, waiting up nights for each . . . can it be that the thing is getting fashionable . . . first *Countee Cullen* and *Yolande Dubois* [sic] . . . with *R. Schlick* and *Pamela* . . . following closely . . . now *Bruce* and *Faire* . . . it shouldn't be long now before *Clint Moore* allies himself with some charming femme of the collar and tie specia."[20]

This tolerance of semiprivate homosexuality among the worldly Harlem elite did not extend to all segments of the African American community's leadership. In 1929, for example, Adam Clayton Powell Sr., pastor of the Abyssinian Baptist Church, initiated a vigorous crusade against homosexuality.[21] In the same vein, W. E. B. Du Bois dismissed Augustus Granville Dill as business manager of *Crisis* after Dill was arrested for homosexual activity in 1928. Du Bois was perhaps motivated as much by the potential negative reaction of his readership as by his own personal disapproval, and he later expressed regret at the injustice he had done Dill.[22] His reaction is understandable; most elite African Americans were intent on maintaining a hyper-respectable public image as a means of personal and racial advancement.

Indeed, distaste for the homosexual undercurrents in the Harlem scene may have contributed to the negative response of some African American critics to the Harlem group. For example, Sterling Brown, a Howard University professor and poet whose stature many consider equal to that of Langston Hughes, said in an interview,

> I have no relationship to any Harlem Renaissance. When they [the writers and artists of that era] were down there flirting with Carl Van Vechten, I was down south talking to Big Boy [a principal informant in Brown's lifelong study of folklore]. One of the most conceited things I can say is I am proud that I have never shaken that rascal's hand. . . . He corrupted the Harlem Renaissance and was a terrible influence on them. He was a voyeur. He was looking at these Negroes and they were acting the fools for him. And the foolisher they acted, the more he recorded them.[23]

The sexual innuendo in Brown's remark is clear.

Nugent's relationships with certain Harlem Renaissance figures who shared his sexual interests—Alain Locke, Richmond Barthé, Wallace Thurman, L. S. Alexander Gumby, and Harold Jackman—illustrate the complexity of the Harlem social environment.

Dr. Alain Locke (junior year Phi Beta Kappa, Harvard Ph.D., the first African American Rhodes Scholar, and professor of philosophy at Howard University) was one of the six "midwives" of the Harlem Renaissance—the men and women whose proselytizing and connections with publishers and patrons made the Harlem Renaissance possible.[24] He was also a self-identified gay man: his erotic interests were exclusively directed toward other men, those interests were central to his sense of self, and he perceived himself as different from the majority on that account.[25] He gathered about him a coterie of brilliant and

Alain Locke. The inscription reads, "For Bruce. Sincerely, Alain Locke 1929." Photograph by James L. Allen.

good-looking young men of color that evolved into a kind of secret society.[26] Moreover, his sexual interests were often a factor in his choice of protégés, even when they were not members of this group.

Langston Hughes was among the protégés in whom Locke had a sexual interest. His campaign to seduce Hughes in 1923 and 1924 is detailed in Arnold Rampersad's biography of Hughes.[27] It began when Countee Cullen, extolling Hughes's virtues, wrote to Locke suggesting that Locke write Hughes. Cullen himself was sexually attracted to Hughes, but he had been unsuccessful in arousing any reciprocal interest. Locke initiated a correspondence with Hughes early in 1923. Hughes responded warmly. As the correspondence continued, Locke eventually made his sexual interests quite clear; Hughes, on the other hand, maintained a studied ambiguity, evading Locke's attempts to arrange a meeting. In an extraordinary correspondence with Countee Cullen, Locke gave a blow-by-blow description of his efforts.[28] Finally, in the summer of 1924, he succeeded in catching up with Hughes in Paris. Later that summer, they met again in Italy and spent several days in Venice together. Did Locke's passion remain unrequited? There is no way of knowing. What is known is that Hughes's passport was stolen, and Locke left him in Genoa to make his own way back to America.

A cryptic entry in Carl Van Vechten's daybook from 31 October 1925 provides an interesting postscript to this affair: "Alain Locke comes in (at 3:00 P.M.). He stays till six—talking about the collection of African sculpture in Brussels & then he discusses the character of Langston Hughes at some length. Telling me extraordinary things about Countee Cullen (adopted by the Rev. Cullen at the age of 12) about Claude McKay etc. I liked him much better than I ever have before."[29]

Alain Locke was also sexually attracted to Nugent. In a taped interview, Nugent reported that on one occasion he was visiting Locke at his home in Washington, and "Locke offered me his body. A professor of philosophy and a person old enough to be your father doesn't lie on a bed in their shorts and say, 'Do anything you want.' What can you do except be embarrassed? And be a little disappointed in the person who did it. I was a lot disappointed. I was traumatized by it."[30]

Despite this event, Nugent accepted Locke as a friend/mentor in whom he could confide his intimate thoughts, as he did in this November 1928 letter.

> I feel the need of someone to lean on *so* bad. What I think would be a cure seems to be such an impossibility. Am I so impossible that I can not get a friend of the sort I want. Everyone else seems to have one close friend who thinks of all the small niceties and petty things except me. With me they all either use me without reciprocation or depend on me until I feel it incumbent upon me to create something in me for them to lean on. And it's sapping all of me away that's all. I know I *should* feel it makes me stronger and I do but I want some—*need* something still. After all I'm not full grown. Don't they ever realize that a prop (of nothing more than honest affection) might help me too?
>
> Please write me soon.
> Love,
> Bruce[31]

Angst such as Nugent expresses here stands in sharp contrast to the unflappable persona he presented to the world at large.

In February 1929 Locke, playing the role of matchmaker, wrote Nugent about Richmond Barthé, another handsome young artist:

Fate ordained that I should receive it [your last letter] just as Barthé and I got back from dinner. . . . Now you have the friend whom you needed — and if there is further need, my own friendship in the background standing in understanding guardianship and benediction.

Out of my own sorrow I am quite sure I know what you have suffered, and I am glad to say that it is without jealousy or envy that I can be happy in your joy — for I love you both — and look forward to warming my own soul a bit at the fire of your youth and at least realizing by proxy some of my own unfulfilled ambitions. For I too wish to create — only as I told Richmond, I only too often do it by proxy. . . .

Barthé I always liked — & I instantly sensed his genius. But after 10 days of quiet intimacy here/ he has just left — I am more sure than ever — and satisfied and happy that he is my friend and yours. . . .

Good night, Bruce. Be happier.

Love,

Alain[32]

On April 25 Locke wrote again to Nugent, who was on tour with *Porgy* in London at the time: "Intermittently since, I have had vivid recalls of the last night we spent together, and send you, along with the usual cordial thoughts, my warm thanks for your part in it."[33]

Richmond Barthé was the most talented and prolific African American sculptor of his generation. A native of Bay St. Louis, Mississippi, he became the houseboy of a wealthy New Orleans family who summered there. In New Orleans Barthé attracted the attention of the family's neighbor Lyle Saxon, a member of the New Orleans cultural elite. Impressed with Barthé's talent, both Saxon and Barthé's pastor sponsored his education at the Art Institute of Chicago. In 1928 Barthé attended a performance of *Porgy* in which Nugent appeared. Fifty years later he wrote to Nugent:

Dear David:

I've learned that David means beloved. How right. You have been my beloved friend since 1927 [*sic*] when the curtain went up on you in the center of that stage in Chicago. I love you with the kind of love that will last forever . . .

As ever, with love,

Your

Jonathan[34]

Despite Barthé's passion and Locke's matchmaking, Nugent and Barthé either did not become lovers or, if they did, did not remain lovers for long. A few reasons suggest themselves. For one thing, Nugent was promiscuous, and Barthé would likely have demanded fidelity. For another, the ambitious Barthé was exceedingly circumspect about his sexual orientation, never revealing his attraction to men to anyone who wasn't also "in the life." Nugent, on the other hand, loved to make known in a wide variety of social circumstances the fact that he found men sexually attractive. For Barthé, an extended liaison with Nugent would have amounted to a public declaration of his sexual interest in men—a declaration he never made in his lifetime.

There were also differences in temperament. In later correspondence with Nugent, Barthé described at great length the accolades he had received, such as an award given by the Governor of Mississippi and the fact that the city of Pasadena had renamed his street "Barthé Drive." Barthé's need for public recognition of this sort exasperated Nugent; he found pursuit of it distasteful.[35]

Wallace Thurman, another of Nugent's closest friends, shared with Nugent both his rented rooms and a taste for "rough trade."[36] But they were not lovers. A brilliant editor, Thurman wrote two of the major Harlem Renaissance novels, *The Blacker the Berry* and *Infants of the Spring*. The latter was a thinly disguised portrayal of real life in Niggeratti Manor in which the characters Paul Arbian (Nugent) and Raymond (Thurman) trade witty barbs for the benefit of, and sometimes at the expense of, their compatriots. Nugent's parallel roman à clef presents them in the same kind of relationship—a shared recognition of superior intelligence combined with underlying strains of competitiveness.

Like Barthé, Thurman hid his erotic interest in men from others—even from some of his confidants. Indeed, despite the fact that he was arrested for illicit sexual activity in a public restroom shortly after he first arrived in New York in fall 1925, Thurman may not have thought of himself as gay. He described the harrowing incident four years later in a letter to William Jourdan Rapp, a white playwright who collaborated with him on *Harlem,* their hit Broadway play. Thurman claimed that the other man had made advances, which he accepted only for the money that was offered. He steadfastly denied being a homosexual.[37] In the same letter Thurman described the break-up of his marriage, denying rumors that it had been due to homosexuality on his part and blaming his wife's sexual inadequacies. (Thurman had married Louise Thompson, a beautiful and brilliant graduate of the University of California at Berkeley. For all intents and purposes the marriage ended after a few months, al-

Sculptor Richmond Barthé with his bust of Toussaint L'Overture. The inscription reads, "To Richard, with best wishes for success. Barthé, 1929."

Wallace Thurman (circa 1929)—Nugent's roommate, editor of *FIRE!!*, and author of *The Blacker the Berry* and *Infants of the Spring*.

though they never divorced.) Nugent, however, stated on many occasions that Thurman did in fact engage in sexual activities with other men.[38]

Yet another member of Nugent's network of gay friends was L. S. Alexander Gumby. An autodidact and a truly memorable personality, Gumby was notorious for his hilarious, sexually explicit sonnets and his atrocious spelling. Born in 1886 in Maryland, he arrived in New York around 1906. A man of studied elegance, he supported himself as a bellhop, waiter, and, during WWI, as a postal worker. Throughout the 1920s, his income was supplemented by the support of Charles W. Newman, a wealthy white stockbroker with whom he had become friends in 1910.[39]

Gumby collected books. When they crowded him out of his apartment, he installed himself "Village style" in a "studio" at 2144 Fifth Avenue in Harlem—a converted commercial space on the second floor with large windows overlooking the street. A grand piano and Persian carpets provided the setting in which he could impress young men with his erudition, silver, and Spode. He held receptions and teas, sometimes renting out the space for recitals, exhibitions, or parties. At one time or another, almost every luminary of the Harlem Renaissance crossed his threshold. His gatherings were reported in the columns of *The Amsterdam News* and *The Inter-State Tattler*. An especially noteworthy stag party was held in 1930 on the occasion of Countee Cullen's return from two years in Paris. Eminences like Heywood Broun, Walter White, and Arthur Schomburg attended that affair.[40]

Inspired, perhaps, by the examples of *FIRE!!* and *Harlem* (Thurman's second effort at literary publication in New York), Gumby set out in 1930 to produce a literary journal entitled *The Gumby Book Studio Quarterly*. It was to have included one of Nugent's "Bible Stories"—"The Tunic with a Thousand Pleats." Unfortunately, the project did not get past the page-proof stage, as Gumby's patron, Newman, had lost millions in the stock market, and Gumby contracted tuberculosis. He was hospitalized for four years, which forced him to give up his studio. In 1931, mindful of the significance of Gumby's collections, his many friends organized a benefit Arts Ball at the Renaissance Casino. The event was sponsored by an amazing roster of Harlem social leaders, writers, actors, and entertainers, including Paul Robeson, Zora Neale Hurston, Langston Hughes, Bill Robinson, Rose McClendon, Hubert T. Delany, W. C. Handy, Bessye Bearden, Walter White, Arthur Schomburg, and Roscoe Conklin Bruce, as well as the downtown hostess of high bohemia, Muriel Draper. The principals of the Cotton Club Review and Noble Sissle performed. Evidently Gumby's sexual predilections, which were widely known, had done little harm to his social respectability, at least in this segment of the community.

In addition to collecting books relating to African Americans, Gumby created an enormous number of scrapbooks on the subject, which he donated to Columbia University in 1951, an arrangement that included his employment as curator for a time. The collection is a gold mine of information about the Harlem Renaissance—especially about those who were "in the life" (this volume, 223). In 1951 Gumby wrote Nugent about the attractions of Columbia:

> Bruce I am not exaggerating when I say that Columbia University is like a harem, there are types there that would make a Narcissus or a Hermes look like a scare-crow. And yet only one of them have dared to rate over the two stares [stars] with me; and that one only went a half star better, altho we spent the best part of the night along togather in my room. . . .
>
> In writing this letter to you; I have the coff-pot going, and feel like I am talking to you, you are the one person I don't hafter pull my punches with, and not afraid to reveal your own escapade;—not like Jackman, if he only knew that I know about a party up in the Bronx where he not only let his hair down, but went much father. I know the guy he had and I cant say I blaim him. He is a two-way brown-skin kid, was about 19 when I tried and failed. [Gumby's atrocious spelling is much in evidence here.][41]

"Jackman" in this letter is Harold Jackman; he and Nugent served as Gumby's executors on his death in 1961. An enormously attractive and socially adept man, Jackman made a point of introducing his innumerable acquaintances to each other. (It was Jackman, for example, who introduced Nugent to Claude McKay.) Intimately familiar with both refined high life and low-down Harlem hideaways, the distinguished-looking Jackman enthralled visiting European aristocrats and white visitors from downtown. He sustained a lifelong friendship with Countee Cullen. Their friendship was such that when Cullen sailed for France three months after his wedding to Yolanda Du Bois, only Jackman and Cullen's father accompanied him—his new bride followed later. There is, however, no firm evidence of a sexual relationship between Cullen and Jackman. Although they were the closest of friends for decades and both were sexually active with other men, those facts do not in and of themselves establish that Cullen and Jackman were ever physically intimate with each other. Like Thurman, both were quite circumspect. Harlem's poet laureate married again in 1940 and remained married until he died in 1946; Jackman never married.

Poet Countee Cullen (left) and his best friend, Harold Jackman, who was a teacher and was often described as one of the handsomest men in Harlem. Cullen's photo is inscribed, "For Bruce—who without this might forget, Countee." Photographs by James L. Allen (circa 1929).

Cullen and Jackman corresponded extensively, with Jackman reporting at length during the late twenties on the doings of Nugent, Wallace Thurman, Edward Perry, Caska Bonds, Claude McKay, Richmond Barthé, Alain Locke, Carl Van Vechten, and Eric Walrond.[42] This network of relationships among men sexually attracted to other men renders tangible the observation that the Harlem Renaissance was "surely as gay as it was black, not that it was exclusively either of these."[43] The network also connected those involved in the Harlem Renaissance with the (white) bohemian elite; the international avant-garde; the worlds of theater, popular entertainment, jazz, and blues; the streets; and the underworld. The extent to which shared sexual interests made possible some of the breakthroughs of the era is a subject that deserves further research.

Before and after *Porgy*, Nugent made art. His work was published in *Opportunity* and featured in *Ebony and Topaz*, a large-format anthology edited by Charles S. Johnson and published by *Opportunity* in 1927 (66–70, 247). However, there were very few venues in which African American artists could exhibit their work. Indeed, the situation was so desperate that the residents of Niggeratti Manor organized their own exhibition on the premises in April 1927.[44] The show launched the career of African American portrait photographer James Allen (who was himself extremely photogenic). He, like Nugent, apprenticed with the catalog firm of Stone, Van Dresser & Co.[45] His importance has only recently been recognized; Yale University Gallery of Art mounted a one-man show of his work in 1999 (for examples of Allen's work, see 23, 30).

An oasis in Harlem's artistic desert was the Harmon Foundation, which, in the late twenties and early thirties, organized traveling exhibitions of the work of black artists. Nugent entered the juried competition, with four of his works being listed in the catalog of the 1931 exhibition, which also included contributions from such now-esteemed artists as Augusta Savage, William Henry Johnson, Archibald Motley, Richmond Barthé, James Lesesne Wells, and Hale Woodruff.

Not content to limit himself to any particular aspect of the arts, Nugent was also involved in one way or another with many of the early efforts to develop African American concert dance companies. He danced occasionally with Hemsley Winfield in the twenties and with Asadata Dafora in the thirties. (Winfield achieved a measure of celebrity when he danced the role of Salome in drag with his troupe, the New Negro Art Theatre, at the Cherry Lane Theater in 1929.)

In 1933 Nugent appeared as a dancer in *Run, Little Chillun,* a "Negro Folk Drama" written by Hall Johnson, in which a "pagan religious cult" invades a "normal Southern village," challenging the town's revivalist Christian faith. Nugent, of course, was among the savages. He recalled having been coached for the show by Doris Humphrey, who was pregnant at the time and rather irritable. He did not find her simpatico—although he *was* enthralled with her partner, Charles Weidman—and was pleased when José Limon, a Humphrey-Weidman protegé, replaced her as his coach.

The play was actually something of a pageant. The action was accompanied by the Hall Johnson Choir, which Johnson, a classically trained violinist, had organized in 1925. (It was Johnson's setting of "Fire," a poem by Langston Hughes, for his choir that suggested the name *FIRE!!* to the Niggeratti for their 1926 publication.) Two of *Run, Little Chillun's* four acts were devoted to "spectacular and stunning" reproductions of the religious services of the two competing cults. The production played four months on Broadway and then went on tour. The critical consensus, as summarized in *Literary Digest,* was that *Run, Little Chillun* was "noble and magnificent, superb and orgiastic, startling and ecstatic, savage and appealing, frenzied and moving, elemental and emotional, an example of group acting the Moscow Art Theater in its heyday could not have improved upon."[46]

In the middle and late thirties Nugent's precise whereabouts are hard to trace. True to form, he drifted from place to place and man to man. Sometimes he stayed with his mother, who then lived in the Bronx. We do know that in 1936, Carl Van Vechten took photographs of Nugent in New York, posing him with a bust of Antinous, Emperor Hadrian's favorite (227). Also, there is some indication that he spent time in Chicago and studied art there.

In 1937 one of Nugent's most important short writings, "Pope Pius the Only," was published in Dorothy West's little magazine, *Challenge* (244). The teen-aged West had been a frequent visitor to Niggeratti Manor. She had acted with Nugent in *Porgy* and sailed with the company to England in 1929. In the early thirties she journeyed to Russia with a group of black writers, among them Langston Hughes and Louise Thompson (Wallace Thurman's estranged wife), to make a Soviet-sponsored film about African Americans. Although the film never materialized, everyone involved had the experience of a lifetime. On her return West founded the modest periodical, *Challenge,* which was intended, perhaps, to be a less flamboyant sequel to *FIRE!!* Although *Challenge* appeared only irregularly for several years, its roster of writers was impressive: Langston Hughes, Pauli Murray, James Weldon Johnson, Countee Cullen, Claude McKay, Frank Yerby, Zora Neale Hurston, Carl Van Vechten, Parker Tyler, Charles Henri Ford, Owen Dodson, and Edouard Roditi, among others, appeared in its pages. The last issue, renamed *New Challenge,* was opened to "a young Chicago group" of writers, with Richard Wright as associate editor. The issue was spectacular, with contributions from Wright, Ralph Ellison, Alain Locke, Margaret Walker, and Sterling Brown. West, however, felt pushed aside and was uncomfortable with the rather stridently leftist views of her new collaborators. Therefore, she closed the magazine and moved to Martha's Vineyard, where she lived for the rest of her life. In 1946 her first novel, *The Living is Easy,* appeared. Nearly fifty years later her second novel, *The Wedding,* became a best-seller. She died in 1998 at the age of ninety-one.

In the late thirties Nugent experienced a rare period of steady employment when he was hired by the Federal Writers' Project (FWP), where his coworkers included Ralph Ellison, Claude McKay, and Waring Cuney, a fellow Washingtonian. Working under Roi Ottley, he wrote biographical sketches of black notables, as well as articles on the history and current condition of blacks in New York (147–56, 211–30). He also researched and wrote biographical profiles of residents from colonial times ("Colonial Worthies"). While he never abandoned his apolitical posture as an aesthete, the rush of the intelligentsia to the left in the thirties had its effect on him: he went so far as to become a shop steward in the union that represented FWP employees.

During this FWP period, Nugent became a good friend of now-obscure artist Henry "Mike" Bannern. Bannern and Charles "Spinky" Alston maintained a studio designated as the site for a Works Progress Administration mural project—a place where younger artists from the community congregated and worked. Jacob Lawrence, Romare Bearden, Norman Lewis, and Charles White were among the members of the "306 Group," so named because the studio was located at 306 West 141st Street. Nugent had tremendous respect for Bannern as an artist and in later years often said that he did not think Bannern had received his due.

In the early forties Nugent joined the Negro Ballet Company, which was founded in 1939 by Wilson Williams, who had studied with Helen Tamiris and probably with Martha Graham and Charles Weidman as well. The company appeared at the Humphrey-Weidman studio theater in 1941 and 1942. It was headquartered in the upper studios of Carnegie Hall, where some of its members, including Nugent, lived for a time. When the Williams troupe went broke, Nugent and other members of the company, hoping to save it by staying together, took a cold-water flat on Charles Street in Greenwich Village. Later, after the group dissolved, Nugent moved into the Jane Street apartment of Warren Marr II and his sister, Grace Marr. Warren Marr, who had been a publicist for the Wilson company and part of the group on Charles Street, became editor of the NAACP magazine, *Crisis,* in the 1970s.

Nugent, like many other Americans, performed his patriotic duty during World War II: he corresponded at length with members of the armed forces. Nugent certainly did not find this particular obligation burdensome, reflecting as it did his interest in young men so well. Among his correspondents was Mario Monteforte Toledo, a Guatemalan writer in exile who served for several months in the U.S. Army in 1945 and 1946. Nugent, who knew Monteforte before he was inducted, collaborated with him in translating one of his poems—"Cabagüil," a Mayan creation myth—into a ballet in English. After his discharge from the army early in 1946, Monteforte returned to Guatemala to participate in the fledgling democracy, which had in 1944 replaced a failed dictatorship. Within the year, he became head of the majority party and was

Grace Marr Nugent in 1951. She was Bruce's wife from 1952 until her death in 1969.

elected to the unicameral Guatemalan congress. For a time he served as president of Congress, which put him first in the line of succession to the Guatemalan presidency. In 1950 he became disillusioned with conflict within his party and declined to stand for reelection. In 1954 the democracy was replaced by a new, CIA-sponsored dictatorship, and Monteforte was arrested and went into exile again. After many years in Mexico, he returned to Guatemala in the 1980s. Having written many books — novels, poetry, and literary criticism — as well as a landmark study of Guatemalan sociology, Monteforte is among the most eminent living figures in Hispanic-American letters.

In the close quarters of the Greenwich Village apartment Nugent shared with the Marrs, a highly romantic but platonic relationship developed between Nugent and Grace, who had graduated from Harlem Hospital School of Nursing in 1941 and was studying nursing education at Teachers College, Columbia. A brilliant and beautiful woman, she earned both B.A. and M.A. degrees there. In 1944 she was appointed instructor in nursing education at Columbia, where she taught microbiology. At the time she was the only African American on the Columbia faculty. In 1949 she returned to Harlem Hospital as educational director of nursing. After two years she left to become supervisor of nursing education with the New York State Department of Education, an achievement that was another "first" for African Americans. In 1952 Grace Marr returned to New York City from Albany and, much to the surprise of many of their friends, married Nugent. The marriage lasted seventeen years.

In the years before the Gay Liberation Movement, it was not uncommon for men who had sex with other men to marry. Often, homosexual activity was kept hidden from the wife. In other cases the marriage was a convenient "cover" for the extramarital sexual activities of both parties. The Nugent-Marr marriage fell into neither of these categories. Deeply in love with Nugent, Grace Marr was fully aware of his homosexuality but decided to marry him anyway. She apparently hoped she could "change" him and that eventually the marriage would be physically consummated. Her hope remained unfulfilled. Bruce maintained a studio separate from the residence he shared with his wife and quite openly continued to have liaisons with other men.

Even so, it is no exaggeration to state that, for Bruce at least, marriage was literally a lifesaver. Grace provided stability and support during a period in which the physical and emotional consequences of his relentlessly Bohemian lifestyle might otherwise have come crashing down on him.

In 1953, shortly after her marriage, Grace Nugent became assistant executive secretary of the American Nurses' Association (ANA), working in the Intergroup Relations Unit. She held this post until 1959, when she abandoned her promising career to devote herself to "Operation Democracy," a project that she conceived during her years with the ANA and that preoccupied her for the rest of her life. Daughter of a clergyman, Grace was profoundly idealistic. She came to abhor all of the social conditions that blocked the realization of each person's full human potential—poverty, discrimination, and the dehumanizing conditions of work in modern society. Her project aimed to effect broad and comprehensive—but vaguely defined—reform. While it attracted some initial support from her friends, her ANA contacts, and the Interdenominational Ministers' Alliance of Brooklyn and Long Island, it soon foundered due to a lack of focus and a failure to identify concrete, achievable goals. For years she carried on alone, supporting herself and her project on her meager earnings as a per-diem and private-duty nurse, berating herself for not putting even more effort into promoting her cause.

During the sixties Grace and Bruce drifted ever further apart. In 1969, frustrated both in her humanitarian aspirations and in her marriage, Grace Marr Nugent committed suicide.

From the forties on, Nugent worked as a freelance artist and portraitist. This

Nugent in the 1950s.

activity did not support him. Occasionally he took "regular" jobs, at one time tending the night desk at the Brevoort hotel and, from 1957 through the 1960s, working part-time for a hardware supply company in lower Manhattan. He also wrote several novels, none of which were published. Thus, he was left to survive on the wages of his wife and the kindness of friends.

One such friend was Bernard Kay, a native of New Hampshire whom Bruce had known since the twenties. A person of exceedingly diverse talents, Kay was a successful actor, director, and producer, as well as a practicing psychologist and a translator. His omnivorous and cultivated intellect, good looks, and sincere empathy drew many young men of genius into his circle, including the actor Earle Hyman and Samuel R. Delany, the writer. Kay directed the teenaged Marlon Brando in his first Broadway appearance (*Bobino*, a children's play). Nugent created his "Gilgamesh" drawings for a Kay production that never came to fruition (see 240–41).

Raymond Jenkins also helped sustain Nugent over the years. A talented African American artist and native of the Bronx, Jenkins chose the security of New York City civil service employment as a draftsman over the vicissitudes of a career in the arts. He and Nugent met in the thirties and remained close until

Nugent's death. Although Jenkins was about ten years younger than Nugent, his death followed Nugent's by only a few months.

In the late sixties Nugent joined other prominent African American artists and concerned citizens to form the Harlem Cultural Council, on which he served for a time as co-chairman and for many years as a member of its board of directors. The group functioned as a conduit for municipal and federal funds for the support of the arts. It sponsored the highly successful "Jazzmobile" and "Dancemobile" projects, in which major artists performed on Harlem streets from stages constructed on flatbed trucks. The council was instrumental in organizing political support for the construction of a new building for the Schomburg Center for Research in Black Culture, the division of the New York Public Library that houses the Western world's most important collection of materials relating to Africa and the African diaspora. The council also took a leading role in mobilizing the community protest against exclusion of black artists from a central role in planning the Metropolitan Museum of Art's landmark exhibition, "Harlem on My Mind." Nugent was particularly proud to have been directly involved in the council's confrontation with museum director Thomas Hoving in 1969.

Also in the late sixties Nugent began a collaboration with young poet Abba Elethea (James W. Thompson) on a cultural history of Harlem. Elethea was a member of the "Umbra" group of writers active at the time on New York's lower east side—a group that included Tom Dent, David Henderson, Calvin Hernton, Raymond Patterson, and Ishmael Reed. Nugent and Elethea prepared a book outline that received high praise from their prospective publisher, but an advance sufficient to complete the project was not forthcoming.

After his wife's death, Nugent scraped together funds for a trip to Rome. He had always been fascinated by Italian men and had studied the language off and on. Rome enthralled him, and he returned each summer for several years. During his first trip in 1971, he met a handsome young Roman with whom he became deeply involved, maintaining yet another of his extensive correspondences, laboriously translating his own letters into Italian. Their relationship continued from summer to summer, even after the young man became engaged and was married, ending only in 1979 (plate 17).

Throughout the seventies Nugent maintained his studio, which he also used as a residence, in the upper reaches of 150 Nassau Street in New York's financial district. The building was locked on weekends, during which time he was essentially homeless. He began staying with a friend who owned an apartment

Nugent in Central Park in 1984. Photograph by Thomas H. Wirth.

Nugent in the Madison Café at Fourteenth and Washington Streets in Hoboken in 1982. Photograph by Thomas H. Wirth.

building in Hoboken, finally moving into an apartment there and closing the Nassau Street studio.

The seventies brought the first serious scholarly study of the Harlem Renaissance, and Nugent became an important resource. His personal recollections have informed many historical and biographical studies of the era. In 1971 he was interviewed by Robert Hemenway for a biography of Zora Neale Hurston. Interviews with David Levering Lewis (1974, 1977) and Arnold Rampersad (1984) followed. His 1982 interview with James V. Hatch was published by the Hatch-Billops Collection in their series, *Artists and Influences*. An interview with Nugent also appears in Jeff Kisseloff's *You Must Remember This: An Oral History of Manhattan from the 1890s to World War II* (1989). In his widely hailed book, *When Harlem Was in Vogue*, Lewis acknowledged his debt to Nugent: "Somewhere in Hoboken, New Jersey, Richard Bruce Nugent lives. To him, above all, this book owes whatever quality it may have of being written from inside of its subject, for many portraits of personality and unravelings of complex relationships were possible largely because of his astonishingly accurate memory and the objective perceptions of the past which he helped to create."[47]

The eighties brought a wave of post-Stonewall interest in gay history, and here, too, Nugent was an important resource. He appeared in the 1986 video documentary *Before Stonewall*. A Nugent interview was published in Joseph

Beam's *In the Life: A Black Gay Anthology*. Isaac Julien, the black gay British filmmaker, used "Smoke, Lilies and Jade" as the basis for a significant portion of his important 1989 film *Looking for Langston*.

I was introduced to Bruce Nugent by Arnold Rampersad in 1981. By this time Nugent was past retirement age and living on very modest Social Security benefits. As a book collector specializing in African American literature and as a gay man, I found him fascinating. He was a world-class conversationalist. Soon we were brunching regularly at the Madison Café at Fourteenth and Washington Streets, around the corner from his Hoboken apartment. We went to conventions of the College Language Association and the National Association of Black and White Men Together. We attended a conference on the Harlem Renaissance at Hofstra University and a black bibliophiles' conference at Howard. We went to gallery openings, where he renewed acquaintances with old friends and colleagues. (I shall always remember Bruce's elation when he met the ninety-eight-year-old Erté for the first time at the Dyansen gallery in Soho and acknowledged the older artist's influence on his own early work.) In 1982 Bruce found a copy of *FIRE!!* in his files, and we published a facsimile edition, which gave *FIRE!!* a renaissance of its own.

Bruce was an unregenerate Bohemian to the very end. His unkempt apartment was more than some visitors could take. His sexual interests never flagged. Young men from the neighborhood were always welcome, and many took advantage of his open door. After his eightieth birthday Bruce began to slow down. In March 1987 he was hospitalized. On 27 May 1987 he died of congestive heart failure, having outlived by many years most of his Harlem Renaissance compatriots. A memorial service in celebration of his life was held on his eighty-first birthday, 2 July 1987, at the Schomburg Center in Harlem.

II

As a writer Nugent stands at the intersection of two separate literary traditions—black and gay. For his significance to be properly assessed, he must be viewed simultaneously from both perspectives. The wider context—American culture as it evolved during the first third of the twentieth century—must be considered as well.

Nugent's seminal work was his pioneering prose composition "Smoke, Lilies and Jade," published in *FIRE!!* in 1926. Its homoerotic perspective is explicit. Alex, the protagonist, encounters a man on the street at four o'clock in the morning. They retire to Alex's room, and "as they undressed by the blue dawn . . . Alex knew he had never seen a more perfect being . . . his body was all symmetry and music . . . and Alex called him Beauty . . . long they lay . . . blowing smoke and exchanging thoughts . . . and Alex swallowed with difficulty . . . he felt a glow of tremor . . . and they talked and . . . slept" (this volume, 75).

Such an explicit, sympathetic treatment of same-sex desire was not yet acceptable to mainstream publishers. In the late teens, Henry Blake Fuller, an established writer, was unable to find a publisher for his genteel comedy of manners, *Bertram Cope's Year;* the male-male romantic interests at the core of the plot were too obvious. The book was finally published by a friend in 1919.[48] Robert McAlmon's book of stories *Distinguished Air* was published in 1925 — not in the United States but privately in Paris.[49] In England, publication of such material could have led to criminal prosecution in the long-lived aftermath of the Oscar Wilde affair; E. M. Forster's novel *Maurice*, written in 1913–14, was not published until 1971.[50] Five years passed after the appearance of "Smoke, Lilies and Jade" before Liveright published Blair Niles's *Strange Brother*, a novel featuring a homosexual as a leading character, in 1931.[51]

Even in the context of underground homoerotica, which was by then well established, "Smoke, Lilies and Jade" was unique — a forthright, uncoded invitation to the reader of any sexual orientation to enter the interior consciousness of a bisexual man and assume a homophilic subjectivity. There is none of the guilt and anguish that had previously characterized most writing about male same-sex desire and that would continue to dominate gay literature for many decades. "Smoke, Lilies and Jade" celebrates sexual attraction between men with exquisite sensitivity, without apology or prurience.

As a gay writer, Nugent began squarely in what might be characterized as the tradition of perfumed decadence. This line of development began with the publication of Joris-Karl Huysmans's notorious novel, *A rebours*, in Paris in 1884, continued with Oscar Wilde and his contemporaries in England in the 1880s and 1890s, and flowered in the United States in the 1920s in the novels of Carl Van Vechten. Associated with this literary tradition were artists like Aubrey Beardsley, the illustrator of the written version of Wilde's play *Salome*, and Erté, the Russian-born Parisian who dominated the pages of *Harper's Bazaar* during the 1920s.

Nugent's connection with these influences is clear. Not only was he personally acquainted with Van Vechten, he also read Van Vechten's novels, which were then bestsellers.[52] Moreover, Wallace Thurman's *Infants of the Spring* explicitly sets forth Nugent's awareness of and enthusiasm for the work of Huysmans and Wilde. Paul Arbian (the character based on Nugent) wrote a novel entitled *Wu Sing: The Geisha Man* dedicated to:

> Huysmans' Des Esseintes and Oscar Wilde's Oscar Wilde
> Ecstatic Spirits with whom I Cohabit
> And whose golden spores of decadent pollen
> I shall broadcast and fertilize.[53]

Like Nugent's "Smoke, Lilies and Jade," Huysmans's novel includes a homo-erotically charged street encounter. Huysmans's protagonist, Des Esseintes, having exhausted the capacity of numerous mistresses to arouse him sexually, meets a young man "wretchedly dressed in a little cheviot jacket too tight round the hips and barely covering the small of his back, [and] close-fitting black trousers," whose "face was disquieting; pale and drawn . . . it was lit up by great liquid eyes," with a mouth which "though small, was bordered by thick lips divided down the center with a groove, like a cherry." The young man's "arm brushed that of Des Esseintes, who slowed his pace as he thoughtfully considered the young man's mincing walk." A "mistrustful relationship" followed, which "lasted for months; Des Esseintes could no longer think of it without a shudder; never had he submitted to a more seductive, more compelling servitude, never had he experienced such dangers, yet never had he felt more painfully fulfilled."[54]

Carl Van Vechten injected these "decadent" European sensibilities into American letters with the publication of *Peter Whiffle* in 1922. In this novel he transposed Huysmans's *A rebours* from the Parisian world of the Comte Robert de Montesquiou (the real-life model for Des Esseintes) into the milieu of affluent and well-traveled Americans like Mabel Dodge, who, during the decade before the Great War, had formed the nucleus of America's first avant-garde. Both novels center on wealthy, effete young men drifting indecisively through life without emotional ties to anyone but themselves. Both contain lengthy catalogs of exquisitely described fabrics, flowers, furnishings, books, jewels, and perfumes.

Van Vechten was by no means so explicit in *Peter Whiffle* about the homosexual inclinations of his protagonist as Huysmans was in *A Rebours*. The closest thing to a sexual encounter in the novel is the protagonist's long pause before Donatello's statue of David in Florence, described by Van Vechten as "that exquisite soft bronze of the Biblical lad, nude but for his wreathed helmet, standing in his adolescent slender beauty with one foot on the head of the decapitated giant," which Whiffle, the eponymous protagonist, declares to be "the most beautiful object that the hand of man has yet created."[55] But the implications of this and certain other scenes are hardly obscure. In one, Whiffle is described as wearing "green trousers, a white silk shirt, a tie of Chinese blue brocade, clasped with a black opal, and a most ornate black Chinese dressing gown, around the skirt of which a silver dragon chased his tail. He was combed and brushed and there was a faint odour of toilet-water. His nails were manicured and on one of his little fingers [was] a ring."[56] In the coded language of fin de siècle literature, every one of these details implies sexual interest in other men.

Several fey characters appear in Van Vechten's next novel, *The Blind Bow-Boy* (1923) and its sequel, *Firecrackers* (1925). In the former book, the character Paul Moody appears as "a young man with curly golden hair and blue eyes and a profile that resembled somewhat Sherril Schell's photograph of Rupert Brooke, a young man with slender, graceful hands which he was inclined to wave rather excessively in punctuation of his verbal effects . . . smoking a cigarette in a jade holder of a green so dark and so nearly translucent that it paraphrased emerald."[57] The same Paul spends the first part of *Firecrackers* in pursuit of a supremely graceful and physically ravishing young man who was hired by Paul's wealthy wife to repair the furnace. Another character in *The Blind Bow-Boy*, Ronald, Duke of Middlebottom, has inscribed on his stationery the motto, "A thing of beauty is a boy for ever."[58]

In one sense, these are peripheral details. As Van Vechten wrote to Mabel Dodge, "My intention in writing is to create moods, to awaken unconscious echoes of the past, to render to shadows their real importance. I don't think I ever think of sex at all. It plays around here and there, but that's not what my books are about. They seem to me to be books about a man who is alone in the world and is very sad."[59] Who, however, is this figure, alone and sad, but Van Vechten himself? And, where does this figure appear? In *Blind Bow-Boy* and *Firecrackers*, the most likely Van Vechten character is female: Campaspe Lorillard. She is an independent, imperious figure who, like Van Vechten himself, is intent on maintaining control of her life even as she seeks out the erotic and the bizarre. While Lorillard incorporates the persona of Mabel Dodge as well as of Van Vechten, it is Van Vechten speaking through her when she says, "How was it possible to read an author who never laughed? For it was only behind laughter that true tragedy could lie concealed, and only the ironic author who could awaken the deeper emotions. The true tragedies of life were either ridiculous or sordid. The only way to get the sense of this absurd, contradictory, and perverse existence into a book was to withdraw entirely from reality. The artist who feels the most poignantly the bitterness of life wears a persistent and sardonic smile."[60]

As Byrne Fone has pointed out, "What Van Vechten describes here is his own method." Here, according to Fone, "are the central mechanisms of camp, the application not of the transcendent or of the profound but of the surface sublime, to make real life unreal and hence bearable and understandable."[61] Thus, it can be argued that these novels are, in their very essence, performances in drag.

Nonetheless, Van Vechten's treatment of homosexuality is elegantly indirect. Although the closet door may be more or less transparent, his characters do remain in the closet. With the exception of *Nigger Heaven*, he never explicitly discusses their erotic lives. Moreover, his exquisitely polished prose style is quite traditional in that it consists of straightforward narrative (save for the omission of quotation marks and his penchant for archaic words).

In "Smoke, Lilies and Jade," Nugent appropriates from Van Vechten and the European aesthetes their coded vocabulary: his protagonist celebrates the "joy of being an artist and of blowing blue smoke through an ivory holder inlaid with red jade and green." But Nugent differs from Van Vechten in two respects. He lifts the veil to reveal, and invites the reader to share, the protagonist's (largely homosexual) erotic sensibilities. And he employs a modernist prose style—stream of consciousness, phrases separated by ellipses, fleeting impressions strung like beads in lines across the page.

> . . . his lips were so beautiful . . . quizzical . . . Alex wondered why he always thought of that passage from Wilde's Salome . . . when he looked at Beauty's lips . . . I would kiss your lips . . . he *would* like to kiss Beauty's lips . . . Alex flushed warm . . . with shame . . . or was it shame . . . he reached across Beauty for a cigarette . . . Beauty's cheek felt cool to his arm . . . his hair felt soft . . . Alex lay smoking . . . such a dream . . . red calla lilies . . . red calla lilies . . . and . . . what did it all mean . . . did dreams have meanings . . . Fania said . . . and black poppies . . . thousands . . . millions . . . Beauty stirred . . . (this volume, 83)

It is a style that could not be more appropriate to the transgressive content of "Smoke, Lilies and Jade."

"Smoke, Lilies and Jade" placed Nugent in the avant-garde. It foreshadowed Charles Henri Ford and Parker Tyler's radically experimental novel on a homosexual theme, *The Young and Evil*, but preceded it by seven years. (*The Young and Evil* was published in Paris by Obelisk Press in 1933 and enjoyed the enthusiastic sponsorship of international luminaries Djuna Barnes and Gertrude Stein. Stein declared that it "creates this generation as *This Side of Paradise* by Fitzgerald created his generation.")[62] "Smoke, Lilies and Jade" also preceded another milestone in gay literature, Robert Scully's high-camp, gender-bending, pornographic romp, *A Scarlet Pansy*, which may have been written before 1926 but, like *The Young and Evil*, was not published until 1933.[63]

Nugent, then, was a black gay man who insisted on participating in the most advanced discourse of the dominant culture, even as he defied that culture's norms. In this regard, Nugent was continuing in the tradition of his distant African American literary ancestors; his insistence parallels Phillis Wheatley's effort in prerevolutionary America to participate in order to force (or persuade) whites to recognize black people as fully human.[64] In refusing to accept the supposition that homosexual themes, modernist forms, and "decadence" were off-limits to black writers, Nugent was not trying to "be white." Rather, he was struggling to expand his contemporaries' conceptions of blackness.

Nugent's Bible stories, written in the late twenties after "Smoke, Lilies and Jade" appeared, were stylistically less radical, but in the context of the time, they were, if anything, more transgressive (113–46). The open, uncoded conflation of homosexuality with the gospels in these stories is even now as unsettling to the conventionally minded reader as it is exhilarating to the iconoclast. In writing them, Nugent drew directly from the tradition of the European aesthetes, who also used biblical themes: Huysmans's fascination with Gustave Moreau's painting of Salome dancing before Herod; Wilde's subsequent play on the same theme with its barely coded homosexual subtexts; Beardsley's disturbing and beautiful drawings that accompanied Wilde's published text; and John Addington Symond's poem "The Meeting of David and Jonathan" are obvious examples.[65]

Unlike Symonds and other British homosexual writers, such as Edward Carpenter, who cited biblical or classical references in an effort to make homosexuality respectable by association, Nugent's use of biblical themes is confrontational. Same-sex desire, to him, required no justification—it was a fact of life. His Bible stories directly challenge both homophobia and shallow piety. "The Now Discordant Song of Bells," for example, is a parable of love, but the love is homosexual—between Carus, Herod's catamite, and the magus Caspar. In the end, the formerly decadent youth surpasses the gentle and restrained Caspar in profundity.

Nugent's confrontational stance mirrors the iconoclasm of his friend and fellow Harlem Renaissance writer, Wallace Thurman, the editor of *FIRE!!* Thurman, in turn, was strongly influenced by the leading American iconoclast of the period, H. L. Mencken.[66] Thus, Nugent's work embodies both the European and the American influences on the Harlem Renaissance.

At the time Nugent and his contemporaries began writing, America was a cultural battleground. Since the beginning of the twentieth century, the best American writers had been struggling to emancipate themselves from the stifling weight of Anglophilic, late-Victorian culture. Except in New York and, to some extent, Chicago, established cultural institutions were controlled by corseted opera lovers who took "great books" with their afternoon tea and by men of wealth who lined their libraries with leather-bound sets of the classics. There was no lack of high culture in the heartland—even avant-garde culture. Before World War I, Sergei Diaghilev's brilliant *Ballet Russe* flashed across the country. Isadora Duncan danced, Sarah Bernhardt acted, theatrical companies toured. The result, however, was not to stimulate local centers of creativity but to enhance the allure of the distant metropolis, with T. S. Eliot, Ezra Pound, and Carl Van Vechten leading the exodus from the provinces early in the century. After World War I, the "lost generation"—Hemingway, Fitzgerald, Lewis, Dos Passos, Crane, and Wolfe among them—fled the towns and prairies to Paris or New York.

The younger Harlem Renaissance writers and artists followed the same pattern. Zora Neale Hurston arrived in New York from Florida, via Baltimore and Washington, D.C. Aaron Douglas came from Kansas. Langston Hughes arrived from Missouri, via Kansas, Illinois, Ohio, and Mexico. Wallace Thurman arrived from Salt Lake City via Los Angeles. Nugent, of course, came from Washington, D.C.

This generation was in revolt against Victorian social and sexual proprieties, against the weltanschauung of Horatio Alger and Pollyanna, and against silence as a tactic for dealing with unpleasant realities. Revolt generated reaction, and the reaction within the African American community was, if anything, stronger than that in the dominant culture. Most community leaders, responding to traditional stereotypes of black people as wanton, stupid, and slothful, were deeply offended by realistic treatment of the seamier aspects of African American life. Dedicated to strengthening bourgeois norms as an essential means of "race advancement" and believing that positive images of African Americans were essential to combating prejudice and discrimination, such leaders condemned alike the blues, jazz, the novels of Claude McKay, and the poetry of Langston Hughes. Critics writing in African American newspapers like the *Pittsburgh Courier* and *Amsterdam News* expressed and re-inforced this position. Paradoxically, these leaders and critics found themselves defending the conservative aesthetic values of the old Anglophilic social order, which was decidedly unsympathetic to black aspirations.[67]

The stance of the African American cultural elite that young writers should place their talents at the service of race advancement implicitly required those writers not only to portray black characters in a positive (or at least sympathetic) light but to eschew the modern—the radical—and to concentrate on develop-ing excellence in widely accepted forms that would not alienate a potentially sympathetic (white) audience.[68] In the context of the 1920s, however, this ex-pectation placed a heavy burden on those young writers; the artist who is con-strained to work in forms that have lost their vitality, and who is constrained also to "put his best foot forward" for the sake of race advancement, is seriously handicapped in his efforts to produce work of the first rank.

Some had more sophisticated views. Among them was W. E. B. Du Bois, the pre-eminent African American intellectual of the period. In addition to being editor of *Crisis*, Du Bois had published the lyrical and decidedly nontraditional *Souls of Black Folk* at the beginning of the century. Even before the twenties, he opened the pages of *Crisis* to emerging African American writers. Aware that racial defensiveness and Victorian prudishness had had a detrimental effect on the quality of African American literary efforts, he defended younger artists like Langston Hughes against *Crisis* readers who complained that the work of those artists was too explicit about matters such as prostitution.[69] Still, there were limits to Du Bois's tolerance.

Du Bois believed that in the real world (as opposed to the ideal world of theo-retical philosophy) Beauty could not exist independently of Truth and Right.[70] Accurate depiction of sordid reality might well be beautiful, but only if the moral conclusions conveyed by that depiction were correct. Prostitution limned with pathos was acceptable; prostitution painted as an enticing or ful-filling way of life was not. Thus Du Bois defended Hughes's early poems about prostitutes, but he excoriated Claude McKay's *Home to Harlem* as "filth."[71] Art for art's sake (which Nugent espoused) was an aesthetic which Du Bois em-phatically rejected.[72] He never reviewed *FIRE!!* or "Smoke, Lilies and Jade," but inasmuch as that story glamorized both deviant sex and indolence, Du Bois presumably didn't approve.

Alain Locke was more accepting of the younger generation than Du Bois. His book *The New Negro*—a seminal anthology that created a comprehensive framework for the interpretation of intellectual developments in the African

American community after 1900—presented the younger generation's work alongside that of established intellectuals like Du Bois and James Weldon Johnson. Locke recognized that many younger writers were among "the moderns." He also recognized that the modernist work of white writers and artists like Sherwood Anderson, Eugene O'Neill, and Pablo Picasso had generated much of the white interest in "things Negro" that was so important in sustaining the Harlem Renaissance.[73]

Locke did not agree with Du Bois's emphasis on moral correctness: he did not view art as a means of moral instruction, and he strongly opposed the conflation of art with propaganda. He valued, above all, authenticity of expression. He was interested in establishing artistic traditions in which the sensibilities and life experiences that African Americans shared could be fully and freely expressed. Furthermore, Locke agreed with the school of thought that held that Western civilization had become over-refined and had produced an unhealthy alienation from the body, which was manifest in the restrictive and hypocritical sexual morality of the Victorian era.

> The modern recoil from the machine has deepened the appreciation of hitherto despised qualities in the Negro temperament, its hedonism, its nonchalance, its spontaneity; the reaction against oversophistication has opened our eyes to the values of the primitive and the importance of the man of emotions and untarnished instincts; and finally the revolt against conventionality, against Puritanism, has fought [sic] a strong ally in the half-submerged paganism of the Negro. With this established reciprocity, there is every reason for the Negro artist to be more of a modernist than, on the average, he yet is, but with each younger artistic generation the alignment with modernism becomes closer. . . . Negro elements, culturally transplanted, have, I think, an important contribution to make to the working out of our national culture.[74]

Locke's support for the younger generation, however, was not unqualified. This fact is evident in his review of *FIRE!!* In that magazine, which was in essence the younger generation's manifesto of revolt against the strictures of the bourgeoisie, they in effect proclaimed themselves to be full-fledged modernists. Given his convictions, one might predict that Locke would wholeheartedly approve of *FIRE!!* But, after noting that "the strong sex radicalism of many of the contributions will shock many well-wishers and elate some of our adversaries," Locke wrote,

If Negro life is to provide a healthy antidote to Puritanism, and to become one of the effective instruments of sound artistic progress, its flesh
values must more and more be expressed in the clean, original, primitive but fundamental terms of the senses and not, as too often in this
particular issue of Fire [sic], in hectic imitation of the "naughty nineties"
and effete echoes of contemporary decadence. Back to Whitman would
have been a better point of support than a left-wing pivoting on Wilde and
Beardsley.[75]

This comment is clearly directed at "Smoke, Lilies and Jade," not the other
contents of *FIRE!!* It is especially noteworthy because Locke was, as we have
seen, a self-identified gay man. Nugent, moreover, was a protégé and an object of his sexual desire. Significantly, Locke does not condemn the depiction
of same-sex desire per se. Indeed, his reference to Whitman clearly reveals to
other cognoscenti that he himself was "in the life." Rather, Locke insists here
that such depictions be coded and "wholesome," so as not to alienate the general audience—a strategy of concealment that he had in common with all other
gay Harlem Renaissance writers except Nugent. In his abhorrence of flamboyant "decadence," Locke was typical of middle-class gay men of his time, who
often felt an intense need to differentiate themselves from "fairies," thereby
avoiding the social damage that would inevitably accompany any identification
with that group.[76]

Locke delivered another rebuke to the younger generation in *Harlem*, a fledgling journal that Wallace Thurman edited a year after the first and only issue
of *FIRE!!* appeared. Locke's rebuke was especially pointed because it appeared
in an article that Thurman had invited him to submit. "Not all of our younger
writers are deep enough in the sub-soil of their native materials," he wrote.
"Too many are pot-plants seeking a forced growth according to the exotic tastes
of a pampered and decadent public. It is the art of the people that needs to be
cultivated, not the art of coteries."[77]

Thus, despite his espousal of artistic self-expression, Locke imposed on writ-
ers and artists of color a heavy burden of representation. In a 1937 review of
McKay's *A Long Way from Home*, Locke acknowledged for the record that "art-
ists have a right to be individualists, of course," but made it clear that only
"Negro writers expressing a folk in expressing themselves" deserved praise.
Locke bitterly condemned McKay's "lack of common loyalty" to the race.
Broadening his condemnation to include other unspecified New Negro writers
and artists, he accused them as a group of "spiritual truancy and social irre-

sponsibility" and deplored their "exhibitionist flair." "The program of the Negro Renaissance," he asserted, "was to interpret the folk to itself, to vitalize it from within; it was a wholesome, vigorous, assertive racialism. . . . Negro writers must become truer sons of the people, more loyal providers of spiritual bread and less aesthetic wastrels and truants of the streets."[78] Thirty years later, this principle became the aesthetic foundation of the Black Arts Movement.

If "the people" is defined (as it usually is) to be the "normal" heterosexual majority, it necessarily follows from Locke's line of reasoning that the aesthetic self-expression of gay black sexuality is without validity. Only by rejecting the burden of representing the race as a whole, as Nugent did, or by insisting that "the people" be defined broadly and pluralistically so as to include gay people, among others, have gay black writers been able to emerge.

Of all the male Harlem Renaissance writers who were sexually attracted to other men, only Nugent broke the taboo that Locke, through his critique, attempted to enforce: only Nugent published work that would lead his readers to identify him unmistakably as "queer." Whatever one's friends may have known or suspected, whatever gossip may have circulated in wider circles, one did not proclaim one's homoerotic sentiments in print. This taboo was consistent with the social convention of the "open secret." Other Harlem Renaissance writers did sometimes skate very close to the edge of self-revelation. They included male characters who had sex with men in their books; they portrayed intense male-male emotional ties; they wrote poetry that on close reading expresses the joy and anguish of same-sex love; and they wrote poems that are ostensibly about race but that actually, or simultaneously, address sexual orientation — but the narrative voice in their work either kept its distance or wore the mask of ambiguity.

Wallace Thurman was particularly careful to distance himself from his homosexual characters. In *The Blacker the Berry*, for example, protagonist Emma Lou discovers her exploitative boyfriend, Alva, "sitting on the bed embracing an effeminate boy." Since Thurman here uses homosexual activity as a device to emphasize Alva's descent into degradation, he as narrator is not implicated.[79] In Thurman's second novel, *Infants of the Spring*, homosexuality appears most obviously in the Nugent-based character, Paul Arbian. Although Arbian is sympathetically portrayed, he remains an exotic, well distanced from the narrator. Thurman's autobiographical character, Raymond, forms an intense, interracial friendship with Stephen Jorgensen, the fictional counterpart of Thurman's white lover, Harold Jan Stefansson, but the sexual aspect of the relationship is carefully disguised, with only the subtlest hints of an erotic attraction—"something . . . too preposterous and complex to be recognized or considered."[80]

Claude McKay's first two novels, *Home to Harlem* and *Banjo*, skate closer to the edge; close reading reveals a strong homoerotic subtext.[81] The novels celebrate not only "the irrepressible exuberance and legendary vitality of the black race" but male bonding.[82] *Home to Harlem* is centered around the friendship between Jake, the carefree protagonist, and Ray, McKay's intellectual alter ego. Jake is not shy about expressing his feelings.

> Jake gripped Ray's shoulder: "Chappie, I wish I was edjucated mahself."
> "Christ! What for?" demanded Ray.
> Becaz I likes you." Like a black Pan out of the woods Jake looked into Ray's eyes with frank savage affection.[83]

Later in the novel, it becomes clear to the careful reader that there is an erotic element in this relationship. In one episode, Ray, fighting insomnia, "looked up at Jake, stretched at full length on his side . . . sleeping peacefully, like a tired boy after hard playing, so happy and sweet and handsome." A cocaine-induced fantasy follows: "And he was a gay humming-bird, fluttering and darting his long needle beak into the heart of a bell-flower. . . . Now he was a young shining chief in a marble palace; slim, naked negresses dancing for his pleasure . . . gleaming-skinned black boys bearing goblets of wine and obedient eunuchs waiting in the offing. . . . And he was a blue bird in flight and a blue lizard in love. . . . Taboos and terrors and penalties were transformed into new pagan delights, orgies of . . . cherubs and seraphs and fetishes and phalli."[84]

In another episode, Ray deflects the advances of a prostitute: "The round face of the first girl, the carnal sympathy of her full, tinted mouth, touched Ray. But something was between them. . . . He was lost in some sensual dream of his own . . . like black youth burning naked in the bush . . . like a primitive dance of war or of love . . . the marshaling of spears or the sacred frenzy of a phallic celebration."[85]

The next day, Jake, commenting on Ray's rejection of the attractive "chippie," comes out and says, "Youse awful queer, chappie."[86] But, even this comment retains the ambiguous double meaning of the word *queer*. Nowhere in the novel is there any indication that Ray's implied homoerotic desire for Jake is ever physically consummated.

Banjo narrates the adventures of a group of black vagabonds on the Marseilles waterfront. One critic has aptly described the waterfront as the "site of promiscuous social interaction and continental drift . . . on the margin of the city . . . [and] on the margin of urban social structures."[87] In the era before Stonewall, sailors were widely recognized as potential sexual partners by those inclined to pursue them; the sailor was, in fact, a central figure in the gay subculture.[88]

Without exactly saying so, McKay makes it clear that his vagabonds are a sexy, virile bunch. Banjo, their leader, for example, "was lying flat on his back on one of the huge stone blocks of the breakwater. . . . He had no shirt on and, unfastening the pin at the collar of his old blue coat, he flung it back and exposed his brown belly to the sun. His trousers waist was pulled down below his navel. 'Oh, Gawd, the sun is sweet!' he yawned and, pulling his cap over his eyes, went to sleep. The others also stretched themselves and slept."[89]

"The boys" live among pimps and prostitutes, and are totally free of domestic attachments. Banjo has a long-term relationship with Latnah, one of the prostitutes, but he comes and goes and sleeps around as he pleases. While there is no indication of homosexual activity among the group—their sexual partners are always female—they do tend to follow the impulses of the moment, and it takes little imagination for a gay reader to infer that, given an appropriate inducement, some of them would happily consent to having sex with another man. In a word, they are potential "trade."

Ray, McKay's alter ego in *Home to Harlem,* also appears in *Banjo*—again as the best pal of the major character. Surely the "animal joy [Ray] felt when in company with the boys" has sexual desire as one of its components.[90] At the conclusion of the novel, Ray leaves Marseilles with Banjo, who admonishes, "Don't get soft ovah any one wimmens, pardner. . . . A woman is a conjunction. Gawd fixed her different from us in moh ways than one. . . . Come on, pardner. Wese got enough between us to beat it a long ways from here."[91]

Obvious as they are to the twenty-first-century reader, the sexual undercurrents in these novels are subtle enough that they probably did not register with McKay's contemporaries—except, of course, with those who consciously shared his erotic interests in other men. The first part of the twentieth century was a period in which working-class men were celebrated as paragons of masculinity, as opposed to men of the middle and upper classes, who many observers believed had become "overcivilized" and "soft."[92] In the popular mind, it was middle- and upper-class men who were primarily associated with homosexual activity. The fact, well known to gay men, that many of these "normal" working-class men were susceptible to seduction by other men was not part of the wider public discourse.

McKay was at his most explicit in one of his early poems, "Bennie's Departure."

> Once his cot was next beside me,
> But dere came misfortune's day
> When de pleasure was denied me,
> For de sergeant moved him 'way:
> I played not fe mind de movin'
> Though me heart wid grief be'n full;
> 'Twas but one kin' o' de provin'
> O' de ways o' dis ya wul'.[93]

This piece and "Consolation," another poem in *Constab Ballads,* which was published in London in 1912, describe McKay's affection for and emotional dependence on a fellow recruit. In the words of McKay's biographer, "['Bennie's Departure'] bordered upon a passionate declaration of homosexual love."[94] However, there is no indication that contemporary readers interpreted the poem as deviant. Despite the Wilde affair and the recent emergence of the term "homosexuality" in medical and psychological discourse, romantic feelings between males seem not to have implied sexual desire or physical consummation to most English and Jamaican readers in 1912. Since it was not publicly discussed, the possibility that masculine-appearing men might have sexual relationships with other men seems simply not to have occurred to those who had no personal experience with such situations. Public perceptions were changing rapidly, however, and it is doubtful that the homoerotic implications of these poems would have escaped notice even ten years later. Significantly, the poems never became widely available, nor were they reprinted in McKay's lifetime.

Same-sex desire also pervades the work of Countee Cullen; there, too, it is discreetly clothed in ambiguous imagery. Most of Cullen's poetry about love is ungendered and can therefore be read as an expression of his own erotic interest in other men. While that particular interpretation is not forced on the reader, it is hard to avoid if one knows anything about Cullen's romantic relationships with other men as he revealed them in his letters to Locke.[95] Particularly resonant with the gay experience is the depiction of hidden love:

> So must I, starved for love's delight,
> Affect the mute,
> When love's divinest acolyte
> Extends me holy fruit.[96]

Even (or perhaps especially) in a religious context, Cullen uses passionately romantic imagery in depicting male-male relationships, as in "The Black Christ," in which the narrator laments the death of his brother.

> My Lycidas was dead. There swung
> In all his glory, lusty, young,
> My Jonathan, my Patrocles, . . .[97]

In "Judas Iscariot," Judas is given the task of betraying Christ in order to save mankind:

> Then Judas in his hot desire
> Said, "Give me what you will."
> Christ spoke to him with words of fire,
> "Then, Judas, you must kill
> One whom you love, One who loves you . . .

The poem concludes with the narrator speaking of Judas:

> But I would rather think of him
> As the little Jewish lad
> Who gave young Christ heart, soul, and limb,
> And all the love he had.[98]

Cullen dedicated "More Than a Fool's Song" to Edward Perry, who was one of the gay men who associated with Caska Bonds and Bruce Nugent, and who may have been Cullen's lover.[99] This poem celebrates paradox and inversion of values, and concludes with the following lines, which probably refer to society's prevailing view of same-sex love: "The souls we think are hurtling down / Perhaps are climbing up."[100]

In a few instances, Cullen openly celebrates male-male attachments. Take "Tableau," for example, which he dedicated to his white lover, Donald Duff.[101]

> Locked arm in arm they cross the way,
> The black boy and the white,
> The golden splendor of the day,
> The sable pride of night.
>
> From lowered blinds the dark folk stare,
> And here the fair folk talk,
> Indignant that these two should dare
> In unison to walk.

Oblivious to look and word
They pass, and see no wonder
That lightning brilliant as a sword
Should blaze the path of thunder.[102]

Or consider "Uncle Jim," whose heart is "walled up with bitterness" against "white folks." The poem concludes:

I have a friend who eats his heart
Away with grief of mine,
Who drinks my joy as tipplers drain
Deep goblets filled with wine.

I wonder why here at his side,
Face-in-the-grass with him,
My mind should stray the Grecian urn
To muse on uncle Jim.[103]

One critic has interpreted "Heritage," one of Cullen's best-known poems (which begins, "What is Africa to me" and is dedicated to Harold Jackman), as the narrative of the internal struggle between Cullen's need to maintain public respectability and his illicit homosexual desires. Thus, he must "twist and squirm" on his bed, stopping his ears to keep out the "great drums throbbing through the air," his "dark blood dammed within / Like great pulsing tides of wine," ultimately forcing himself to "quench my pride and cool my blood, / Lest I perish in the flood."[104]

Langston Hughes was perhaps the most circumspect of all. There was no revealing correspondence comparable to Cullen's with Locke. Even Nugent, one of Hughes's closest friends in 1925 and 1926, was unable to state unequivocally for the record whether Hughes was sexually attracted to men or not, although he suspected that Hughes was.[105] Some of Hughes's early poetry can be interpreted as the expression of same-sex desire, but that work is only a tiny part of his enormous oeuvre. Nonetheless, those examples are notable. Consider "Poem [2]."

I loved my friend.
He went away from me.
There's nothing more to say,
The poem ends,
Soft as it began, —
I loved my friend.[106]

The Hughes poem "Boy," loosely quoted in "Smoke, Lilies and Jade," can also be read as an expression of sexual desire (79–80).

> He was somewhat like Ariel
> And somewhat like Puck
> And somewhat like a gutter boy
> Who loves to play in muck.
>
> He had something of Bacchus
> And something of Pan
> And a way with women
> Like a sailor man.
>
> He was straight and slender
> And solid with strength
> And lovely as a young tree
> All his virile length.
>
> He couldn't have been a good man,
> All shut up in a cell,
> 'Cause he'd "rather be a sinner,"
> He said, —"and go to hell."[107]

It has been pointed out that Hughes is especially eloquent on the subject of sailors.[108] "Port Town" is another sexually ambiguous poem about sailors.

> Hello, sailor boy,
> In from the sea!
> Hello, sailor,
> Come with me!
>
> Come on drink cognac.
> Rather have wine?
> Come here, I love you.
> Come and be mine.[109]

The reluctance of male Harlem Renaissance writers publicly to reveal their sexual interest in other men continued into the next generation. Robert Hayden, for example, carefully hid his same-sex desires. Therefore, for thirty years Nugent stood as the only African American to write from the perspective of a man who not only acknowledged but openly celebrated his erotic fascination with other men. Only in 1956, with the publication of *Giovanni's Room*, did James Baldwin emerge as another overtly gay writer.

Critics likewise maintained a long silence on the subject of homosexuality. The fact that a significant portion of the Harlem Renaissance writers had same-sex erotic interests was not generally acknowledged until the 1980s, and it was even later when scholars actually began to take these desires into account in textual analyses.

Nugent the visual artist, like Nugent the writer, drew on both black and gay influences, sometimes combining them in unexpected ways.

He shared with Aaron Douglas and Sargent Johnson the distinction of being among the first African American artists to celebrate their African heritage by utilizing African motifs in their work. Prior to the Harlem Renaissance, black artists shunned the primitive. Ironically, as Alain Locke pointed out in the 1925 "Harlem" issue of *Survey Graphic,* African sculpture had influenced Matisse, Picasso, Modigliani, and other modern European artists; Locke went on to suggest that "surely this art, once known and appreciated, can scarcely have less influence upon the blood descendants than upon those who inherit by tradition only."[110] This issue of the magazine had been illustrated by Winold Reiss, a classically trained Bavarian artist who had an interest in folklore and "ethnic types." He had executed an array of superb portraits of African American leaders and Harlem residents, which were featured in the issue, along with several of his black and white drawings of Harlem life, executed in a manner reminiscent of *Scherenschnitt*—a German folk technique employing black, scissors-cut silhouettes. Aaron Douglas was so impressed that he came to New York, in part, at least, to study with Reiss. He soon developed his own distinctive style, simplifying and strengthening Reiss's technique of drawing in silhouette, and his work was often featured in *Crisis* and *Opportunity*. Nugent, who was a good friend of Douglas and his assistant in executing murals on the walls of Harlem nightclubs, also began to draw in silhouette and to incorporate African motifs into his work. From time to time, Nugent accompanied Douglas to lessons with Reiss.

Nugent's work is both similar to and different from the work of Douglas and Reiss. Like them, for example, Nugent employed dance as a trope to express primitive vitality and freedom from sexual inhibition. But, whereas dance was only an occasional subject for Douglas and Reiss, it was central for Nugent: images of dancers dominate his early drawings and recur throughout his

Weinold Reiss, *Interpretation of Harlem Jazz* (1925).

oeuvre (65, 68–73, 147–55). Nugent displayed extraordinary skill in capturing the shapes of his dancers' bodies and suggesting movement by means of a simple, highly stylized vocabulary. To Nugent, the forms and movements of dance were of importance in themselves, not just as symbols of the primitive.

Whereas Douglas turned to ancient Egyptian art as both a symbolic connection with the ancient African past and a source of ideas about design and representation, Nugent's art evolved under the influence of Beardsley and Erté. The sinuous curves of the lynch victim's body and the surrounding vegetation in the illustration accompanying "Pope Pius the Only" (247), for example, are distinctly Beardsley-esque, as is the use of seemingly peripheral details — the dying flowers, the stringy moss — to reinforce and elucidate the work's theme. (Beardsley's *The Climax*, an illustration for the published version of Wilde's *Salome,* is presented here for comparison.) Indeed, much of Nugent's work is a dialogue with Beardsley. The erect flowers at the base of the figures on pages 65 and 71 are direct allusions to the flower rising from the pool of Jokanaan's blood in "The Climax." The lush foliage surrounding Nugent's

Aubrey Beardsley, *The Climax* (1894).

dancers in these images also mirrors the vines that frame Beardsley's illustrations for *Le Morte Darthur*. Similarly, the three candles that appear in Nugent's drawings of monks (237, 239) unmistakably refer to Beardsley's artistic signature, which appears to the right of the flower in *The Climax*.

Although the techniques and tropes of Beardsley, Douglas, Reiss, and others appear in Nugent's art, the synthesis is uniquely his. No one else brought the fin de siècle aesthetic sensibility so effectively to bear on African or African American subject matter. Few have more skillfully attacked prevailing sexual, religious, and racial norms simply by celebrating the joyous potential of transgressive sexuality.

Especially noteworthy for its originality is Nugent's Salome series (plates 1–7). These images are like nothing anyone else has done. The nudes, mostly women flamboyant in their sexuality, are titled with the names of biblical characters. As in his Bible stories, Nugent's conflation of sexuality and the scriptures is highly transgressive. Equally interesting is the masklike nature of his faces—indeed, of the entire bodies of these women.[111] These figures present

Aaron Douglas, Dancers
(1928).

sexuality as performance, as artifice—as drag. They, like Nugent's persona itself, perfectly express the zeitgeist of Manhattan in the twenties, in which life was lived as theater.[112]

Nugent's open assault on mainstream religious sensibilities is not without precedent in African American culture; it echoes David Walker's devastating attack on hypocritical Christianity in his 1829 *Appeal to the Coloured Citizens of the World*.[113] Nugent's stories are more subtle than Walker's *Appeal*, but they, too, were highly subversive. By placing biblical characters in a context in which traditional Christian assumptions about sexuality and race are violated, Nugent challenged readers to acknowledge that their prejudices were (and are) inconsistent with basic Christian principles. Nugent continued his commentary on religion, the church, and sexuality in his sexually suggestive drawings of monks—drawings that still have not lost their power to shock (234–40).

In the 1940s, Nugent explored further his favorite themes and refined his technique. His draftsmanship rose to a high level of expertise; he augmented his exquisite pen and ink drawings with the transparent Japanese dyes that were used at the time to tint photographs (plates 9–11). During the 1950s, however, Nugent began to turn away from the mannered techniques that had characterized much of his previous work, both literary and visual. Increasingly, his work became a forthright expression of his erotic interests. He drew portraits of exquisite young men in the style of Michelangelo (plates 15–16; 233, 266–67). He wrote realistic, sexually explicit novels exploring the emotional complexities of relationships between openly gay men like himself and the straight men they attract and to whom many of them are attracted.

Some of Nugent's work is in print. "Smoke, Lilies and Jade," his groundbreaking contribution to *FIRE!!*, has been included in several recent Harlem Renaissance anthologies. Some of his images have recently been republished as well. But, because Nugent did not pursue a conventional career as a writer or artist, and because his work profoundly subverted sexual, racial, and religious norms, most of it was never published. What was published appeared in periodicals that are now available only in research libraries. This collection is intended to rectify that situation by gathering together his more important published work, selections from his unpublished manuscripts, and examples of his visual art.

EARLY WORK

This section presents some of Nugent's work from 1925–1932 and later, stylistically related material. Other work from this period—"Gentleman Jigger" excerpts, the Bible stories, the Salome Series drawings, and the poem "Shadow"—is presented in other sections. Much of Nugent's early artwork did not survive because he gave it away to friends and often lacked a permanent residence. His writing seems to have fared better; several early notebooks and manuscripts were in his estate. Even so, there is, for example, no extant sequel to "Smoke, Lilies and Jade," despite the fact that it concludes with "to be continued." Where no publication history is given, the piece in question is published here for the first time.

SAHDJI

"Sahdji," one of Richard Bruce Nugent's first published pieces, appeared in Alain Locke's seminal anthology, The New Negro, *in 1925. By including it, Locke established Nugent's legitimacy as a young writer.*

THAT one now . . . . that's a sketch of a little African girl . . . delightfully black . . . I made it while I was passing through East Africa . . . her name was Sahdji . . . wife of Konombju . . . chieftain . . . of only a small tribe . . . Warpuri was the area of his sovereign domain . . . but to get back to Sahdji . . . with her beautiful dark body . . . rosy black . . . graceful as the tongues of flame she loved to dance around . . . and pretty . . . small features . . . . large liquid eyes . . . over-full sensuous lips . . . she knew how to dance too . . . better than any. . . . .

Sahdji was proud . . . she was the favorite wife . . . as such she had privileges . . . she did love Konombju . . .

Mrabo . . . son of Konombju, loved Sahdji . . . his father . . . fifty-nine . . . . too old for her . . . fifty-nine and eighteen . . . he could wait . . . he loved his father . . . but . . . . maybe death . . . his father was getting old. . . . .

Numbo idolized Mrabo . . . Numbo was a young buck . . . . would do anything to make Mrabo happy. . . .

one day Sahdji felt restless . . . why . . . it was not unusual for Konombju to lead the hunt . . . even at his age . . . Sahdji jangled her bracelets . . . it was so still and warm . . . she'd wait at the door . . . . standing there . . . shifting . . . a blurred silhouette against the brown of the hut . . . she waited . . . waited . . .

maybe . . .

she saw the long steaming stream of natives in the distance . . . she looked for Konombju . . . what was that burden they carried . . . why were they so solemn . . . where was Konombju. . . .

the column reached her door . . . placed their burden at her feet . . . Konombju . . . . . an arrow in his back . . . just accident . . . *Goare go shuioa go elui ruri—* (when men die they depart for ever)—they hadn't seen him fall . . . hunting, one watches the hunt . . . a stray arrow . . . Konombju at her feet . . .

preparations for the funeral feast . . . the seven wives of Konombju went to the new chief's hut . . . Mrabo . . . one . . . two . . . three . . . he counted . . . no Sahdji . . . six . . . seven . . . no Sahdji . . .

the funeral procession filed past the door . . . and Mrabo . . . Mrabo went too . . . the drums beat their boom . . . boom . . . deep pulsing heart-quivering boom . . . and the reeds added their weird dirge . . . the procession moved on . . . on to Konombju's hut . . . boom . . . b-o-o-m. . . . .

there from the doorway stepped Sahdji . . . painted in the funeral red . . . the flames from the ground are already catching the branches . . . slowly to the funeral drums she swayed . . . danced . . . leading Konombju to his grave . . . her grave . . . their grave . . .

they laid the body in the funeral hut . . . *Goa shoa motho go sale motho—*(when a man dies a man remains)—Sahdji danced slowly . . . sadly . . . looked at Mrabo and smiled . . . slowly triumphantly . . . and to the wails of the wives . . . boom-boom of the drums . . . gave herself again to Konombju . . . the grass-strewn couch of Konombju. . . .

Mrabo stood unflinching . . . but Numbo, silly Numbo had made an old . . . old man of Mrabo.

Drawing, probably from the 1930s.

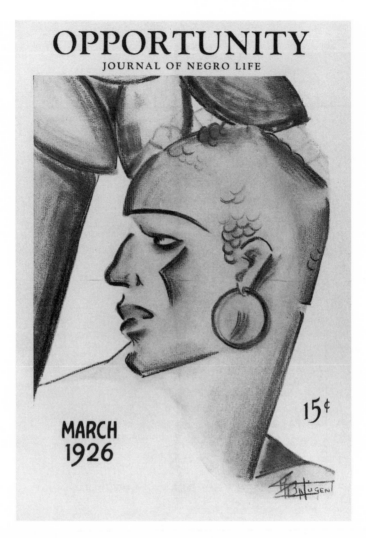

OPPORTUNITY

JOURNAL OF NEGRO LIFE

MARCH
1926

15¢

Nugent's March 1926 cover of *Opportunity* was a real coup for a nineteen year old who had been part of the scene in Harlem for only a few months. *Opportunity*, edited by Charles S. Johnson, was the magazine of the National Urban League. Masquerading as a palm tree, the large phallus on the left is surely one of the more audacious jokes ever to be perpetrated on the editors and readers of a mass-circulation magazine. And, is the young man really a denizen of the jungle, or is he perhaps a Harlemite in drag?

Drawings for Mulattoes—Number 1 (1927). The Drawings for Mulattoes series was included as a four-page spread in *Ebony and Topaz,* an important anthology edited by Charles S. Johnson and published by the Urban League. *The New Negro* and *Ebony and Topaz* were the two anthologies that helped define the Harlem Renaissance. Johnson used several other Nugent graphics to illustrate *Opportunity* articles in 1927 and 1928.

Drawings for Mulattoes—Number 2 (1927).

Drawings for Mulattoes—Number 3 (1927). This is Nugent's most widely reproduced image; it has been used as a cover design for several books in recent years.

Drawings for Mulattoes—Number 4 (1927).

Drawing (1948). This graphic of women dancing in silhouette is an extension of the style of *Drawings for Mulattoes*, although it was executed two decades later. The black images were once outlined in transparent blue dye, which gave the illusion of motion. Unfortunately, the blue has faded on the original.

Drawing (date unknown).

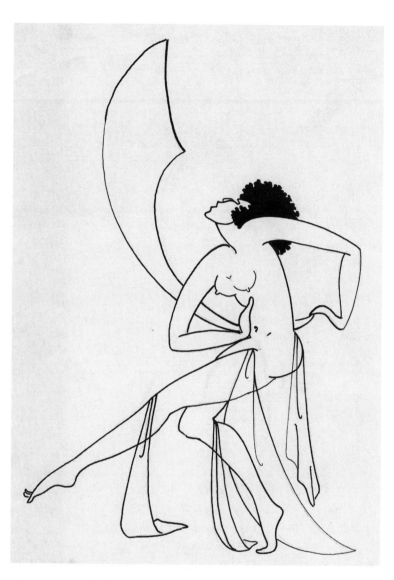

Drawing (date unknown).

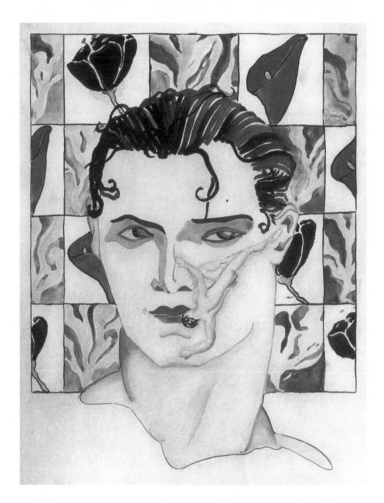

Smoke, Lilies and Jade (circa 1926). This image, which is in the collection of the Howard University Gallery of Art, was not published in *FIRE!!*, even though Nugent undoubtedly created it as an illustration for the story of the same title published there. It was donated to the institution by Alain Locke and included in the 1999–2001 touring exhibition *To Conserve a Legacy: American Art from Historically Black Colleges and Universities.*

SMOKE, LILIES AND JADE

"Smoke, Lilies and Jade" is Nugent's most important work. Published in the first and only issue of FIRE!! *in November 1926, its explicity homoerotic content was unprecedented and, together with stories by Zora Neale Hurston and Wallace Thurman, established* FIRE!! *as the younger generation's declaration of artistic independence from their Harlem Renaissance elders.*

He wanted to do something . . . to write or draw . . . or something . . . but it was so comfortable just to lie there on the bed . . . his shoes off . . . and think . . . think of everything . . . short disconnected thoughts . . . to wonder . . . to remember . . . to think and smoke . . . why wasn't he worried that he had no money . . . he *had* had five cents . . . but he had been hungry . . . he *was* hungry and still . . . all he wanted to do was . . . lie there comfortably smoking . . . think . . . wishing he were writing . . . or drawing . . . or something . . . something about the things he felt and thought . . . but what did he think . . . he remembered how his mother had awakened him one night . . . ages ago . . . six years ago . . . Alex . . . he had always wondered at the strangeness of it . . . she had seemed so . . . so . . . so just the same . . . Alex . . . I think your father is dead . . . and it hadn't seemed so strange . . . yet . . . one's mother didn't say that . . . didn't wake one at midnight every night to say . . . feel him . . . put your hand on his head . . . then whisper with a catch in her voice . . . I'm afraid . . . ssh don't wake Lam . . . yet it hadn't seemed as it should have seemed . . . even when he had felt his father's cool wet forehead . . . it hadn't been tragic . . . the light had been turned very low . . . and flickered . . . yet it hadn't been tragic . . . or weird . . . not at all as one should feel when one's father died . . . even his reply of . . . yes he is dead . . . had been commonplace . . . hadn't been dramatic . . . there had been no tears . . . no sobs . . . not even a sorrow . . . and yet he must have realized that one's father couldn't smile . . . or sing anymore . . . after he had died . . . everyone remembered his father's voice . . . it had been a lush voice . . . a promise . . . then that dressing together . . . his mother and himself . . . in the bathroom . . . why was the bathroom always the warmest room in the winter . . . as they had put on their clothes . . . his mother had been telling him what he must do . . . and cried softly . . . and that had made him cry too but you mustn't cry Alex . . . remember you have to be a little man now . . . and that was all . . . didn't other wives and sons cry more for their dead than that . . . anyway people never cried for beautiful sunsets . . . or music . . . and those were the things that hurt . . . the things to sympathize with . . . then out into the snow and dark of the morning . . . first to the undertaker's . . . no first to Uncle Frank's . . . why did Aunt Lula have to act like that . . . to ask again and again . . . but when did he die . . . when did he die . . . I just can't believe it . . . poor Minerva . . . then out into the snow and dark again . . . how had his mother expected him to know where to find the night bell at the undertaker's . . . he was the most sensible of them all though . . . all he had said was . . . what . . . Harry Francis . . . too bad . . . tell mamma I'll be there first thing in the morning . . . then down the deserted streets again . . . to grandmother's . . . it was growing light now . . . it must be terrible to die in daylight . . . grandpa had been sweeping the snow off the yard . . . he had been glad of that because . . . well he could tell him better than grandma . . . grandpa . . . father's dead . . . and he hadn't acted strange either . . . books lied . . . he had just looked at Alex a moment then continued sweeping . . . all he said was . . . what time did he die . . . she'll want to know . . . then passing through the lonesome street toward home . . . Mrs. Mamie Grant was closing a window and spied him . . . hallow Alex . . . an' how's your father this mornin' . . . dead . . . get out . . . tch tch tch an' I was just around there with a cup a' custard yesterday . . . Alex puffed contentedly on his cigarette . . . he was hungry and comfortable . . . and he had an ivory holder inlaid with red jade and green . . . funny how the smoke seemed to climb up that ray of sunlight . . . went up the slant just like imagination . . . was imagination blue . . . or was it because he had spent his last five cents and couldn't worry . . . anyway it was nice to lie there and wonder . . . and remember . . . why was he so different from other people . . . the only things he remembered of his father's funeral were the crowded church and the ride in the hack . . . so many people there in the church . . . and ladies with tears in their eyes . . . and on their cheeks . . . and some men too . . . why did people cry . . . vanity that was all . . . yet they weren't exactly hypocrites . . . but why . . . it had made him furious . . . all these people crying . . . it wasn't *their* father . . . and he wasn't crying . . . couldn't cry for sorrow although he had loved his father more than . . . than . . . it had made him so angry that tears had come to his eyes . . . and he had been ashamed of his mother . . . crying into a handkerchief . . . so ashamed that tears had run down his cheeks and he had frowned . . . and someone . . . a woman . . . had said . . . look at that poor little dear . . . Alex is just like his father . . . and the tears had run fast . . . because he *wasn't* like his father . . . he couldn't sing . . . he didn't want to sing . . . he didn't want to sing . . . Alex blew a cloud of smoke . . . blue smoke . . . when they had taken his father from the vault three weeks later . . . he had grown beautiful . . . his nose had become perfect and clear . . . his hair had turned jet black and glossy and silky . . . and his skin was a transparent green . . . like the sea only not so deep . . . and where it was drawn over the cheek bones a pale beautiful red appeared . . . like a blush . . . why hadn't his father looked like that always . . . but no . . . to have sung would have broken the wondrous repose of his lips and maybe that was his beauty . . . maybe it was wrong to think thoughts like these . . . but they were nice and pleasant and comfortable . . . when one was smoking a cigarette through an ivory holder . . . inlaid with red jade and green . . . .

he wondered why he couldn't find work . . . a job . . . when he had first come to New York he had . . . and he had only been fourteen then . . . was it because he was nineteen now that he felt so idle . . . and contented . . . or because he was an artist . . . but was he an artist . . . was one an artist until one became known . . . of course he was an artist . . . and strangely enough so were all his friends . . . he should be ashamed that he didn't work . . . but . . . was it five years in New York . . . or the fact that he was an artist . . . when his mother said she couldn't understand him . . . why did he vaguely pity her instead of being ashamed . . . he should be . . . his mother and all his relatives said so . . . his brother was three years younger than he and yet he had already been away from home a year . . . on the stage . . . making thirty-five dollars a week . . . had three suits and many clothes and was going to help mother . . . while he . . . Alex . . . was content to lay and smoke and meet friends at night . . . to argue and read Wilde . . . Freud . . . Boccacio and Schnitzler . . . to attend Gurdjieff meetings and know things . . . Why did they scoff at him for knowing such people as Carl . . . Mencken . . . Toomer . . . Hughes . . . Cullen . . . Wood . . . Cabell . . . oh the whole lot of them . . . was it because it seemed incongruous that he . . . who was so little known . . . should call by first names people they would like to know . . . were they jealous . . . no mothers aren't jealous of their sons . . . they are proud of them . . . why then . . . when these friends accepted and liked him . . . no matter how he dressed . . . why did mother ask . . . and you went looking like that . . . Langston was a fine fellow . . . he knew there was something in Alex . . . and so did Rene and Borgia . . . and Zora and Clement and Miguel . . . and . . . and . . . and all of them . . . if he went to see mother she would ask . . . how do you feel Alex with nothing in your pockets . . . I don't see how you can be satisfied . . . Really you're a mystery to me . . . and who you take after . . . I'm sure I don't know . . . none of my brothers were lazy and shiftless . . . I can never remember the time when they weren't sending money home and when your father was your age he was supporting a family . . . where you get your nerve I don't know . . . just because you've tried to write one or two little poems and stories that no one understands . . . you seem to think the world

owes you a living . . . you should see by now how much is thought of them . . .
you can't sell anything . . . and you won't do anything to make money . . . wake
up Alex . . . I don't know what will become of you . . . .

it was hard to believe in one's self after that . . . did Wilde's parents or Shelley's
or Goya's talk to them like that . . . but it was depressing to think in that vein . . .
Alex stretched and yawned . . . Max had died . . . Margaret had died . . . so had
Sonia . . . Cynthia . . . Juan-Jose and Harry . . . all people he had loved . . . loved
one by one and together . . . and all had died . . . he never loved a person long
before they died . . . in truth he was tragic . . . that was a lovely appellation . . .
The Tragic Genius . . . think . . . to go through life known as The Tragic Genius
. . . romantic . . . but it was more or less true . . . Alex turned over and blew
another cloud of smoke . . . was all life like that . . . smoke . . . blue smoke from
an ivory holder . . . he wished he were in New Bedford . . . New Bedford was a
nice place . . . snug little houses set complacently behind protecting lawns . . .
half-open windows showing prim interiors from behind waving cool curtains
. . . inviting . . . like precise courtesans winking from behind lace fans . . . and
trees . . . many trees . . . casting lacy patterns of shade on the sun-dipped sidewalks . . . small stores . . . naively proud of their pseudo grandeur . . . banks . . .
called institutions for saving . . . all naive . . . that was it . . . New Bedford was
naive . . . after the sophistication of New York it would fan one like a refreshing
breeze . . . and yet he had returned to New York . . . and sophistication . . . was
he sophisticated . . . no because he was seldom bored . . . seldom bored by anything . . . and weren't the sophisticated continually suffering from ennui . . . on
the contrary . . . he was amused . . . amused by the artificiality of naiveté and
sophistication alike . . . but maybe that in itself was the essence of sophistication or . . . was it cynicism . . . or were the two identical . . . he blew a cloud of
smoke . . . it was growing dark now . . . and the smoke no longer had a ladder
to climb . . . but soon the moon would rise and then he would clothe the silver
moon in blue smoke garments . . . truly smoke was like imagination . . . .

Alex sat up . . . pulled on his shoes and went out . . . it was a beautiful night
. . . and so large . . . the dusky blue hung like a curtain in an immense arched
doorway . . . fastened with silver tacks . . . to wander in the night was wonderful . . . myriads of inquisitive lights . . . curiously prying into the dark . . . and
fading unsatisfied . . . he passed a woman . . . she was not beautiful . . . and he
was sad because she did not weep that she would never be beautiful . . . was it
Wilde who had said . . . a cigarette is the most perfect pleasure because it leaves
one unsatisfied . . . the breeze gave to him a perfume stolen from some wandering lady of the evening . . . it pleased him . . . why was it that men wouldn't

use perfumes . . . they should . . . each and every one of them liked perfumes . . . the man who denied that was a liar . . . or a coward . . . but if ever he were to voice that thought . . . express it . . . he would be misunderstood . . . a fine feeling that . . . to be misunderstood . . . it made him feel tragic and great . . . but maybe it would be nicer to be understood . . . but no . . . no great artist is . . . then again neither were fools . . . they were strangely akin these two . . . Alex thought of a sketch he would make . . . a personality sketch of Fania . . . straight classic features tinted proud purple . . . sensuous fine lips . . . gilded for truth . . . eyes . . . half opened and lids colored mysterious green . . . hair black and straight . . . drawn sternly mocking back from the false puritanical forehead . . . maybe he would make Edith too . . . skin a blue . . . infinite like night . . . and eyes . . . slant and gray . . . very complacent like a cat's . . . Mona Lisa lips . . . red and seductive as . . . as pomegranate juice . . . in truth it was fine to be young and hungry and an artist . . . to blow blue smoke from an ivory holder . . . .

here was the cafeteria . . . it was almost as though it had journeyed to meet him . . . the night was so blue . . . how does blue feel . . . or red or gold or any other color . . . if colors could be heard he could paint most wondrous tunes . . . symphonious . . . think . . . the dulcet clear tone of a blue like night . . . of a red like pomegranate juice . . . like Edith's lips . . . of the fairy tones to be heard in a sunset . . . like rubies shaken in a crystal cup . . . of the symphony of Fania . . . and silver . . . and gold . . . he had heard the sound of gold . . . but they weren't the sounds he wanted to catch . . . no . . . they must be liquid . . . not so staccato but flowing variations of the same caliber . . . there was no one in the cafe as yet . . . he sat and waited . . . that was a clever idea he had had about color music . . . but after all he was a monstrous clever fellow . . . Jurgen had said that . . . funny how characters in books said the things one wanted to say . . . he would like to know Jurgen . . . how does one go about getting an introduction to a fiction character . . . go up to the brown cover of the book and knock gently . . . and say hello . . . then timidly . . . is Duke Jurgen there . . . or . . . no because if one entered the book in the beginning Jurgen would only be a pawnbroker . . . and one didn't enter a book in the center . . . but what foolishness . . . Alex lit a cigarette . . . but Cabell was a master to have written Jurgen . . . and an artist . . . and a poet . . . Alex blew a cloud of smoke . . . a few lines of one of Langston's poems came to describe Jurgen . . . . .

Somewhat like Ariel
Somewhat like Puck

Somewhat like a gutter boy
Who loves to play in muck.
Somewhat like Bacchus
Somewhat like Pan
And a way with women
Like a sailor man . . . .

Langston must have known Jurgen . . . suppose Jurgen had met Tonio Kroeger . . . what a vagrant thought . . . Kroeger . . . Kroeger . . . Kroeger . . . why
here was Rene . . . Alex had almost gone to sleep . . . Alex blew a cone of smoke
as he took Rene's hand . . . it was nice to have friends like Rene . . . so comfortable . . . Rene was speaking . . . Borgia joined them . . . and de Diego Padro
. . . their talk veered to . . . James Branch Cabell . . . beautiful . . . marvelous . . . Rene had an enchanting accent . . . said sank for thank and souse for
south . . . but they couldn't know Cabell's greatness . . . Alex searched the smoke
for expression . . . he . . . he . . . well he has created a fantasy mire . . . that's it
. . . from clear rich imagery . . . life and silver sands . . . that's nice . . . and silver
sands . . . imagine lilies growing in such a mire . . . when they close at night
their gilded underside would protect . . . but that's not it at all . . . his thoughts
just carried and mingled like . . . like odors . . . suggested but never definite . . .
Rene was leaving . . . they all were leaving . . . Alex sauntered slowly back . . .
the houses all looked sleepy . . . funny . . . made him feel like writing poetry
. . . and about death too . . . an elevated crashed by overhead scattering all his
thoughts with its noise . . . making them spread . . . in circles . . . then larger
circles . . . just like a splash in a calm pool . . . what had he been thinking . . .
of . . . a poem about death . . . but he no longer felt that urge . . . just walk and
think and wonder . . . think and remember and smoke . . . blow smoke that
mixed with his thoughts and the night . . . he would like to live in a large white
palace . . . to wear a long black cape . . . very full and lined with vermilion . . . to
have many cushions and to lie there among them . . . talking to his friends . . .
lie there in a yellow silk shirt and black velvet trousers . . . like music-review
artists talking and pouring strange liquors from curiously beautiful bottles . . .
bottles with long slender necks . . . he climbed the noisy stair of the odorous
tenement . . . smelled of fish . . . of stale fried fish and dirty milk bottles . . .
he rather liked it . . . he liked the acrid smell of horse manure too . . . strong
. . . thoughts . . . yes to lie back among strangely fashioned cushions and sip
eastern wines and talk . . . Alex threw himself on the bed . . . removed his shoes
. . . stretched and relaxed . . . yes and have music waft softly into the darkened

and incensed room . . . he blew a cloud of smoke . . . oh the joy of being an
artist and of blowing blue smoke through an ivory holder inlaid with red jade
and green . . .

the street was so long and narrow . . . so long and narrow . . . and blue . . . in the
distance it reached the stars . . . and if he walked long enough . . . far enough
. . . he could reach the stars too . . . the narrow blue was so empty . . . quiet . . .
Alex walked music . . . it was nice to walk in the blue after a party . . . Zora had
shone again . . . her stories . . . she always shone . . . and Monty was glad . . .
everyone was glad when Zora shone . . . he was glad he had gone to Monty's
party . . . Monty had a nice place in the village . . . nice lights . . . and friends
and wine . . . mother would be scandalized that he could think of going to a
party . . . without a copper to his name . . . but then mother had never been to
Monty's . . . and mother had never seen the street seem long and narrow and
blue . . . Alex walked music . . . the click of his heels kept time with a tune in his
mind . . . he glanced into a lighted cafe window . . . inside were people sipping
coffee . . . men . . . why did they sit there in the loud light . . . didn't they know
that outside the street . . . the narrow blue street met the stars . . . that if they
walked long enough . . . far enough . . . Alex walked and the click of his heels
sounded . . . and had an echo . . . sound being tossed back and forth . . . back
and forth . . . someone was approaching . . . and their echoes mingled . . . and
gave the sound of castanets . . . Alex liked the sound of the approaching man's
footsteps . . . he walked music also . . . he knew the beauty of the narrow blue
. . . Alex knew that by the way their echoes mingled . . . he wished he would
speak . . . but strangers don't speak at four o'clock in the morning . . . at least if
they did he couldn't imagine what would be said . . . maybe pardon me but are
you walking toward the stars . . . yes, sir, and if you walk long enough . . . then
may I walk with you . . . I want to reach the stars too . . . perdone me señor tiene
usted fósforo . . . Alex was glad he had been addressed in Spanish . . . to have
been asked for a match in English . . . or to have been addressed in English
at all . . . would have been blasphemy just then . . . Alex handed him a match
. . . he glanced at his companion apprehensively in the match glow . . . he was
afraid that his appearance would shatter the blue thoughts . . . and stars . . . ah
. . . his face was a perfect compliment to his voice . . . and the echo of their steps
mingled . . . they walked in silence . . . the castanets of their heels clicking accompaniment . . . the stranger inhaled deeply and with a nod of content and a
smile . . . blew a cloud of smoke . . . Alex felt like singing . . . the stranger knew

the magic of blue smoke also . . . they continued in silence . . . the castanets of their heels clicking rhythmically . . . Alex turned in his doorway . . . up the stairs and the stranger waited for him to light the room . . . no need for words . . . they had always known each other . . . .

as they undressed by the blue dawn . . . Alex knew he had never seen a more perfect being . . . his body was all symmetry and music . . . and Alex called him Beauty . . . long they lay . . . blowing smoke and exchanging thoughts . . . and Alex swallowed with difficulty . . . he felt a glow of tremor . . . and they talked and . . . slept . . .

Alex wondered more and more why he liked Adrian so . . . he liked many people . . . Wallie . . . Zora . . . Clement . . . Gloria . . . Langston . . . John . . . Gwenny . . . oh many people . . . and they were friends . . . but Beauty . . . it was different . . . once Alex had admired Beauty's strength . . . and Beauty's eyes had grown soft and he had said . . . I like you more than anyone Dulce . . . Adrian always called him Dulce . . . and Alex had become confused . . . was it that he was so susceptible to beauty that Alex liked Adrian so much . . . but no . . . he knew other people who were beautiful . . . Fania and Gloria . . . Monty and Bunny . . . but he was never confused before them . . . while Beauty . . . Beauty could make him believe in Buddha . . . or imps . . . and no one else could do that . . . that is no one but Melva . . . but then he was in love with Melva . . . and that explained that . . . he would like Beauty to know Melva . . . they were both so perfect . . . such compliments . . . yes he would like Beauty to know Melva because he loved them both . . . there . . . he had thought it . . . actually dared to think it . . . but Beauty must never know . . . Beauty couldn't understand . . . indeed Alex couldn't understand . . . and it pained him . . . almost physically . . . and tired his mind . . . Beauty . . . Beauty was in the air . . . the smoke . . . Beauty . . . Melva . . . Beauty . . . Melva . . . Alex slept . . . and dreamed . . . . .

he was in a field . . . a field of blue smoke and black poppies and red calla lilies . . . he was searching . . . on his hands and knees . . . searching . . . among black poppies and red calla lilies . . . he was searching and pushed aside poppy stems . . . and saw two strong white legs . . . dancer's legs . . . the contours pleased him . . . his eyes wandered . . . on past the muscular hocks to the firm white thighs . . . the rounded buttocks . . . then the lithe narrow waist . . . strong torso and broad deep chest . . . the heavy shoulders . . . the graceful muscled neck . . . squared chin and quizzical lips . . . Grecian nose with its temperamental nostrils . . . the brown eyes looking at him . . . like . . . Monty looked at Zora . . . his hair curly and black and all tousled . . . and it was Beauty . . . and Beauty smiled and looked at him and smiled . . . said . . . I'll wait Alex . . . and

Alex became confused and continued his search . . . on his hands and knees
. . . pushing aside poppy stems and lily stems . . . a poppy . . . a black poppy . . .
a lily . . . a red lily . . . and when he looked back he could no longer see Beauty
. . . Alex continued his search . . . through poppies . . . lilies . . . poppies and
red calla lilies . . . and suddenly he saw . . . two small feet olive-ivory . . . two
well-turned legs curving gracefully from slender ankles . . . and the contours
soothed him . . . he followed them . . . past the narrow rounded hips to the tiny
waist . . . the fragile firm breasts . . . the graceful slender throat . . . the soft
rounded chin . . . slightly parting lips and straight little nose with its slightly
flaring nostrils . . . the black eyes with lights in them . . . looking at him . . . the
forehead and straight cut black hair . . . and it was Melva . . . and she looked at
him and smiled and said . . . I'll wait Alex . . . and Alex became confused and
kissed her . . . became confused and continued his search . . . on his hands and
knees . . . pushed aside a poppy stem . . . a black-poppy stem . . . pushed aside
a lily stem . . . a red-lily stem . . . a poppy . . . a poppy . . . a lily . . . and suddenly
he stood erect . . . exultant . . . and in his hand he held . . . an ivory holder . . .
inlaid with red jade . . . and green . . . .

and Alex awoke . . . Beauty's hair tickled his nose . . . Beauty was smiling in
his sleep . . . half his face stained flush color by the sun . . . the other half in
shadow . . . blue shadow . . . his eyelashes casting cobwebby blue shadows on
his cheek . . . his lips were so beautiful . . . quizzical . . . Alex wondered why
he always thought of that passage from Wilde's Salome . . . when he looked at
Beauty's lips . . . I would kiss your lips . . . he *would* like to kiss Beauty's lips . . .
Alex flushed warm . . . with shame . . . or was it shame . . . he reached across
Beauty for a cigarette . . . Beauty's cheek felt cool to his arm . . . his hair felt soft
. . . Alex lay smoking . . . such a dream . . . red calla lilies . . . red calla lilies . . .
and . . . what could it all mean . . . did dreams have meanings . . . Fania said . . .
and black poppies . . . thousands . . . millions . . . Beauty stirred . . . Alex put out
his cigarette . . . closed his eyes . . . he mustn't see Beauty yet . . . speak to him
. . . his lips were too hot . . . dry . . . the palms of his hands too cool and moist
. . . through his half-closed eyes he could see Beauty . . . propped . . . cheek in
hand . . . on one elbow . . . looking at him . . . lips smiling quizzically . . . he
wished Beauty wouldn't look so hard . . . Alex was finding it difficult to breathe
. . . breathe normally . . . why *must* Beauty look so long . . . and smile *that* way . . .
his face seemed nearer . . . it was . . . Alex could feel Beauty's hair on his forehead . . . breathe normally . . . breathe normally . . . could feel Beauty's breath
on his nostrils and lips . . . and it was clean and faintly colored with tobacco . . .
breathe normally Alex . . . Beauty's lips were nearer . . . Alex closed his eyes

. . . how did one act . . . his pulse was hammering . . . from wrist to finger tip . . . wrist to finger tip . . . Beauty's lips touched his . . . his temples throbbed . . . throbbed . . . his pulse hammered from wrist to finger tip . . . Beauty's breath came short now . . . softly staccato . . . breathe normally Alex . . . you are asleep . . . Beauty's lips touched his . . . breathe normally . . . and pressed . . . pressed hard . . . cool . . . his body trembled . . . breathe normally Alex . . . Beauty's lips pressed cool . . . cool and hard . . . how much pressure does it take to waken one . . . Alex sighed . . . moved softly . . . how does one act . . . Beauty's hair barely touched him now . . . his breath was faint on . . . Alex's nostrils and lips . . . Alex stretched and opened his eyes . . . Beauty was looking at him . . . propped on one elbow . . . cheek in his palm . . . Beauty spoke . . . scratch my head please Dulce . . . Alex was breathing normally now . . . propped against the bed head . . . Beauty's head in his lap . . . Beauty spoke . . . I wonder why I like to look at some things Dulce . . . things like smoke and cats . . . and you . . . Alex's pulse no longer hammered from . . . wrist to finger tip . . . wrist to finger tip . . . the rose dusk had become blue night . . . and soon . . . soon they would go out into the blue . . . .

✹

the little church was crowded . . . warm . . . the rows of benches were brown and sticky . . . Harold was there . . . and Constance and Langston and Bruce and John . . . there was Mr. Robeson . . . how are you Paul . . . a young man was singing . . . Caver . . . Caver was a very self-assured young man . . . such a dream . . . poppies . . . black poppies . . . they were applauding . . . Constance and John were exchanging notes . . . the benches were sticky . . . a young lady was playing the piano . . . fair . . . and red calla lilies . . . who had ever heard of red calla lilies . . . they were applauding . . . a young man was playing the viola . . . what could it all mean . . . so many poppies . . . and Beauty looking at him like . . . like Monty looked at Zora . . . another young man was playing a violin . . . he was the first real artist to perform . . . he had a touch of soul . . . or was it only feeling . . . they were hard to differentiate on the violin . . . and Melva standing in the poppies and lilies . . . Mr. Phillips was singing . . . Mr. Phillips was billed as a basso . . . and he had kissed her . . . they were applauding . . . the first young man was singing again . . . Langston's spiritual . . . Fy-ah-fy-ah-Lawd . . . fy-ah's gonna burn ma soul . . . Beauty's hair was so black and curly . . . they were applauding . . . encore . . . Fy-ah Lawd had been a success . . . Langston bowed . . . Langston had written the words . . . Hall bowed . . . Hall had written the music . . . the young man was singing it again . . . Beauty's lips

had pressed hard . . . cool . . . cool . . . fy-ah Lawd . . . his breath had trembled
. . . fy-ah's gonna burn ma soul . . . they were all leaving . . . first to the roof
dance . . . fy-ah Lawd . . . there was Catherine . . . she was beautiful tonight . . .
she always was at night . . . Beauty's lips . . . fy-ah Lawd . . . hello Dot . . . why
don't you take a boat that sails . . . when are you leaving again . . . and there's
Estelle . . . everyone was there . . . fy-ah Lawd . . . Beauty's body had pressed
close . . . close . . . fy-ah's gonna burn my soul . . . let's leave . . . have to meet
some people at the New World . . . then to Augusta's party . . . Harold . . . John
. . . Bruce . . . Connie . . . Langston . . . ready . . . down one hundred thirty-
fifth street . . . fy-ah . . . meet these people and leave . . . fy-ah Lawd . . . now to
Augusta's party . . . fy-ah's gonna burn ma soul . . . they were at Augusta's . . .
Alex half lay . . . half sat on the floor . . . sipping a cocktail . . . such a dream
. . . red calla lilies . . . Alex left . . . down the narrow streets . . . fy-ah . . . up the
long noisy stairs . . . fy-ahs gonna bu'n ma soul . . . his head felt swollen . . .
expanding . . . contracting . . . expanding . . . contracting . . . he had never been
like this before . . . expanding . . . contracting . . . it was that . . . fy-ah . . . fy-ah
Lawd . . . and the cocktails . . . and Beauty . . . he felt two cool strong hands on
his shoulders . . . it was Beauty . . . lie down Dulce . . . Alex lay down . . . Beauty
. . . Alex stopped . . . no no . . . don't say it . . . Beauty mustn't know . . . Beauty
couldn't understand . . . are you going to lie down too Beauty . . . the light went
out expanding . . . contracting . . . he felt the bed sink as Beauty lay beside him
. . . his lips were dry . . . hot . . . the palms of his hands so moist and cool . . . Alex
partly closed his eyes . . . from beneath his lashes he could see Beauty's face
over his . . . nearer . . . nearer . . . Beauty's hair touched his forehead now . . .
he could feel his breath on his nostrils and lips . . . Beauty's breath came short
. . . breathe normally Beauty . . . breathe normally . . . Beauty's lips touched his
. . . pressed hard . . . cool . . . opened slightly . . . Alex opened his eyes . . . into
Beauty's . . . parted his lips . . . Dulce . . . Beauty's breath was hot and short . . .
Alex ran his hand through Beauty's hair . . . Beauty's lips pressed hard against
his teeth . . . Alex trembled . . . could feel Beauty's body . . . close against his
. . . hot . . . tense . . . white . . . and soft . . . soft . . . soft . . . .

&

they were at Forno's . . . everyone came to Forno's once . . . maybe only once
. . . but they came . . . see that big fat woman Beauty . . . Alex pointed to an
overly stout and bejeweled lady making her way through the maze of chairs . . .
that's Maria Guerrero . . . Beauty looked to see a lady guiding almost the whole
opera company to an immense table . . . really Dulce . . . for one who appre-

ciates beauty you do use the most abominable English . . . Alex lit a cigarette
. . . and that florid man with white hair . . . that's Carl . . . Beauty smiled . . .
The Blind Bow-Boy . . . he asked . . . Alex wondered . . . everything seemed so
. . . so just the same . . . here they were laughing and joking about people . . .
there's Rene . . . Rene this is my friend Adrian . . . after that night . . . and he
felt so unembarrassed . . . Rene and Adrian were talking . . . there was Lucrecia
Bori . . . she was bowing at their table . . . oh her cousin was with them . . . and
Peggy Joyce . . . everyone came to Forno's . . . Alex looked toward the door . . .
there was Melva . . . Alex beckoned . . . Melva this is Adrian . . . Beauty held
her hand . . . they talked . . . smoked . . . Alex loved Melva . . . in Forno's . . .
everyone came there sooner or later . . . maybe only once . . . but . . . .

❧

up . . . up . . . slow . . . jerk up . . . up . . . not fast . . . not glorious . . . but slow
. . . up . . . up into the sun . . . slow . . . sure like fate . . . poise on the brim . . .
the brim of life . . . two shining rails straight down . . . Melva's head was on his
shoulder . . . his arm was around her . . . poised . . . the down . . . gasping . . .
straight down . . . straight like sin . . . down . . . the curving shiny rail rushed up
to meet them . . . hit the bottom then . . . shoot up . . . fast . . . glorious . . . up
into the sun . . . Melva gasped . . . Alex's arm tightened . . . all goes up . . . then
down . . . straight like hell . . . all breath squeezed out of them . . . Melva's head
on his shoulder . . . up . . . up . . . Alex kissed her . . . down . . . they stepped
out of the car . . . walking music . . . now over to the Ferris Wheel . . . out and
up . . . Melva's hand was soft in his . . . out and up . . . over mortals . . . mortals
drinking nectar . . . five cents a glass . . . her cheek was soft on his . . . up . . . up
. . . till the world seemed small . . . tiny . . . the ocean seemed tiny and blue . . .
up . . . up and out . . . over the sun . . . the tiny red sun . . . Alex kissed her . . .
up . . . up . . . their tongues touched . . . up . . . seventh heaven . . . the sea had
swallowed the sun . . . up and out . . . her breath was perfumed . . . Alex kissed
her . . . drift down . . . soft . . . soft . . . the sun had left the sky flushed . . . drift
down . . . soft down . . . back to earth . . . visit the mortals sipping nectar at five
cents a glass . . . Melva's lips brushed his . . . then out among the mortals . . .
and the sun had left a flush on Melva's cheeks . . . they walked hand in hand
. . . and the moon came out . . . they walked in silence on the silver strip . . .
and the sea sang for them . . . they walked toward the moon . . . we'll hang our
hats on the crook of the moon Melva . . . softly on the silver strip . . . his hands
molded her features and her cheeks were soft and warm to his touch . . . where
is Adrian . . . Alex . . . Melva trod silver . . . Alex trod sand . . . Alex trod sand . . .

the sea *sang* for her . . . Beauty . . . her hand felt cold in his . . . Beauty . . . the
sea *dinned* . . . Beauty . . . he led the way to the train . . . and the train dinned
. . . Beauty . . . dinned . . . dinned . . . her cheek *had* been soft . . . Beauty . . .
Beauty . . . her breath *had* been perfumed . . . Beauty . . . Beauty . . . the sands
had been silver . . . Beauty . . . Beauty . . . they left the train . . . Melva walked
music . . . Melva said . . . don't make me blush again . . . and kissed him . . .
Alex stood on the steps after she left him . . . and the night was black . . . down
long streets to . . . Alex lit a cigarette . . . and his heels clicked . . . Beauty . . .
Melva . . . Beauty . . . Melva . . . and the smoke made the night blue . . .

Melva had said . . . don't make me blush again . . . and kissed him . . . and the
street had been blue . . . one *can* love two at the same time . . . Melva had kissed
him . . . one *can* . . . and the street had been blue . . . one *can* . . . and the room
was clouded with blue smoke . . . drifting vapors of smoke and thoughts . . .
Beauty's hair was so black . . . and soft . . . blue smoke from an ivory holder . . .
was that why he loved Beauty . . . one *can* . . . or because his body was beautiful
. . . and white and warm . . . or because his eyes . . . one *can* love . . . .

. . . To Be Continued . . .

NARCISSUS

"Narcissus" was originally published in Trend: A Quarterly of the Seven Arts, *a
very elegant little magazine embellished with tipped-in block prints and published in
New York by the Society of Teachers and Composers. The issue in which "Narcissus"
appeared included contributions from Michel Fokine, the dancer/choreographer, August W. Derleth, the writer, and Countee Cullen. Edward Perry was on the editorial
board of* Trend.

—And as he gazed there seemed to grow
The sound-soft beauty of pale Echo;
Petaled breasts began to show
On the image pictured below.

And the beauty of it pained him so,
The smile so double sexed and slow,
Faint fair breasts and pale torso,
Male into female seemed to flow,—

SCHEME

"Scheme" appeared in Dorothy West's "little magazine," Challenge, in 1936 under the pseudonym "Gary George." "Gary" and "George" were the maiden names of Nugent's grandmothers.

Ecurb Y. Drahcir is the name he told me. And the myths, of which the following is one, he spouts at the slightest provocation. A strangely strange-looking lad he was, and I met him at the Cafe Royal. Ecurb Y. Drahcir he said was his name. A literary device I'm sure, for he told me that I might repeat any of his tiny tales if I did so after his manner. I have tried.—Gary George

Truly there had never been a man who wanted to die so little as he. There was still so much of Life he had not known; so much of Life he had known. He loved Life with a tenacity that prevented for a great while the usual procedure of things as they should be. For Life and Death dovetailed with mathematical precision and intricate detail, and he quite upset their pretty design with his consistent refusal to collaborate like all other things which live and die. For he stubbornly held on to Life.

He loved Life. Loved Life with the passionate and also passive affection bred from habit. He knew Life too well and Death was new. He had played and wept and laughed and loved and hated. He had lived with Life. He had lived and was living, and Life he knew, so he clung tenaciously to all that was familiar. He held stubbornly to Life. And the scheme of things was upset by this selfish procedure.

Of course Life was flattered that such love should be so evident, but he was a worn-out man, and Life was through with him and had quite discarded him. But he would not be discarded, and Life was annoyed. And Death was piqued that abhorrence of Her should be made so manifest. After all, there were many who welcomed Death, and everyone accepted Her. Everyone save this one, who clung so fervently and with so little pride to Life. It was most insulting to Death and quite upset the pattern of things as they are.

So Life and Death plotted to outwit this puny thing, whose selfish whim and foolish affection disrupted so completely Their well-laid plans. And when for a moment the man slept, Death took him. Life sighed a small sigh of momentary regret, turned for diversion to the litter side of a black alley cat, tweaked the tails of the fourteen kittens, and felt quite proud of such fine work.

And Death put him aside till the moment when, after the worms and the elements had worked their tasks, Time could find a spare moment to give Her the finished product, wrought from dust returning to dust etc. And Death, marking in blue that this man was to be won over to love of Her, when she could find time, sighed in pleasant anticipation and swooped prankishly to take from the arms of a queen her first-born son.

So the worms worked their will and rejoiced in Life. A fisherman dug them up and speared them through and used them for bait. Death accepted them casually. When Time got around to it, He followed his usual procedure and dust was dust etc.

The man was dead. How long he was dead he never knew, but Death was sweet. A little strange at first, exotic, but after a while, when he had learned Her ways, he loved Her, became accustomed to Her, and all was well. For long lengths and a great while things were as they were. Then he was seized with a great queerness and knew that the dreaded moment was coming when he would have to leave Death, leave all with which he was familiar. He was afraid. It meant leaving all he knew and loved and was accustomed to. So he clung tenaciously to Death. And Death was flattered, but Death had tired of him, had become bored with his affection. Besides, he was upsetting the preconceived Plan of things as they should be, and that was annoying, for the Plan was orderly and largely the creation of Habit. And so she relinquished him, disposed of him.

And he liked not at all the manner in which he was disposed. For he was bewildered by the darkness and the organic smells and his close quarters, and twisted and turned and gave his mother great trouble at his Birth.

BASTARD SONG

This and the following poem express the angst underlying young Nugent's brave exterior. H. F., to whom this poem is dedicated, is probably Hank Fisher, who was a lover of Nugent's in the period around 1930.

For H. F.

Since I am neither truly one, nor really true the other,
Can you not see that I must be the third—the first two's brother?
For it is true I am not black and just as true not white,
But when the day gives sudden way, dusk stands 'tween it and night

And dusk is just as true a thing as either night or day
And if the dusk smells faint of musk, turn not its scent away—
Night perfumes dusk's pallor—day etiolates the night:
My love for you is love for you though neither black nor white.

Yes, it's love I offer you and hope that you will keep.
This love you see is true, from me;—but no—it is to weep,
For you—pale white—cannot trust love from whom you've loved too long
And yet deride with untaught pride—my love is far too strong
So what thing can I offer you? What gift is there to give?
Not even dreams, or so it seems—for you refuse to live.
So this I offer now to you is weak with right and wrong—
Half dark, half light, half black, half white—a truly Bastard Song.

WHO ASKS THIS THING?

I walk alone and lone must be
For I wear my love for all to see—
It matters not how close our hearts appear to be.
Since I tell my love in song for all to know—
It matters not how close our hearts may seem to grow—
Love must not be blind or small or slow,
But that I wear my heart for all to see
Means I am bound while he is, sadly, free.
He walks alone who walks in love with me.

GEISHA MAN *(excerpt)*

In Wallace Thurman's 1932 roman à clef about the Harlem Renaissance, Infants of
the Spring, *Richard Bruce Nugent is a major character—Paul Arbian (R.B.N.) by
name. The novel concludes with Paul's flamboyant suicide. He is found dead, wrists
slashed, in an overflowing bathtub with the pages of his novel,* Geisha Man, *strewn
across the floor. The flood had rendered the manuscript illegible.*

Infants of the Spring *is unfaithful to reality in only a few respects. One of these
is that Nugent did not, in fact, commit suicide but lived to the ripe old age of 80.*

The other is that the manuscript of Geisha Man *survived among Nugent's papers. Presented here is an excerpt from that manuscript.*

(Written in black ink on a silver ribbon)
Is it wrong to love bodies? Just bodies? To cover myself with the sight of bodies, like I clothe myself in magnolia scent? Bodies call. Often, a body passing in night mystery will pierce my vision with the poignancy of a gull's cry. Of course, a gull's cry leaves a void even as it fills. But why not play a wonderful song on bodies, like one plucks the strings of a zither? Music is beauty in tones, and a body is one tone. Oh, to make a searing chord! A searing chord of bodies garnered from the night. A chord of the beautiful sight and feel and smell of bodies.

I am a song; I would be sung on the tones of many bodies. On the graceful curve of that lad, his contours showing through his trousers as he sits on the bench, beauty rippling his sleeve as he moves his arm. On that man — on the calves of his leg and the warm movement of his thigh suggested beneath his clothing. Or on that man — on the flow of muscles and the play of light on his cheek and forehead. On the light powdering of gold that the sun and down paint on his wrists. On the silver of his veins.

I would sing — sing a short sharp song. . . . . But the song would be Beauty. I would be a virgin — a nun giving myself to God. *Ease, oh Pulcreado!* The song of Beauty sung through the streets of night, in the baths and on the bodies of men is too beautiful. It is a black flame welling forth to drown me.

I passed beneath a light. On the dusk-hidden benches youths sat in couples, arms around each other, oblivious to the snickers and innuendoes of passing couples of men and women. Courage. Or was it lack of shame? In the darkness I walked and felt tall, reaching the stars almost. But there was so much of night. Little circles of light pried into the secrets of the couples on benches. They were fearful little lights. Malicious cowardly lights.

Under one lamp I could see beautiful legs and hands. The young man was leaning against the post, bent forward slightly as though trying to glimpse his toe. His face was in shadow, but his hand was pregnant as he flicked the ash from his cigarette. He was a beautiful forgotten note about to be sung. As I approached, he tossed back his head. His face was pale and olive, hidden in smoke from his cigarette. And I remembered. As I passed, he smiled vaguely. A flame soothed my throat. I walked slowly toward a bench and sat. My knees trembled and my eyes felt dark. I sat and waited. Smoked and waited — waited with knees aquiver and eyes the color of opals. He sauntered easily over and sat. For a while we both sat. Silent. Then he changed his position. His knee touched mine. I felt a tremor start at the base of my throat, and I looked at him. We both looked at the same moment. We smiled. We had been surprised behind our look.

He lit a fresh cigarette and placed an arm behind me. Then he lit another from the first and placed it between my lips. He allowed his hand to caress its way from my lips over my chin to my throat. His touch painted greens with my emotions. Piercing greens. And blues—burning blues. And seas of vermilion. His air was of calm possession, of assurance. But at the same time, it was an air of helplessness.

He: You don't mind, do you?

Me: No.

He: You like it, don't you? My name is Don.

Me: Mine is Kondo—Kondo Gale.

Oh, Gale is a beautiful name, and my mother named me Gale.

Don: Kondo Gale—a lovely name. Gale is a beautiful name.

Silence wrapped around us like the coolness of four fathoms of green sea.

Don: Do you live near here? I'd love to kiss you—your throat and . . . ears.

Oh, the thought of him! Kissing *me*! Passion caught in my throat like a dry martini straight. I felt inadequate—naive—sitting there in silence.

Don: Wouldn't you like to have me kiss you . . . Gale?

Me: Maybe you would care to have a drink with me.

It sounded so unnecessary! I was spoiling it. I was covering moon silver with purple black.

Me: Yes. I would. More than anything, except . . . I once saw you on Broadway, under a light, just for a moment. I remember you. You—you are the rose.

I felt foolish even as I said it. The buses rumbled by so loudly. The lamps cut such sharp circles in the dark.

Don: The rose. The rose . But—

Me: If I could smell a rose, I might remember. Just . . . well. Just if I could. And you . . .

Don: So I'm a rose.

And his laugh was so warm, so tangible beside me.

Don: Gale, you are a queer person. By God, you are beautiful! I can *feel* your beauty like a . . . a . . .

Me: Shall we go? It's not far.

We walked off, out of soft black into hard circles of light and into soft black.

Oh, I wanted him always! Just to walk beside me. Just to look at and feel and want and smell.

Me: Pulcreado is a God to be proud of. He has redeemed his blue porcelain hoofs. I would like to weave a life around you, Don. "Don" is such a soft, beautiful sound. And the life would be beautiful. Colors—reds and whites and greens and mauves. All moving and merging like colors thrown on a screen by a color organ. A symphony of colors, and they would merge and make more colors. And on and on and . . . but I must be boring you. Don't mind what I say. I just talk and talk.

Don: Go on. Your words are strange . . . and beautiful. I like them.

Me: These colors would move as on a screen. Only . . . they would be like the sea. And I would cover myself with them and drown a million times. And the sea would be you. Only—well, I won't allow myself to drown in the sea of you. I'll just dream about it, because your face is too handsome and your body too perfect. I will only wet myself and allow the memory of you to perfume me.

Don gripped my arm.

Don: You say strange things, Gale. I can't understand them. But they sound nice. They make my muscles quiver. They make me want to kiss you. And hurt you . . . and myself.

Me: My thoughts are always strange, but I . . . well, I can't tell whether they are thoughts or emotions or . . .

We walked through sharp circles of light. As we walked out of a hard light, Don stopped me in the dark and kissed me. Kissed me with his arms around me. Then stood off and looked at me as though he wanted to speak. Just looked and swallowed visibly. Then kissed me again. Hungrily.

Me: Don't. Someone might come. And besides, we're nearly home.

Don: Go on, talk. Just talk. I love to hear you.

His face was serious and beautiful. Burn incense of orchids before Pulcreado! Let pale green smoke veil his haggard, handsome man's face and torso. And let the orchid scent be praised! Pulcreado has sent me a soonlove.

Me: This is where I live . . . Don.

We walked through the hallway, and as I put the key in the lock, he kissed me. I felt warm gooseflesh prickle my neck. Inside I sat him before the fireplace and laid out liqueurs and pajamas. He watched my every move.

Me: Don't hesitate to go to bed when you are sleepy. Here are pajamas, and the bedroom is there.

We changed into pajamas, and I sat on the lounge before the fireplace. Soon he came and sat beside me. Oh, the hot feel of him through the silk! Why can't one be *aware* of all of one's selves? I would have liked to live in the I that had Don near him forever. Only . . . I can remember legs so shapely that . . . Gale is a . . . I can't fill myself with Don. He can enter me and pour all of himself into me, but there will still be void. Although he fills more than . . . well . . . he and the rest will whirl 'round and 'round in the vortex of me, but only Gale can calm the whirlpool.

(Written in scarlet ink on silver paper)
The sunlight hung in the room like a mist—like the mist infused in moon-stones. His pale arm lay on me, and the faint perfume of warm breath fanned my cheek. I turned and looked at him. Don was so beautiful! So vital! Never before had I desired to see and touch and feel anyone so. To caress and protect. To play with and keep. I wanted to walk with him and shout, "He is mine!" To be him and yet be me, so I could see and feel him. *Ohutsuchi no-kami* my God is great and kind and cruel!

Don opened his eyes. For a moment they wandered over me. Then his hand caressed me as his eyes had. With a swift movement he leaped out of bed all alive with the sun and beauty. He stood before a mirror, and, raising his arms, pranced and posed, admiring his own perfection. Reveling in himself.

Then I knew. I could love him and go when I liked, because nature had provided him armor—defense mechanisms. His beauty was a song. A dream.

Sing a dream
Sing a dream
Sing a dream
Flame!

I am building a room around a stained glass window. If only I could live in my Shintos without knowing they had to be built. But I am greater than God. *I keep.*

As Don admired himself in the mirror and dressed, he would whisper a tune. Buttoning his shirt, he would stop before me and, bending over, brush me with his lips as he smiled slightly. And I could hear

Se ti puta cite mora
Si mi ri ni veti udo gia.

Va le me il che cadale
Celo more, more celo.

Then he would move away and glance at himself in the mirror. Then glance at me, smiling strangely, blow me a kiss, and hum the words again. They bothered me—they and that smile. So I asked him what they meant. He only smiled and hummed. Smiled at me in the mirror and hummed in English.

If I have kissed thee, what hast thou gained?
My soul is consumed with fire
Dance lightly, more gently and more gently still.

His shirt fit snugly his slender waist, and his trousers caressed his legs as he danced a step or two and laughed at my seriousness. His laughter and his movements were warm and tangible. The perfection of him and the words made me love him. As I dressed I could hear him humming still that haunting tune:

Va le mi il che cadale
Celo more, more celo.

But I am greater than God. *I keep.* I would build me a Shinto of smoke wherein to pray. But the wind caused by Pulcreado's flight might abolish it. Or the air currents made as I walk back and forth performing a sendōmairi might cause it to career and tremble and disappear in tiny blue, gray-gold clouds.

Oh sing me a song
On the slender strings of silver violins
On the beveled edge of a crystal cup
On the muted tremors of scarlet sins
On the perfumed smoke that spirals up
But sing me a song!

Don's face was so beautiful. His body so perfect. His face was beautiful because nearly every expression depended upon the angle of his eyelashes to his eyes. When he was drunk, his eyes became very wide and open, and he looked like a beautiful precocious child as he spouted his little conceits. That when he desired history, he read Rabelais. Or when he felt sentimental, he read Shakespeare. Or when tired, Wilde's trivial poetry. Or when he desired poetry, he read Wilde's *Salomé*. And he would look at me and smile and say, "Come sit near me, Gale. Your skin gives me pleasure, and I would have you kiss me . . . only I prefer to kiss you."

He would be beautiful and maudlin, and I would love him so much that my ears would become warm and my fingers cold and my throat filled. Oh, Don was perfection, but . . . Gale is a beautiful name. And I was but a vessel, and

Don could not *fill* me. There was too . . . too . . . Still, Don was perfection. His lips were firm and his muscles smooth. His eyes held perfumes and nights and silks from Lahore . . . black diamonds from Hindoostan . . . yellow cobras from India . . . obsidian masks from Malaya. His lips tasted slightly of tobacco and toothpaste. His cheek brushed mine. His breath crossed mine as I lay on the smooth firmness of his arm, against the hard whiteness of his chest. He had once admired my faint body odor of musk and damp orchids. Don was perfection.

(Written in mauve ink on canary paper shot with black and gold)
Don once took me to a party. All men. I sat there not knowing anyone and a little uncomfortable. Everyone talked about someone else whom everyone else knew. Drinks were passed. And more drinks. The men became amorous, and public caresses became more and more frequent. Hemsley was dancing nude in the front room. I looked for Don . . . and saw him sitting on a lounge in the other room, kissing a boy. The dance ended. Still more drinks—drinks with the pale green of cucumber floating beautifully through sparkling opal tints. Someone suggested that we go up on the roof. We trooped up the stairs onto the roof in pairs, laughing and talking. Only I was alone. Don was nowhere around. The view was all housetops and sunset and distance. And there, in one corner, was Don kissing a lad—a different lad.

It was the first time I had ever experienced that sort of shame. Downstairs again. I was being made a fool of. More drinks. The doorbell rang. I was being made a fool of. The newcomer was tall and large and loud. I wondered why he was there. He seemed so out of place. I became suddenly ashamed to be seen there. I abhor lack of refinement, and there was something a little crude in those men being so flagrant. I went over to the window and gazed down. Don was making me appear a fool. I felt cheapened just to be there.

A voice behind me spoke. It was the newcomer.

He: Lonesome?

Me: No.

He: Aren't you having a good time?

Me: Well . . . of course I am.

He: But all alone . . . I mean . . .

I felt myself blushing.

He: Well, I mean . . . ah . . . ah . . . what are you doing here? You know you don't like all . . .

Me: Oh it's all right, only . . .

He: My name is Adam.

Me: I'm Kondo.

Adam: Can I sit here and talk to you? The others are acting . . . well, just a little foolish.

Me: I'd be very glad if you did. No one else seems able to talk, and . . .

Adam: Kondo. That's not American, is it? I like it, though.

He sat on the lounge, and I sat beside him.

Adam: This sort of thing (he waved his hand) . . . does it amuse you?

Me: I don't know yet. I . . . I've never been to anything like this before.

Adam: I mean, just the mere pressing of lips. The mere rubbing of bodies. The tasting of bad breaths. All before the eyes of others. Does it seem . . . well, does it seem . . .

Me: No . . . not to me. They might say, "Why hide things?" And I agree. Only . . . why exhibit them? It's all right to let the world know a man cares for another man. It's all right to show the *world*. But . . . well, refinement. Maybe it's my mother, but . . . well . . .

Adam: I know. You object to its being public.

Me: No I don't. Only to the promiscuity. It's very possible for one person to care for more than one. But just to kiss because one can . . . I don't know . . .

Adam: But you're still a child, Kandy.

Me: *You* may kiss me. No one has ever given me a "nickname" before. And besides, you smile with your eyes.

Adam slipped a hand under my shirt and kissed me. Pressing hard with his lips and leaning on me. His tongue probing, searching between my lips, his eyes half closed. His breath was warm. His leg crossed over mine. He drew away slowly with a peculiar look in his eyes. I liked him. I was afraid that I had fallen in his estimation because he had kissed me. Yes, I liked him.

Adam: God, kid!

My face still tingled from the feel of his rough chin. I looked up. Behind him was Don, flaming with anger. Beautiful.

Don: Well, I'll be damned. What the hell is this?

Don was unsteady on his feet. I was embarrassed. I looked at Adam. Then, deliberately before Don, I kissed him full on the lips and whispered,

Me: Give me your card, please, and say nothing to Don. . . .

I rose with the card in my palm.

Me: Let us go, Don. And oh, pardon me. Don, this is Adam. Named for the first man. Good night, Adam.

Adam: Good night, Kandy.

(Written on opaque crimson paper in pale gray ink)
I sat beside Don, silent in the jouncing taxi, glancing at him from time to time.
Beautiful. I thought of a few lines of one of Cummings's poems

> nearer:breath of my breath:take not thy tingling
> limbs from me:make my pain their crazy meal
> letting thy tigers of smooth sweetness steal
> slowly in dumb blossoms of new mingling:
> deeper:blood of my blood:with upwardcringing
> swiftness plunge these leopards of white dream
> in the glad flesh of my fear:more neatly ream
> this pith of darkness:carve an evilfringing
> flower of madness on gritted lips . . .

Gale is a beautiful name. Don sulked in the corner and was beautiful. I kissed
him, smiling slightly. But he moved the straight firm softness of his lips away.
He allowed them to curl as though in scorn of my caresses and lowered his
eyebrows to shade the sulky smoldering dusk of his eyes. With beautiful movement of too-delicate hands, he made gestures of frustrated anger, crossing his
leg away from me with a petulant superbness of shape and suggestion. He was
beautiful. I whispered,

> Iitai guchi rayé
> Kao miriya kiyété
> Tokaku namidaga
> Saki ni deru

Don flushed. Coldly he turned to me.
Don: You have, I believe, a knowledge—a fair knowledge of English. And
also, I hope, a faint intimation as to what comprises politeness.
His face was white and hard; his lips scarcely darker. All color had fled his
features, all light his eyes, all expression his voice.
Me: (folly I wanted to utter)
Seeing his face, at once the All melted out of my thought (and somehow
the tears came first). Again Don flushed, and again he turned away. I took his
hand. We rode on, silently. Past swaying houses and lamps and fences and cats.
Over jolts, faster and more silently. All was a fascinating farrago of thoughts
and emotions and darkness and light. Don sat silent. I felt superior. I knew
exactly what to do, how to act.

Me: Parted from you, my beloved, I go alone to the pine field. There is dew of night on the leaves; there are also a few tears.

I looked at Don. He still sat motionless.

Me: Things never changed since the Time of the Gods—the flowing of waters, the Way of Love.

I smiled slightly. I was so sure of myself!

Then Don turned and, seeing the smile, struck me full in the face. A stinging, insulting blow. A shattering blow to my vanity. A parody, causing my emotions to slide into certain abysmal reaches of utter emptiness. My whole body instinctively contracted. I drew myself into a knot in a far corner of the cab and hid my face. I had no idea how to retaliate. I had no desire to strike Don. I felt no anger. I only curled there. I was seized with a fit of ague. I could attribute it to no cause. I did not fear Don, nor was I angry or belittled or really even insulted. I just curled up vaguely, trembling, watching Don from the corners of my eyes. He was beautiful. His profile was white and hard and chiseled, set with cold against the warmth of the lights and darkness that filed past in quick succession in the square of the window. He turned and looked at me, aloof and cold. What to do? He looked very steadily and long. His face flushed slightly. His lips trembled. He made a halting gesture with his hands. Then his lips set firm again, and with a slight lifting of his eyebrows, he turned to the window. We rode on. Past more lights and buses and fences and cars in the noisy night-silence. He turned toward me again, and regarded me with very strange eyes. Long. Long. He wet his lips, and ran slender, nervous fingers through his hair. Hesitatingly he laid a hand on me.

Don: Gale?

I tried to answer, but my voice had left, and my throat was filled with the same nervous quiver that held my body. He spoke again and very softly lifted my face. He eased an arm behind me, and I lay there against him trembling, inhaling his smell—warm tobacco and wool.

"Gale, Gale," he whispered over and over.

I was very happy and comfortable. But his whisper made me think of another man—a man who had struck me in the face with the hard palm and knuckles of his hand. A man who had left a taste of blood on my lips. A man who had never spoken to me since, and whom I had only seen once again.

Gale is a beautiful name: that expression had grown to be the remembering of the man. And my mother named me Gale. One couldn't think such thoughts. But my father was American. He left us before I was born. And my mother named me after him. Gale is a beautiful name.

Don was very kind and gentle to me from then on. But sometimes he would become jealous of someone I looked at or spoke to, and his emotions would assert themselves in various ways. I think I enjoyed his tempers. He was so contrite after all was over.

(Written in blue ink on gold paper worked with a spiderweb motif)
The room was filled with poppies. Silver poppies, large and small. Hundreds of silver poppies. A seamstress was sitting in a chair sewing silver poppies onto a silver base. She was making a costume. For me. Don and I were going to a masked ball, and I had designed a gown of silver poppies. There . . . it was finished. She rose to her feet and shook her skirt free from the bits of silver thread and stems and petals. With the sweep of a brush, she gathered the fragments from the shining black floor and with a curtsy left the room.

I could hardly wait. Not since I had been a geisha in Osaka had I felt the swirl of silks around me. I pulled on transparent silver hose. Slid into silver slippers with very high heels. The uncertain balance delighted me. With trembling fingers I donned the underdress of silver cloth that fit as tightly as my hose, slipping my arms through the straps and allowing the stream of flowers of varying sizes to cascade over my left shoulder. Then I stepped into the skirt and snapped it around my waist. It fell in heavy folds of blossoms to my ankles and trailed in a silver moon a yard behind me. I pirouetted back and forth before the mirror. Admiring myself. Prancing. La Maitresse de Pavots d'Argent.

Very carefully I sat on the couch to allay the trembling of my knees, spreading the gown around me, allowing it to trail along the floor. I lay back among the black and silver cushions and closed my eyes. I could see myself in the black-draped room, with its black floors and silver-relieved black furniture reflected in the two full-length mirrors. I smiled and was happy. If only I had been born a woman! To dress in flowing silks and silver and colors always, with a modish mannish look and gestures. With perfumes and lace. And attention. Maybe Gale would have loved me then. I dozed off into polyglot dreams and fancies.

The ball. We arrived late, and the dance floor was a single chaotic mass of color. Abbreviated ballet skirts of pink, blue, silver and white dancing with Arab sheiks in fantastic colors . . . Turks with bright ballooned trousers, curled pointed boots and turbans with sweeps of brilliant feathers and sparkling glass gems . . . pirates in frayed trousers, bloody shirts, headbands, earrings and tattoos . . . houri girls . . . fashion girls. . . . Apache Indian, Spanish, Dutch and Japanese girls. One man resplendent in the third-dynasty costume of a Chinese bandit king. Court dresses of Louis XIV . . . hula girls and boys . . . clowns and deaths and pirouettes . . . Indian temple dancers . . . evening gowns and the black and white of full dress. Boys dressed as girls and simpering sadly. Girls dressed as boys and bulging in places. Corked clowns and stage take-offs. A peacock gown with a train of iridescent green being broken if held and trampled if not. Flame kings and snow queens. Bathing beauties and Greek Gods. I recognized an Eastern prince as an Armenian acquaintance. Laughter, noise, petulance, brawls, perfumes; dust, dim lights, slippers, floors, arguments—perspiration. Trampled handkerchiefs, bits of costumes, swishing of silks, caress of fans, coquettish glances, bare knees, empty liqueur bottles . . . overturned glasses, wetted straws, cigar bands and cigars, jangle of bracelets. Pit-pit-p-p-pit of broken beads striking the floor, rolling and bouncing . . . then crack and crunch as they were ground under heels. Laughter and perfume and costumed greetings . . . heavy overtone of voices, clink of ice in glasses, blare of an orchestra and the scrape and thud of many feet.

It was intoxicating. Don was lost at once. And I was accosted by men. For a dance. May I see you home? All alone? Lonesome? Beautiful costume! Entering for the prize? Myriad remarks and stares, flattering in their very crudeness.

I was dancing with a handsome Turk. He was whispering little exciting breaths in my ear and surreptitiously kissing me. The feel of his muscles! His thighs darted into the folds of silver poppies, connecting with electric simplicity ever so often through the metallic flowers. The body feel of him! I was floating on music and sensuality.

"Kandy!" a voice called. I turned. Only Adam called me Kandy. And there he was. Big and white and blond. Dressed as a Viking. I floated toward him. I hadn't trod earth all evening. Adam and I. All around us was noise and weird, intoxicating beauty. We sat at a table near the dance floor, drinking—watching the ever-changing throng. Adam said many nice things. Don danced by with a Sappho. A clown and a courtesan. Everything just a little too intense, a little too foolish, a little too painted. A little too unreal. I turned to speak to Adam, and . . . a flame caught at my throat. Coming toward us was Gale.

He wore immaculate evening clothes. His face was set and determined. A black flame welled forth to drown me. He stopped at our table and looked down at me, one hand fidgeting nervously in his trouser pocket, the other flicking ashes from his cigarette. *Oh, Pulcreado!* Would he never speak? I could not take my eyes from him. His eyes were smoldering. Gray over gray like billows of smoke.

"Hello, Gale."

I wondered at the natural sound of my own voice. This, the man for whom I had created a God. This, the man whose face had remained an empty ache for a year. Whose voice I had remembered perfectly but vaguely—as one *knows* a tune without the power to recall it. Whose tense body beauty had beaten beaten beaten at my memory and dreams, as had the feel of his blow and the sarcasm of his voice and the curl of his hair and the muscles of his legs and . . .

"Hello," he answered, and his voice was still hard and sarcastic and beautiful. "May I disturb you? I'd like to. May I dance?"

His voice!

"Pardon me, Adam."

I was already walking off as he replied, "Certainly, Kandy."

We were dancing. Gale held me unnaturally. Painfully.

Gale: Kandy. So that's what you are called. I wondered.

He had thought of me, then.

Gale: But how did you know my name?

Me: From a card in the purse.

Gale: And you remembered it despite the . . . the . . . er . . . ah . . . many people you must have met.

Me: But I liked you.

Gale: Liked me . . . ?

He planted an awkward kiss on my eyebrow.

Gale: I must have . . . listen . . . Kandy . . . I can't talk well. Just this. I've been sorry . . . damn sorry . . . I haven't been able to forget you . . . even through Marseilles. Paris. Budapest. Vienna . . . Monte Carlo . . . Cairo . . . and the rest.

Poor Gale. But it was nice of him to pretend.

Gale: And . . . ah . . . Kandy, I want to prove how much I do care.

Me: Care?

Gale: I mean . . . Kandy, won't you come live with me?

He was very much embarrassed. Very drunk. I nodded and he guided me through the maze of kaleidoscopic dancers, into a car. It was all quite unreal. He evidently thought he must act a part and promptly began caressing, whispering, kissing. *Oh, Pulcreado!* Just the feel of him! Just the breath of him. Just the damp contact of his perspiring forehead with my cheek. Just the tingling scrape of his chin. *Pulcreado!* He was whispering an unconnected tale through which ran the words, "remember . . . love . . . marry . . . alone," punctuating it from time to time with hard kisses and unintended caresses with his knees. Oh, the firmness of him! He was saying it would serve her right if he married someone else. Married me. He was through with women. And he was intoxicated.

We drove long cool miles into the country. Across a ferry. Long cool miles of damp leaves and darkness. And I was two. My one instinct was proud—to scorn this pseudo-love visited on me in a moment of pique. My other instinct was to accept this gift, however false, with intense gratitude and profound humility—to accept this semblance of my strongest desire. For,

> I have seen the tense length of my mother's lover
> White with strain near the body of her child;
> Damp with passion beside ivory softness;
> Hot with desire to be cooled with soft coolings:
> Have felt hot breath breathe short on the soft lips of me;
> Felt taut muscles flinch at the feel of cool softness;
> Sensed damp, curly hair brush with tremors my forehead;
> Felt dry lips that fumbled in pained passion searching;
> Felt hard whiteness damp with thin-lipped desire
> For the soft satiation of the smooth cooling ivory
> Of the body of the child of my mother and her lover.

We stopped before a grand house set far back from the road. The moon made silver patterns on the lawn and gilded the rhododendrons. Gale helped me from the car. Somehow, I felt disappointed. I could not encompass my emotions in their entirety. We stood on the porch. Gale rang the bell. It echoed and re-echoed through the silence. The moon had painted my dress white—dazzling, unreal white. And my hands—all I could see was a pale, dreamy, yet transparent green. I must have been very weird and ghostly and beautiful—a pale green apparition in a dazzling white dress. A pale green, oval face punctuated with slant, gray eyes and mauve lips hemmed with blue-highlighted black hair. Tiny white slippers accentuating the blue shadows cast by my skirt.

Gale must have felt the weird beauty of me and the surroundings, because he urgently drew me into his arms and bit my lip. Once. Softly. Then again and again till I whimpered. He kissed the hurt tenderly. Again and again. His arm muscles contracted. His lips drew my breath from me. Then he bit my lips again. Harder. Harder. He was beautiful and strong and strange with moon and passion.

The door opened, and we were ushered in. But I was thinking of a night in Osaka . . . a night in Paris . . . a night in New York . . . and Gale. The tense whiteness of his leg muscles . . . the curl in his hair . . . his firm lips and narrow hips . . . his voice. I was thinking of moon and passion. But especially of moon. My head was filled with pale green and silver and blue. Filled with blue and the moon and fumes of gin. Fumes of gin and the feel of Gale. Moon making life dazzling white and transparent milky green. And blue. My head was filled with the long, soft ride through black and silver, filled with the smell and feel of Gale. Filled with remembrance of tense muscles and hair with curls. Gale's ring on my finger. His repetition of the statement that we were married "in the sight of man and God." All unbelievable and impossible. As impossible as the white and green and blue of the night. What could be more fitting than that my wedding gown be of silver poppies? Les pavots d'argent.

Past a sleepy butler into a foyer of marble and brass. Up many steps to an apartment above. This house was Gale's home. My home. And there came to my mind an old marriage song of ancient Athenai:

Oh gently, gently, ye silver horses
Stay your courses
For a little while.
Let darkness cover
The loved and lover,
And lamp warm shadows the maid beguile.

They will not hearken
The rain drops darken
The star-bright waters of the well-head clear.
No sound shall hasten their strict embraces
Their ardent faces
Shall find no fear.

With stingless arrows shall love possess them
His wings caress them,
That close they lie.
Oh fair the wedding,
And fine the bedding,
The Gods' own Eros will satisfy.

And we would enter a cart with gilded wheels drawn by two white mules. And singing and garlands and night . . .

Soft rugs strewed the floors—hard, plain floors. Dark, massive, roughly-carved tables and chests and chairs. A river-rock fireplace and walls covered with burlap and mahogany strips. Many tiny-paned windows. A ship's lantern and a heavy leather easy chair. Books. Gale had gone into another room, and I sat in the easy chair and picked up an open book from the stand beside me—a beautifully bound book. The *Kama Sutra* by Vatsyayana. I glanced at the opened page. Gale reading The *Kama Sutra*? I don't know why that surprised me, but . . . I glanced at the marked place. "Of the Auparishtaka" was the heading of the chapter. I glanced over the words and phrases, some of which forced themselves through the fog of poppies and moon and alcohol that whirled my head round and round. "Eunuchs" . . . "Some masquerade as women" . . . "Under the pretense of shampooing" . . . "Auparishtaka," or "converse by mouth." The eight steps of the process, numbered and named.

Suddenly the room ceased to revolve. Each board of the floor was horribly straight and correct, vanishing off in perfect and precise perspective. I noticed how mellow and silver the folds of my gown seemed against the floor and the chair. Gale must have been reading the *Kama Sutra* only just before he came to the ball. It made things all so clear and horrible and muddled. As clear and muddled as those straight and perfect boards vanishing off into perfect and precise perspective. As clear as . . .

Gale had entered the room and was standing behind me. He laid his hands on my shoulders and arms and, bending over, kissed my forehead. I lay my head back on the chair, the better to feel his lips—to feel the sandpaper of his chin as he lightly passed it over my closed eyes and forehead. He led me into the bedroom. Lying in bed, he watched me as I undressed. I unsnapped the skirt, and it fell in a pool around my feet. Then I removed my slippers . . . my stockings. I was very uncertain and undecided. What was expected of me? Gale lay there flat on his back, eyes closed and breathing heavily. What was I to do? Was I expected to make advances? *Should* I? The *Kama Sutra* whirled through my head with the memory of Gale in Osaka, entwining itself with the memory of that olive-brown lad I had encountered in Paris. I had given the lad money. Was this the way he had felt? Did he, too, have doubts as to what was expected of him?

My eyes were beginning to smart and fill with tears. It was too foolish. But I did so want to do the right thing. I did love Gale so! I switched off the light and crept into bed. Gale did not move. I was afraid to touch him. I wanted to feel him so! I wanted to please him. Keep him. *Oh, Pulcreado.* Please! I lay there rigid. What *was* I to do?

But this was the wrong way to approach things. I had never felt uncertain before. Was this loving Gale? This tumble jumble of desires and fears? If only I had not seen that opened *Kama Sutra*! If only Gale would move! Make *some* move. Was it just curiosity? I couldn't believe he loved me. Was it Auparishtaka? I would even practice Auparishtaka for him. Only . . . would he be satisfied? Or satiated and disgusted? Would he ever kiss me again? I lay there in the blackness. Hours and hours it seemed. *Pulcreado!* I made you God. Help me! Me—the Maker of God.

Suddenly I became aware that my every muscle ached from tension. I relaxed. Physically. Only the soft, even breathing of Gale answered. He was asleep. Or was he asleep? Was he just feigning to see what I would do? I turned over, straining very hard so as to make no movement on the bed. I raised my hand slowly. Slowly, slowly to touch his chest. Hours and hours it seemed. Then I felt him beneath my hand, warm and soft and hard. The steady rise and fall of him. *Was* he asleep? I kissed him. His lips were partly opened. I sank back from my strained position and lay with my head on his shoulder. Lay there wide-eyed and comfortable. Breathing the taste of his neck and cheek and hair. I slept.

How long I slept, I do not know. But I awoke feeling his hands caressing my body and face and hair. Feeling his lips on me. Feeling his breath. Feeling his body against me. I feigned sleep. I turned. For a while he lay very still, and then I could feel his hand, vainly attempting to be unfelt, caressing me again. I could feel his short, hot breath on my neck and hear his little whispered words. Maybe I had feared Auparishtaka for no cause. He placed a cool, hard-muscled leg over mine and drew me to him. Relentlessly. Strongly. Gently. Pulcreado is a great God!

For a long time afterwards we lay in each others arms, whispering and kissing.

(Written on rose taupe paper in crimson ink)
I awoke staring into small gold squares. There were small gold squares on the bed—and on Gale. Light streamed through the windows. Gale was asleep, breathing quietly, his hair in beautiful, damp curls. Just the feel that he was actually here beside me was enough. That I had but to reach out a hand a few inches to touch the curve of his neck! Had but to incline my head just ever so slightly to kiss the soft, damp curl from his forehead!

Gale was smiling in his sleep. It was all too impossible. I must reassure myself. I leaned toward him and tasted the warm breath from his parted lips. Press softly. Press. The tangible feel of his teeth under his lips! The pulsing of his chest just touching mine! *Oh, Pulcreado!*

The moon was a song
And the boy could sing
Sing a dream
Sing a dream
Sing a dream
Flame!

Gale stirred ever so slightly and turned his head. With a few incoherent whispers he put an arm fumblingly around me and settled back to sleep. It had happened. Gale is a beautiful name. I lay with the pleasant personal smell of his neck in my nostrils and the intimate tickle of his ear on my cheek . . .

Oh the moon was a gong
For the boy to ring
Sing a dream
Sing a dream
Sing a dream
Flame!

Softly I disengaged myself and got out of bed. There was a dressing robe flung over a chair near the bed. I put that on and went into the bathroom. Then, while the water was running, I wandered around the apartment to learn Gale's home. I was actually becoming maudlin about anything he had touched. I loved him so! I went into the bathroom and turned off the water. I stepped into the tub and allowed the steaming water to tingle me. Oh cover me with the waters of Gale!

It was so pleasant to lie there in warm water and think of Gale. Remember his little movements and gestures. The feel of him! His voice, the curl in his hair. His firm thin lips and his eyes that had become so warm and piercing and beautiful. They withheld something, though. One could not get behind them. But they were so beautiful.

And his white body—his beautiful white body with its soft sculptured curves of hard muscle! The flexing of muscles bringing them into sudden but expected prominence. The feel of his leg over mine, of his moist warm hands caressing my coolness. The taste of his breath and the damp intimate warmth of his forehead and eyelids and nose and neck and ears. The tingling roughness of his cheek and chin.

One should just lie passive and allow him to rub one's eyelids and cheeks and nose with his rough chin. Allow him to press the blood of one's lips into a crimson line against the teeth under the feel of his as he draws a sobbing breath from one. Allow his hands to grip one so forcibly as to hurt and make one wince into a proffering attitude, until his chest presses like a wall and his warmth measures itself and covers one's coolness. Allow oneself to feel the cording of hard muscles under a soft skin press against one until it hurts. One should allow oneself to be hurt by Gale.

Oh the warm feel of water!

Gale had slapped me long ago with his palm and knuckles and left only the taste of blood on my lips and the remembrance of his hair and his feel and his smell all mixed with hurt and pride and God. Oh, I've done well to fashion me a God! Pulcreado is a worthy God.

The water cooled. I stepped from the tub and dried myself before the mirror. Creator of a God! A powerful God.

Adam was so nice. But why should I think of Adam? He had been so astonished at something in the one kiss I had offered him. But so had Don and the olive brown lad and even the lad in need of money. So had Gale. How would he feel this morning?

Flowers on both hands—flowers of plum and cherry:
Which will be, I wonder, the flower to give me fruit.

I put on the silver stockings and absurd silver slippers. With the dressing gown wrapped around me and these silver-clad ankles and feet showing, I looked very strange. When I reached the bedroom, Gale still lay there, giving beauty to the lines of the covers. I went to the chifforobe and, standing on tiptoe, was able to see to comb my hair.

The *Kama Sutra*. Auparishtaka. Had I done right? Gale is a beautiful name.

I turned and tipped toward the bed. Gale's profile was a clean line of beauty in the sun. Just kiss his eyelids. For some reason my own eyes had become full of tears as I watched him, and a black flame caught my throat. I leaned forward and kissed him—lightly, so as not to awaken him.

Suddenly his eyes were open. They held several depths—each clouding and obscuring the next, softly but relentlessly shutting him off from me. I felt very silly under his gaze—silly and hurt. Then suddenly his eyes became warm and hard and held a smile as he reached a hand out and drew me to him. God, the feel of his lips! And nose. I could not open my eyes. I was afraid of what they held—or withheld. But I was happy.

We drew apart. After looking at me for a moment, he sprang from bed with a laugh—a laugh that warmed me and destroyed the depths in his eyes. Singing, he went into the bathroom. I could hear his voice above the water. I could hear his song become submerged and drown as he washed, then burst forth suddenly again in cheerful snatches.

At breakfast we kept up a lively chatter. After the coffee and a cigarette, he turned to me bewildered and asked what one did to secure fitting clothes for one's wife. So I explained that he should simply buy a plain dress, size sixteen, a chemise, step-ins, and shoes and stockings to match the dress. Then he left me.

(Written with cerulean blue ink on orange paper)
The many days of buying. Dressing. The charming things one could buy. And the dinners in large dining rooms, with Gale proud to exhibit me. I was always the most chic woman in the room. And Gale's friends. The amusing little incidents because I was Gale's wife. And the nights and mornings with Gale. He was very lovely to me, but frequently absent behind the clouded depths of his eyes.

At odd moments I wrote. I had a feeling of contentment that enabled me to take much time and many pains with my writing and painting. I had minor successes. I was the first Negro ever to have written a ballet. I lived in the feel of women's clothes—in the caress of silks and velvets and the feel of high-heeled shoes—and in the memories of Gale's moments of love. For as the months passed, Gale became more distant.

Every so often he would remember me and make a pretense of love, but . . . God made Gale normal and Gale was only decent. *Ohutsuch-no-kami* help me bear my resentment. I hated to kiss Gale and discover him in some little gesture of disgust or boredom. I resented even more his trying to hide his feelings—but oh, the memory of his muscled leg! I resented his inadvertent sigh as I kissed him and—but soft Pulcreado, the curl in his hair! The hastily hidden dislike and pity that crossed his face—*ease Pulcreado!* The memory of the warm smell of him, of the firm pressing of his lips! Pulcreado, Pulcreado—is there no way?

I wandered about the roof garden. New York lay pale and hard in the moonlight. Is there no way, Pulcreado? No way to keep the curl of his hair and the chiseling of his brow and nose, the warm personal feel of him pressed against me? The moon passed behind a cloud.

Ah, coward moon, to quit the shores of this exquisite hell, to quit this phallic city of silvers and blues and leave only the phalli of gray, of stone and steel and black—hard cold phalli dead and jeering against a happy sky! There must be some way. I would *make* Gale be nice. But could he ever I—? I would leave a photograph—the picture of a handsome American youth of sixteen or seventeen—where he could see its inscription, where he could read, "For Yetsin (Gale), to keep my place while I'm away." Then he could read the painfully-drawn Japanese character for love. I would hurt him—hurt him for standing in my life like a stone and steel phallus hard and gray against a happy sky. Because there is no moon to color his hardness with silvers and blues. *God, Pulcreado!* I would kill myself.

I went into the house and threw on a wrap. Out into the street. Down Fifth Avenue, never to go back. Always leave a dream unfinished! Past an open barouche and four taxis parked near the curb. A group of four young men— very delicate, very elegant, and very rouged. High unpleasant voices and . . . Because if ever one should finish a dream, one would be dead. Past Child's Restaurant and twelve young men—very delicate, very rouged, very elegant. Past two sailors. A man and a woman. A taxi creeping in the gutter. A lad in "knickers." A "lady" with too-red lips and too-tight hips. Strange how mortals find hidden truth without knowing it. One only needs to dream well. Only dreams are true. Life is the dream. How is it that no one has noticed that the existence one calls life never ends either? Past Harriman National Bank. Four young men with mincing gait and well-rouged lips and cheeks and voices. A police officer. A gentleman and a lady. A gentleman. A girl and boy with arms and bodies mingled. A Special Police officer. A fireplug. Schrafft's. Strange that no one has realized that if one completes *either* a dream or life, one will die. There is no sleep in this life. Past Huyler's Lunch and Grill. Seven laborers under an arc light. Three young men with shrill voices and gestures. A charwoman on her way to work. Forty-Second Street. The Public Library and two snobbish stone lions. A north-bound bus. Knox's hat store. Avedon. A bare-faced mansion. Ovington's, with a table in the window spread with snowy, lace-edged linen and laid for eight, with beautiful greenglass plates, water glasses, wine glasses, cocktail glasses, liqueur glasses and silver and candles and napkins. And then maybe death is only another existence in which one "lives" and "dreams" and confuses the two and decides that "death" is the sleep one was refused in that existence. Past two young men with too-nicely manicured hands and voices and features. Two inebriated men supporting between them a third, whose hat was lost and whose hair fell in a shock of yellow curls over his reddened face and swollen eyes. A policeman. A taxi. Two policemen. Thirty-Fourth street and the Waldorf with slatternly charwomen seen through the window, busily scrubbing the dining room floor. Gale was so beautiful.

Musk kisses
Beauty looked into his mirror at morning
And turned from her own shadow
To love the musk of his nakedness.

Gale is a beautiful name but . . . Past—past a man with a pale blue shirt. An ogling taxi driver. A worker dressed in white, cleaning brass. A night watchman. A sign reading "All Busses Stop Here." Metropolitan tower, the clock chiming eleven. A streetcar. Dreams are Shintos built of smoke and the coward moon, sinking, whispers a breath and destroys the prayer house and rears a city of stark gray phalli against a happy sky. Turn down Broadway. Past clothing firms and a Special Policeman. One light. Two lights. A curbstone. Many lights and many curbs. But to live with even a dream destroyed. And the damp curl had been so beautiful on his forehead! Stone and steel phalli. *Oh Pulcreado!* The world has died a million deaths. What matter that I die? Life is but a series of deaths. Gods die. Yes, Pulcreado, gods die. As they live, they die. Never dead, but always dying. And Life. Life is eternal only in its deaths. It dies a million times, and each minute brings a million deaths. Life is personal. As men see it one minute—even one tiny fraction of time—it never is again. And time—dying also. As men know it. And each bird and flower and ant and tree. Yes, even life dies and is eternal—dying. Do words—the invention of man—mean just the opposite? So what matter if the death I feel one minute be so painful and . . . and felt. A million deaths pass with a laugh. A caress. A whisper. Or a tear. A sob. An ache. I dance. And each step lives but briefly. And with each step *a part of me dies.* Gods die. Even gods. The Jews gave birth to a religion that died in its birth. But yet lives. On and on. For other men it lives. The only eternal thing is worship. Man must worship—the gods or this or that. And many deaths to each. Single deaths. Deaths abstract and concrete. *Oh Pulcreado!* Everlasting God. Created by the death of gods. Created by my death with gods. Created by my birth from deaths. Born of life born of death. Living eternally in dying, because in your life I learned the secret of death. *Oh Pulcreado*—golden God with silver wings and hoofs of frail blue porcelain! Help me to know the secret of life! Or is it death? Or life. Or death. Or both? Life or death or life and death or life or . . .

THE BIBLE STORIES

Written in the late twenties and early thirties, Nugent's Bible stories were unfortu-
nately not accessible to readers of that time. Four of the five stories for which manu-
scripts survive are included here. More were planned and may have been written, but
if so, they have been lost.

BEYOND WHERE THE STAR STOOD STILL

"Beyond Where the Star Stood Still" was first published in a very limited, privately
printed edition in 1945. Later, in 1970, the story appeared in Crisis *magazine, but*
attracted little notice. Warren Marr II, Nugent's brother-in-law, was editor of Crisis
at the time.

It was the birthday of the King of Ethiopia. For eleven years he had ruled over
the scattered tribes, and today he would be twenty. Everything was in readi-
ness. The tables had been laid on the roof of the palace; Samos glass and Egyptian gold shone in the brilliant evening sun and glowed under the canopy of
white and scarlet stuffs. The opal cups stood beside the crystal plate and cast
back the fires of the exotic fruit, so extravagant in color and form. The snow
was melting in the painted tubs and the wine vessels half-floated in the chilled
water. The flowers were beginning to wilt and turn brown where the petal edges
curled. The visitors and patricians and the members of the palace were warm,
and their white and blue robes showed gray where they clung damply to perspiring bodies. The peacock had lain beneath its blanket of iridescent plumage
until it had ceased to give off its warm steam of savory aroma, and the feathers
were beginning to cling, dejected and dull. The pasties were cold, the water was
warm, the guests were nervous, and still Caspar had not put in an appearance.

Nor could he be found anywhere. He was not in the baths, or in the palace,
or its gardens, or the city. And there was no speck on the desert as far as eye
could see.

The fowl was removed, and hungry eyes followed its brilliant passage as cul-
tured lips continued to smile and utter polite mouthings. The musicians ceased

to play, and no one noticed, for slaves were removing vessels of wine. Dancers came, danced, and left unseen. The red sun sank exhausted in the desert; the cold night was sudden and blue. The guests drew their cloaks around them and descended the ramps into the palace.

And here was set another feast, a continuation of the first. There were great cushions and tiny tables scattered around the large hall. There were snow-cooled wines and chilled fruits and cold meats and breads. And pipes. Dancers as black as ebony, from tribes said to eat human flesh, painted with white and blue and yellow, danced to the incessant throb of drums and gourds. Brown dancers in red skirts turned and spun as they circled the room to the tireless beat of drums pounded with fists. Turned and spun with their red skirts stiff on the air around them, until they looked like crimson plates, and one became dizzy with watching. Became dizzy with watching and leaned back against the pillars of black, smooth stone inlaid with colored clays, and wondered. For Caspar had not yet appeared.

Not since Isis had come to claim his hand-maiden, the beautiful Queen Nar-the-is, had a king of Ethiopia failed to observe the ritual feasts of the twenty-first year. That failure had portended great change: Egypt had been born to grow and become the world power it now was, taking to marry into its new and ruling house the ancient blood of Ethiopia, absorbing Ethiopia's culture and its knowledge. Now again, after centuries, a king had not appeared at the feast given for his entry into the third cycle of life.

Caspar sat in a small round room and gazed through the crystal ceiling. Around him sat the astronomers of his kingdom. For Caspar was as learned in the meaning of the stars as he was in the religion of Persia. And as he sat in the room with its conic walls and gazed up through the double crystal that was the ceiling, a mighty event was being staged in the heavens, focused by the magnifier.

Jupiter and Saturn were in the sign of the fish, and Mars had come to complete the trigon in Pisces. But then appeared the phenomenon. For, at the foot of Ophiuchus, between Saturn and Mars, appeared as a comet a new star—a star of great magnitude and like a comet in glory. It was great and white and shed a light in great and white fantailing. But unlike a comet, it stayed with calm and was fixed and rooted there, making white the blue September night.

And Caspar, who was versed in the books of Avesta, knew the star to be the signal of the birth of a new Messiah. Of the Magi surrounding him, one, Bar-Jesus, spoke in corroboration and said:

"It is so. The star doth tell of the birth of a new Messiah. And thou, Caspar, who doth believe, should take unto Him thy gift and welcome, as token of thy faith in Him."

Pacing many times the circular room, Caspar then did ponder through the double crystal the bright light of the star reflecting on his slender black length of limb and making focal his unwitting beauty. Then did he decide to take his offering—myrrh.

It was October when the caravan sighted Alexandria; the star was still before them. There Caspar turned his followers back and rested seventeen days. Then he set out alone on a great white camel across the sands, following still the great star whose blue light made white the cool night.

And there were long days of sleep on the sand in the shadows of hills. The journey following the star was difficult.

One day Caspar was awakened by a burning on his forefinger. It was the heat of the sun refracted through the clear emerald signet on his hand. And he opened his eyes to the brass day to see above him still the cool light of the star. And in the distance a speck was approaching. So Caspar prepared a meager meal of dates and oranges and nuts and honey. And two cool pots of water and two cool pots of wine, which he dug from their buried depth in the sand. For as the spot grew greater, he saw that it was one on such a camel as his, only golden like the sand.

As the stranger neared, Caspar saw that he was likewise resplendent in the garb of a king. His robe was of heavy, bright blue wool—heavy to keep off the heat. From beneath it showed a skirt of pale yellow stuff with a sheen. His sandals were jeweled with stones that gave off a blue light and the trappings on his camel were of blue leather, soft as cloth and woven with a golden thread. When the camel came to a stop in the shadow beside him and kneeled for its rider to dismount, Caspar saw that the man had regal features, flowing beard, and aristocratic carriage.

"Well come." The words came simply from Caspar's purple lips.

"Well come," answered the stranger, touching his turban and forehead with the back of his left hand. Caspar marveled at the whiteness of the stranger's beard, which made a flowing silver frame for his saffron face. And Caspar marveled at the beauty of his hands, so like brass in color, as they accepted the vessel of cooled water.

When they were seated, the stranger spoke. "I am Melchior, Shah of Persia, and I am weary. So I am grateful even more for thy welcome, for I know not how long my journey will be nor where it will end."

And Caspar answered, saying, "I am Caspar, King of Ethiopia. I also know not how far my journey will be, nor whither the star shall lead. For I seek the new Messiah, and the star is my light."

"Then it was fated that we meet, Caspar, for I likewise follow the star, even to the end of the earth, that I might pay homage to the Messiah whom it betokens."

They broke their fast and rested. When evening was blue in darkness and white with the star, Melchior gave to Caspar a bangle of silver to wear, and Caspar gave Melchior a golden chain. Then they rode out across the desert together, the black man and the brown, the gold camel and the white, all becoming bluer shadows in the blue of night.

It was as a December night became suddenly red dawn, and Caspar with Melchior was spreading rugs for sleep, that another met with them. He appeared suddenly around a hill of sand on a great black camel. And his robes were royal and red. The red of the dawn reflected crimson on the silver harness and lighted his pale tan face and pale gold hair. When he approached and greeted them, it was with simple majesty and formal courtesy. His blue eyes were pointed with sleep.

"Well come," spoke Caspar, and his voice was friendly.

"Well come," breathed Melchior, his bronze features remotely hospitable.

"Well come," answered the newcomer, and they sat upon the rugs and cooled their fevered throats. As they broke their fast, they spoke.

"The one of us is Caspar, King of Ethiopia. I am Melchior, Shah of Persia. Our way lies together."

"And I am Balthasar, King of Sheba," replied the newcomer, and he drew aside the garment at his throat that they might see the sign of his royal rank on the locket around his neck. The ruby signet lay vivid on the white of his chest, so much paler than his suntanned face and arms and throat. He hesitated as though uncertain, then spoke.

"There is before me yet a long journey—or perhaps a short one. I know not—"

Balthasar stopped speaking with a question in his voice. Melchior remained silent, and Caspar did likewise. Balthasar wet his lips with wine and spoke again, his deep voice doubtful. "I am troubled inly, and I am hesitant—"

Melchior remained yet silent. But Caspar's eager young voice burst forth, and he said, "We also know the star and live by its light, that we may likewise know the Messiah."

Melchior's hand lay brass on Caspar's ebon one to restrain him as his brown eyes appraised Balthasar. And Balthasar lay his pale tan hand in a pyramid on theirs, and gazing at the two with his clear, blue eyes, he said, "Then the way for the three of us is the same." And the three exchanged gifts, then slept in the bright sun air.

When they reached the end of the desert, they left their camels and bought Arab horses—a white, a black, and a gold. It was in such a way that they came upon Jerusalem.

The three great castles shone white in the wall. The travelers stopped before the first—Hippicus—towering one hundred and twenty feet above its base and built high on the hill above the City of David. Caspar touched the smooth white marble blocks and could not find where they were joined. Melchior marveled at the great ponderous mass; Balthasar believed it was carved of one great stone and polished as a jewel.

They paused before Phasaelus, with its tower of war, and came to Miriamne, named for the queen, Herod's wife, whom he loved and murdered.

Finally they came to Mount Zion and the palace of Herod, with its park walls forty-five feet high, from which, at even distances, rose towers. All this was shining marble. Here they were received with great pomp and ceremony.

Balthasar was shown to chambers with walls of jade and citron, floors of glass and silver, and stuffs of silk and metal. Melchior was taken to chambers of ebony and bronze, the floors of which were brass and marble, the ceiling carved of teak. And Caspar was shown to chambers of creamy marble veined with soft red, the floor being crystal held in formal design by silver bands, the ceiling being cedar wood, giving off a pleasant scent and set with mosaics of gods in beryl and lapis.

From his window Caspar could look out on gardens and formal parks and mazes made from blossoming shrubs, and he could see fountains and pools and porticoes with rare and colorful pillars made with semi-precious stones and rock. It was the sixth day of Thebeth.

In the morning they dressed for their audience with Herod. Caspar donned a sleeveless undergarment of palest yellow that fell to the ankles and was weighted with opals that, holding occasional reflections of his solid color, gave off purple lights. Over this was drawn a garment of faint cerulean blue, edged and bordered with crystal beads and made with great flowing sleeves. Over his head so that it fell to his shoulders and framed his face, a soft white scarf was held firmly with a cap of woven silver thread fitting close to his rounded skull. Around him as a cloak he held a great square of royal bright red. On one ankle he wore the silver gift of Melchior, and in his cap Balthasar's beryl signet.

Melchior (circa 1950).

Melchior donned pleated trousers that clasped at the ankles beneath his blue leather shoes. His great trousers hung like fabulous bags, and where the blue pleats broke at the ankle-fold, the gold lining could be seen. Around his waist was a broidered sash of deeper blue; its ends were weighted with polished brass signs of the heavens. Into his folds he tucked Balthasar's mosaic flask. His silken blouse of blue so pale as to seem white in the sun had great sleeves that were caught at the wrists with silk- and topaz-tasseled cords. His vest was night-blue wool and his turban built high and conic of transparent stuffs in every shade of blue, with a great soft fold of deeper blue and white edging its head-line and making his face seem more brass above his silver beard. And on his wrist he wore the golden chain that had been Caspar's.

Balthasar wore narrow orange trousers that disappeared in the green leather leg wrappings and soft leather stockings that emphasized the beauty of his muscular calves. Over this, and hanging halfway to his knees, he wore a yellow shirt tight across his massive chest and shoulders, the long tight sleeves of which had been twisted into creases and folds to the wrists. Around his waist was wound a sash of ruby red, and on the bosom of his shirt his ruby signet glowed. On his tanned hand was an onyx ring. A cloth of orange like his trousers hung to his shoulders over his head, held in place by a twisted green cloth worn as a circlet on his brow; the cloth was pierced by an agate pin.

Herod, wan and eaten by disease, received them in the lotus garden, lying on a sumptuous litter. There was an odor of degeneracy coloring his sallow sunken face which his excessive finery emphasized. At his right stood Carus, who was the most beautiful boy of his age. He was fourteen, and fabulously white, with long green eyes and carefully tangled auburn curls. His eyebrows had been shaved and others drawn with an up-slanting line of indigo. He was the favorite of Herod, loved above the murdered Alexander and Aristobulus and Miriamne.

Herod was crafty, for rabbis had spoken with him and said, "A King will rise from his children's children and the Son of David will be born." And Herod had heard of the reason for the Magi's journey. So he said to them as they feasted, "Well come."

"Well come," they replied.

And Herod flattered them with gifts and said, "When thou hast discovered the place of the new Messiah, thou wilt inform me that I likewise may do him homage."

And they were pleased and answered, "It shall be even so."

When they set upon their journey at dusk, the star still above them, they

Carus. This image was published in the privately printed
version of "Beyond Where the Star Stood Still" in 1945.

were stopped at the gate by Carus leading an ass laden with a great box made of the rich, red wood of Lebanon. Carus went straight to Caspar, whom he drew aside, and to whom he spoke, saying, "Thou wilt take me with thee, Caspar? For 'tis love for thee that hast loosed my tongue till I warn thee: do not return to Herod! He fears this new-born king and would discover him only to do him ill."

When Caspar did not speak, Carus continued. "But thou must take me with thee. For Herod will know I have warned thee, and my life will be of little value. And also, Caspar, thou must take me because it was sight of thee that caused me to forego the luxury that I know so I might warn thee and be with thee."

When Caspar still did not speak, Carus' childly lip quivered and his eyes were bright and moist as he lay a trembling, transparent hand on Caspar's firm black arm.

"I might even help thee know Him, Caspar. For today as I was passing through the upper city, I saw a woman and her child and heard a prophet stop them and ask, 'Thy child was circumcised today? And what is he called?' And the woman answered, 'Jesus.' Then did the prophet speak yet again, saying, 'Thy child is destined for the fall of many an Israel, for many will reject him, but also for the rising up again of many who will believe.' And I asked their whereabouts and was told they came here from Bethlehem. So thou seest, Caspar, thy star was right, and eight days before, on the seventeenth day of the Jewish month Chislen was this child born. And I give you these seventeen stones for his birthday." And Carus gave him a handful of garnets.

"See, Caspar, I have brought with me all of my wealth, for if thou dost not take me with thee, then must I turn from Herod and seek safety elsewhere. And I know not much of the world." And Carus was weeping.

Caspar drew Carus to himself as he would a babe and consoled him. And they set off for Bethlehem, where the star stood still.

THE NOW DISCORDANT SONG OF BELLS

Published posthumously in Wooster Review *in 1989.*

The room was long and spacious and made with three walls. The fourth side was open from wall to wall and ceiling to floor and looked out on the palace gardens. The sun shone fully in, picking out glittering points of mica in the polished granite floor. It was a chamber of great taste and luxury, with rugs and foreign skins strewn about the divans and lounging-platforms. The walls were paneled with mosaic pictures in brilliant though subdued colors and banded with alabaster, through which the light showed translucently. The ceiling and the furniture were ebony with ivory inlays. The urns and vessels were Grecian and simple.

Carus lay on a divan in the opening, full in the sun and fresh from his bath. His long, auburn curls were still damp and scented. On the low table at his side were many cups of different wines, from which he sipped tiny tastes. Cluttered among them were rings and necklaces and bangles. His slender white body stretched in its beauty with a sensuous luxury very much like that of the cat which lay against his hip. He idly scratched the dark brown head as he gazed out to the miniature temple Herod had built for him. It was a strangely Egyptian temple and depicted, in a border near its roof, hundreds of sinuous cats. It was a temple to Pasht.

"If thou wert dead, Sextabius, then might I enjoy the Egyptian ritual that so intrigues me."

Sextabius opened one bright blue eye and closed it slowly and stretched his paws in ecstasy before him, unsheathing his claws from their velvet cases in luxurious flux of tension and release.

"But thou payest me no heed, Sextabius." Carus affectionately smacked the smooth, soft flanks, and the skin crinkled in pleasure, causing nervous waves to part the pale dun fur.

"Thou art flagellist. See how thine ears flatten to thy skull in pleasure, and hear how contented is thy purr. Thou hast a strange beauty, Sextabius. It is no wonder I love thee. Thou art so sleek and slim, so dun and dark. Thou art near as strange with thy unembarrassed blue stare in thy dark face as I. And thou art vain. Look how thou art preening."

For the cat was on its feet, arching its back and yawning. Then it stalked the length of the youth to his armpit and sniffed disdainfully before casually curling itself in the soft hollow there.

"But thou dost not love me, Sextabius, else thou wouldst concern thyself greater with my desire. The temple is thine, and if thou dost not take care—"

Carus hesitated, and his long green eyes narrowed before they opened to his thought.

"Mayhap 'twould be the seemly thing—"

Carus reached to the cluttered table, annoying Sextabius, who, discomfited, sat and gazed his disapproval. And Carus found that for which he searched. It was a slender silver pin with a great pearl at the end of its three inches. Carus was seated upright now, and excitement had caused a glow on his cheeks and drawn his bright young lips into a smile—a smile most innocent and pleasant in contrast with the ancient inscrutability of his eyes. They were flecked with gold and black now and seemed to hold laughter deep behind them.

He picked a bit of candied tangerine from a box and held it out to Sextabius. His voice was pretty and caressing and filled with the teasing laughter of love as he spoke.

"Thou art as fond of my favorite sweet as I, Sextabius. But thou must beg for it. Prettily."

Sextabius blinked slowly before he would condescend to move. Then, slowly and graciously, he approached Carus's lap, and placing one careful foot after another on his thigh, stretched his flat head toward the sweet. As he grasped it with his pointed teeth, showing the graceful line of his throat, Carus, with a swift and silent movement, thrust the pin through where the fur was softest, and before the cat could twitch, had flung it away.

Sextabius was mad with pain and fright, and leapt high and blind in his frantic efforts to rid himself of this thing that pierced his throat and choked his breath. He rolled over again and again, clawing at the two ends of the pin with all four feet. But his efforts only tore more surely the wound in his throat and painted more deeply with blood his tawny underfur. Carus lay back in a fatigue of excitement and nibbled sweets as he watched with glowing eyes and soft curved lips. When the cat was quite dead and had ceased even to quiver, and was lying in a contorted pose with the pearl like an inlaid stud on his pale and blood-colored fur, Carus struck a gong. It was answered by a youthful slave, to whom he said, "Send my barber to me. And notify the priests. My cat has died."

His eyes were filled with tears, and his lips were tremulous, and he seemed childly. As the pitying slave was departing, Carus added, "But send me first the painter of friezes. Send me Bar Shem-El, that he may see the formal design Sextabius makes as he lies there."

The inside of the temple was painted a solemn blue and was lighted by the flickering flames from two brass bowls of fire. These were placed on either side of the blue marble altar that stood at the end directly opposite the entrance. It was a massive slab and highly polished, resting on the heads of four elongated replicas of cats. Towering over and behind the altar was a statue of Pasht, her woman's head as feline above the voluptuously carved breast as the feline half was feminine. There was a broad flight of seven shallow steps that reached the base on which the Goddess crouched. Between her paws was a space in which reposed an alabaster box. The statue of the goddess was itself greatly jeweled, having emeralds for eyes and draped with necklaces of great price. An attendant in flowing white robes entered and silently glided to the great sacrificial altar.

There were many cats about, their eyes phosphorescent in the gloom or opal in the light. The attendant threw a handful of powder into each of the brass bowls of flame, and they gave off a heavy and heady cloud of violet smoke that rose to the roof and hung as a veil below the lapis-inlaid beams. A muffled gong sounded. The ceremonies had begun.

In through the door and from the blue night outside proceeded a group of virgin youths in long, full skirts of transparent yellow. Their faces were painted into identical white-blue masks, and in the center of each forehead a jeweled signet glowed. They entered in pairs, and from their ankles and wrists came the sounds of the tiny silver bells that ornamented them. Each group of bells had a different tone, so that the shaking of an ankle would produce a sound that, combined with the shaking of a wrist, could make a harmony.

In pairs they came until they were twelve; they jingled with pleasant discord as they walked to group themselves in the festive crescent before the great altar. Then they were still. The priests arrived in their long robes of office. The robes were of dark blue and solemn. The three priests stood behind the altar, on the first step to the shrine itself. Facing the Goddess, they invoked in chant and monotone. Each pause was colored by the sounds of wrists and ankles chosen to create chords of fragile beauty.

The first invocation ended. There was a moment of silence, then the High Priest of the Temple entered. Carus's face was white and beautiful above his somber robe. His slender waist seemed yet more slender under its wide, dull-silver sash. Around his neck hung a fabulous necklace of sapphires and his transparent hands seemed fragile in their pale beauty as he fingered it, reciting prayers in occult numbers as he held each stone. His face was strange and flat and feline in its beauty, and the shaved expanse where his eyebrows had been lent his eyes the discomfiting, self-contained stare of a cat. His movements were solemn and silent.

He came to a halt before the altar. Behind him followed two youths with shaven brows and foreheads. One bore a brass cup and a knife, while the other carried a scroll of Egyptian characters and a cushion on which reposed a small covered form. They took their places, one on either side of the altar, facing each other. When all was silent, Carus lifted his childly voice and intoned. And the virgin lads accompanied him in a dance of formal groupings and attitudes to furnish the necessary hymn-tune with their bells.

Then, with beautiful gestures, Carus took from one of the youths a dove and from the other a knife, and he offered the dove for sacrifice to the tune of the dancers' bells and the intoning of the Egyptian characters. One youth caught the blood in a chalice; then Carus flung the dove into a corner. A lean black cat, crouching low to the cobalt floor, stole toward it and spat warning to a slick yellow one that disputed. But none paid them heed, for Carus had neared the Goddess and was slowly ascending the steps.

When he had reached the top step, he laid bare his tender chest and drew thereon an occult figure with a finger dipped in the blood from the chalice and likewise drew between the stone breasts before him a similar sign, intoning all the while. And the dancers danced their hymn of tuneful, chanting bells, becoming wilder and wilder in movement and sound, becoming faster and faster, stranger, but never losing the tune so amazingly created with their moving wrists and legs and arms. Then with great ceremony Carus placed the spiced and linen-wrapped form of Sextabius in the alabaster box between the Goddess's feet. The chant grew to a wail as the dancers and priest became sexual in their ceremonies; heavy breathing and pleasure gasps mingled sensually with the now-discordant song of bells.

It was dusk of the next evening, and Carus lay spent from the last night's excesses, flushed and beautiful with memory. He lay on the divan in the opening of his chambers. Then he saw the Magi for a moment as they entered through the gate. But mostly he saw Caspar.

The next morning, when they were ushered into their audience with Herod, Carus sat with him, his brow painted with indigo eyebrows. Herod lay xanthocroid and ancient, making Carus seem even more incredibly white and young.

Carus heard little of what was said between Herod and the Kings, for he was absorbing the exotic beauty of Caspar and was excited by his unconscious beauty and his blackness. Caspar's voice seemed soft and warm and black also as it fell on Carus's unaccustomed ears, binding them as his eyes were bound by Caspar's slender body. Of all this, Caspar was unaware. But Carus decided he would possess this rarity and could think of no way in which to do so.

When the wise men left through the Flamingo Gate that night, Carus joined them, carrying with him a wealth of jewels. Caspar listened to him and was not aware of the guile Carus practiced, and he took the child with them.

And so they came, the four of them, to Bethlehem and made their shelter beyond the town. Then, when Caspar, Melchior, and Balthasar were ready, Carus spoke and said, "Caspar, wilt thou allow me to offer my homage to thy Messiah also?"

And Caspar said, "No."

But Carus persisted, and flinging open the top of his cedar box to disclose to their view the magnificence therein, spoke, saying, "Hast thou a greater gift than these?"

Whereupon Melchior laid bare his gift, and Carus spoke, saying, "It is but gold."

But Caspar answered, saying, "It is Gold for the King."

And Carus asked again if he might accompany them, and Caspar answered still, "No."

Then Carus drew from around his neck the necklace of great value and, placing the many cords of sapphires with the wealth within the chest, asked, "And is this still no gift for a king?"

Whereupon Balthasar laid bare his gift, and Carus said, "It is but frankincense."

Whereupon did Caspar speak and say, "It is Incense for Divinity."

And Carus pleaded still to go, for he feared that Caspar might in some wise escape him, but Caspar answered yet again, "No."

Carus drew from his sash a flask of rare perfume, saying, "And is this not a fit offering to divinity?"

Whereupon Caspar laid bare his gift, and Carus said, "It is but myrrh."

Once more Caspar answered, saying, "It is the gift of Humanity."

Then did Carus know that he could not impress Caspar, for Caspar was even then unaware of Carus's guile. And Carus's childly lip trembled, and tears fell. Caspar watched him with gentle, immobile eyes, and Melchior watched with tender expression, and Balthasar looked with a strange smile playing on the corners of his beautiful thin lips. Then Melchior spoke, saying, "But these are a fitting gift."

And he smiled as Caspar consoled the youth with a caress. Then they went and laid their gifts before the Infant, and Carus waited beyond the town without fear, because he knew that Caspar would soon return. In the morning they started their return journey—Melchior and Balthasar going their separate ways, Caspar going with Carus to the south. And Caspar told Carus of God.

When they were lying in the cool of a shadow, and the desert was blazing about them, Carus spoke, "And this God of whom thou speaketh, Caspar? What is he?"

Caspar was lying full length on his back and Carus sat beside him. Caspar answered, "God is love."

And Carus, observing Caspar's slenderness, whispered, "Ah, true. Love is God."

Caspar turned his head to view the boy before saying, "Thou hast not heard me."

And Carus, desiring to see the full lips move more and reveal the great blunt teeth, argued, "But thou thyself hath said, 'Love is God.'"

And Caspar answered, "No, Carus. That God is love."

"And yet, Caspar, I can only understand that it is as I have said. If one is the other, is not the other the one?"

And Caspar answered, saying, "Thou art allowing thy words to use thee, Carus."

And Carus had desire to note the contrast his hand would offer on Caspar's ebony one, but, sitting still and childly, continued saying, "But only that thou mayest know, Caspar, that thou awakest God in me."

"I awaken God in thee?" Caspar raised himself to his elbow and gazed at the lad, for there was that in Carus's voice that he did not understand. He questioned, "Thou meanest, I awaken love?"

Carus concealed his excitement at the unconscious awakening in Caspar's voice, shown in Caspar's tone rather than in the question itself. And Carus replied as simply as before, "Is it not as thou art teaching me, Caspar?"

And Caspar answered, "Thou must not make little of my sayings, Carus, when I speak with seriousness to thee."

Carus was pleased with the look in Caspar's eye and the unknowing entreaty in his voice. For Carus had seen like signs before and did not know that Caspar was in truth a simple man. So he was bold beneath his childly innocence as he asked, "Is it light speech to say I love thee?"

And Caspar, in his earnest zeal, placed a hand over Carus's hand where it lay on the sand, and his speech was impetuous, "But see thou, Carus, the love of which thou speakest is an active thing, and that of which I teach thee is a name."

And Carus's pulse was faster beneath his still sincerity as he answered, "Then, if to me thou art love, is it correct that I think of thee as God?"

And Caspar answered quickly, "No, Carus."

To which Carus answered quickly also, "Yet thou hast told me God is love."

And Carus knew his guile was successful, for Caspar argued now. "When thou callest me God, because I am to thee love, thou art saying, love is God."

And Carus, secure in belief of his victory, said, "Then I am no good at learning."

Caspar gazed at him for a moment in silence, then spoke, saying, "But more than excellent at argumentation."

There was that in his voice that caused Carus to doubt. And he answered quickly, to keep the quiver of fear from his voice. "'Tis because, when thou art serious with me, I am reassured that thy concern may be love for me."

Caspar's voice was changed and slightly impatient as he answered. "But, Carus, thou knowest I love thee. As a brother. Nothing can alter that." He lay back again and turned on his side away from Carus, saying, "Not even thy childish coquetting."

Carus knew that he was unhappy in this first encounter, and he sat long, gazing out across the desert through tears that were not alone of disappointment.

Carus's fondness for Caspar became even love, and Carus knew he had never loved before. And when they were in Ethiopia, Carus stayed in the palace and was friend to Caspar and listened to his teachings and grew wise. And Carus grew into manhood and became gentle through his love — so gentle and wise in religious meaning that when he was twenty-one, Caspar decided to send him to Cyrene to be friend and teacher to Simon, who was cousin to Caspar, and who would someday rule Cyrene.

The day that Caspar told Carus of his plan was bright and hot. Caspar was lying full in the sun on the palace roof, his beautiful black body bare and a linen cloth of great whiteness thrown across his loins. Carus was seated under a canopy of red stuff and was tinted by its reflection. Caspar spoke.

"Thou art the world to me, Carus. And thou hast grown so in thy goodness —"

Carus twirled a vessel of wine around in the tub of snow-cold water. He was pleased, as always, when Caspar spoke in this intimate way with him, and the proximity of Caspar moved him now as it had nine years before.

"And thou, Caspar—thou knowest my regard for thee."

Caspar moved sensuously in the brilliant sun. "Thou hast grown so, Carus, that thy love for me is as I would have it."

Carus remained silent as Caspar continued. "And thou canst perform for me a great kindness if thou wilt."

And Carus merely answered, "Thou knowest I would do for thee anything."

Caspar raised one knee and stretched, and his unconscious beauty was poignant to Carus. He continued, saying, "But this is a pleasant thing I would ask thee. I have a cousin, Simon of Cyrene, and I think that thou art the one for his growth. For thou couldst teach him and his twin thy beauty and make great their souls. Thou wouldst always be with them, and their country is beautiful, and thou so lovest beauty that—"

Carus's breath caught in a sob. "Thou meanest, Caspar, that I must leave thee?"

And his voice was so despairing that Caspar looked to him, "But surely, Carus, if thou lovest me, thou wilt leave me."

But Carus was already descending the ramp into the palace. When he reached his chambers he allowed his tears to flow unashamed and his agitation to take form. He paced the floor as some animal whose quarters are unaccustomed and too small. He stopped before a mirror. It had been a gift from Caspar. Carus contemplated himself therein.

"Wherefore am I not comely to this man?" he questioned his reflection.

And the trembling lips in the beautiful face asked also the forlorn question, "Is not my beauty real? Are not these tears sprung from the very soul of my emotion?"

The reflection answered affirmatively even as it mouthed in silence his queries: "And in truth are not these tears sprung from the very emotion of my soul?"

He tore from himself his fine garment and stood before the beauty of his entirety—beauty such as had no parallel anywhere in the world—and he intoned, "Likewise am I not completely beautiful? Can he not know that my love is even yet greater?"

But the reflection offered no solace and showed him only how great was his despair. He felt he could not live, so intense was his sorrow. Then he decided.

Caspar was sitting in the garden near the Gate of the Fish when Carus came and stood before him. And Carus was dressed for travel. When Caspar would speak, Carus raised a hand to silence him, and spoke himself, saying,

"I leave thee, Caspar, to do thy bidding and thy wish. I pray thee speak nothing. I have learned too well thy teachings and shall work thy will wherever I go. But likewise I would have thee understand. Thou hast said, 'God is love.' Now that I leave thee, know thou this likewise. So also is Love God."

And Carus left as Caspar watched—watched and watched until Carus disappeared into the setting sun and tears.

SLENDER LENGTH OF BEAUTY

"Thou art fairer than I, Narcissus, and that is not fitting. Thou art a man, and I— I am a queen."

Narcissus rolled over on his back and shaded his eyes with an alabaster arm.

"Thou art not a queen, Sa-la-ma!"

"Then a princess. Daughter of daughters of queens."

Narcissus's teasing smile pulled the corners of his mouth gently down.

"Thou art not a princess, Sa-la-ma."

"Then I am—"

Narcissus interrupted with his voice as soft as violet night.

"Thou art Sa-la-ma."

"But truly," Salome ceased idly tracing the golden down on his loins, "'tis known to everyone that I am the princess Salome."

"Thou art woman. And thy name means perfect in thy tongue."

Narcissus looked at her until she became confused and said, "Thine eyes are beautiful, Narcissus. So soft and gray, with a slender line to paint the circle."

"And thine are as the blackest dawn, Sa-la-ma, and soft, as with dew."

"But while thine eyes are gray, Narcissus, and thy hair is golden like the midday sun—almost silver—thy lashes are as black as kohl."

"And thine, Sa-la-ma, are as long as thy love and cast a lacy, blue shadow to match the blue lights of thy hair."

Salome stretched her ivory leg out next to his white one.

"But see how rosy-white thou art, Narcissus, while I—I must use pale purple powders and—"

"Thy color is like the heart of the golden roses in thy father's garden, Sa-la-ma, and thou dost give forth as heady a perfume."

"Thou dost love me, Narcissus?"

"Even as thou lovest me, O perfect one."

Salome allowed the shepherd to kiss her rounded breast; she marveled at the cool softness of his mouth and was pleased with the pale pink of his lips upon her arm and throat.

"Are my lips as comely against thy skin, Narcissus, as thine are on mine?"

"Thy lips, Sa-la-ma, are like two rubies for color and like unto sun-warmed persimmons to my flesh."

Salome lay propped on one arm, weaving her dark hair with his pale curls as she spoke.

"But whence comest thou here? Who art thou, Narcissus, that thy beauty should tend my father's sheep?"

"I came here from Gaul and there from Greece. I am a slave of war. That thou knowest."

"But art thou perhaps a prince, Narcissus, in thine own land?"

Narcissus's voice was as far away as his eyes and smiled also in a like manner when he answered.

"I am a twin, Sa-la-ma. And there is a legend that as a twin, I am incomplete. Only together can we be one. And over all the world am I searching."

Salome was quick with jealousy.

"Is this twin a sister? And must thou find her that thou might, for reasons of state, wed her?"

"Art thou jealous, Sa-la-ma? But fear not. I love thee with too great a love to ever love another. No. My twin is a brother."

The lights in Salome's eyes almost laughed aloud as she spoke again.

"Has this twin half thy beauty? For I might find that I love him also."

"Thou lovest me too greatly, Sa-la-ma. Thy coquetry frets me not."

"But a princess may not love a slave."

"Thou art no princess, Sa-la-ma."

"And thou art no slave. But if thy brother hath not thy beauty, how wilt thou know when thou hast found him?"

Narcissus's voice was certain and beautiful when he answered, "I shall know."

"Hast thou ever seen him?"

"Never, Sa-la-ma."

"Has he a mark by which thou canst tell him?"

"I know of none."

"Knowest thou aught of this twin at all?"

Narcissus opened his eyes and looked up at her, and it was as if she were a tablet he sought to read. Then he kissed her.

"Lie here close beside me, Sa-la-ma, that I may feel thee near. And I will tell thee of my mother. I never knew her, but 'tis said she was possessed of a rare, fair beauty. She lived near here in a country of the south; she married and was happy. Her name was Eliza. Eliza-Beth. My father was called Zachariah. We were their only children. The first born was my brother, and the delivery was in the desert as my parents journeyed. And because it was too soon—seven months after conception—it was a miracle. And my father, who was dumb, spoke, and his words were: 'His name is John.' Then did they know that god had indeed singled them out to know the touch of His hand."

Narcissus was seeing far into the past and his eyes were bright with his seeing. His voice had grown tense and soft, and he continued.

"Then did my mother become separated from my father on the desert; my brother was but three months old. Nor had the swelling left my mother's belly. And a band with weapons did set upon her, and she did flee, carrying her son in her arms. Before her was a mountain; escape seemed impossible. So she sobbed to God, and the mountain did open to receive and hide them. There was I born in the cave at the appointed time."

Salome sighed and stirred. "And thy mother called thee Narcissus."

"I was not called." Narcissus turned his lips to her. "For I was sent, with a cousin, into Greece for safety. There we were captured, and I was sold a slave, and my master called me Narcissus—for a flower I resembled."

Salome sat up. "Thou must be very learned. How many tongues dost thou speak?"

"All, Sa-la-ma, since I know thee. For I speak love."

"Then thou wilt speak it when I return. For now I must leave thee, Narcissus. 'Tis the Tetrarch's birthday and I must appear at the feasts. But I shall return before the moon is high, and then thy lips—"

"My lips, Sa-la-ma, will speak a more intimate tongue—"

Salome rose from his arms as she interrupted him.

"But speak now of thyself and thy brother, for 'tis not yet quite dark, and I may stay for a moment longer."

"There is naught to say, Sa-la-ma. We are twins, so neither is complete without the other. Perhaps he feels the warmth of love for thee in his heart likewise—for 'tis said, 'that which pierceth the heart of one twin is felt in the heart of the other. And when one heart does cease to beat, the other does likewise.'"

Salome laughed with upward sound.

"But now thou art coquetting, Narcissus. I find it inconvenient to love a twin. I can imagine strange mishaps should this twin—"

"Then be thou gone, Sa-la-ma, for thy nearness doth cause me to tremble with desire for thee, and thy beauty inflames me."

Salome was happy as she gathered her cloak about her, and Narcissus's eyes were serious and gray, and his lips a slender straight line.

"Then regard thyself like thy namesake until I return, Narcissus. And save thy breath, that thou mayest lose it between my lips when I kiss thee."

And Salome was gone.

Salome stepped into the center of the green marble hall and leaned over a cool marble rail that arose there from the floor. She was as some fabled maid at some mythical well as she peered into the pit which the rail surrounded. A voice came up to her, but she could not hear the words. She looked about the floor for a pebble and, finding none, took from her ear a golden hoop and dropped it through the grating which covered the pit. She gazed below to make sure she had attracted the attention she sought. And the words rose distinct and clear to her.

"O Daughter of an adulteress, repent!"

Salome laughed, and her laughter sounded of the innocence and joy of a child as she answered, "'Tis Salome, granddaughter of the great Herod, daughter of daughters of priests and kings."

"Repent ye, sayeth the Lord." Iokanaan's eyes were gray and inspired and mad. But Salome was happy, and her voice was as clear as music-bells.

"Thy voice, O Prophet, is like that of a poet—like unto one I know well. But Herod may be born of the name Heroditus. And the blood of that poet from Persia may sound in me music that mayhap even thou cannot voice."

Iokanaan's eyes were gray and inspired and mad, and his lips were soft and coral. But his voice was as the snows from the hills that chilled the fruit for the feasts as he spoke.

"Repent ye, daughter of an adulteress, for the wrath of the Lord is mighty, and his fury everlasting. This, the house of thy fathers, is doomed."

"Thine eyes are like a lover's, prophet. And thy lips are near as beautiful. May a princess kiss thee, Iokanaan?"

"Thou art not a princess!"

Salome laughed at his answer, and her voice was hidden as she continued teasing him.

"So is it rumored, prophet. It has been said that I, the daughter of kings, am Sa-la-ma."

"And thou art as thine uncle's wife, thy mother, a temptress even more."

Impatience had not yet spread its fingers in Salome's mood, and she answered, "But thy voice is so vibrant, thine eyes so bright, thy lips so straight, oh prophet! Would thy lips be cool on me also?"

Salome drew away from the rail as she asked this flirtatious question. But Iokanaan was silent. Salome waited a moment, then spoke.

"Wouldst thou suffer a woman to kiss thee, Iokanaan?"

But Iokanaan was silent, and after a moment more, Salome continued on her way and reached her chambers. Her toilet for the night would be elaborate, for she was dancing for Herod Antipas.

She entered a small, sunken room, in the center of which was a dais raised two steps; on it was a couch. There she was first rubbed with lemon to make more white her skin, and as three slaves massaged her, others filled with water to the depth of twelve inches the sunken room. And into it was poured many vessels of perfumes and many boxes of spices. Then were brought in many great stones heated to a great heat, and these were laid on the floor in the water. And a heavy curtain was lowered over the doorway and Salome lay on her couch in the perfumed steam until breathing became difficult.

Then was she carried into another room, heated with many braziers of red coals. Here there was a pool of cool water on which floated the crushed petals of roses and lilies and ginger-flowers. Here beside the pool, she was rubbed with palm and other oils that would make a froth when mixed with water from heated vessels, and she was washed. This robe of froth she rinsed off by a plunge into the pool. Then was she briskly rubbed with linen and camel's-hair stuffs to bring a glow to her skin. Her hair she dried over a censer of coals on which cinnamon had been tossed. The lids of her eyes she carefully painted blue. Her lips and the nipples of her breasts she drew crimson with a paste made of cochineal and the oil from lotus-blooms. The nails on her fingers and toes were likewise made crimson with lacquer. Her lashes she weighted with gold paint smelling of the oil of oranges. Over her whole body she dusted pale purple powder. Into her hair she sifted gold and sparkling dust. From her ears were hung tiny silver bells, and on the first finger of each hand she wore a great ruby ring.

Then she draped around her waist a veil as red as blood, which fell in transparent folds around her feet. Next, she covered her breasts with a second veil—this one of brightest vermilion—which hung in a graceful line to the floor behind her and touched, in front, her ankles. Around her waist she drew a plaited silver cord. Next came a scarf of brilliant orange to clasp on the left shoulder and appear as a flowing sleeve over the right arm. Clasped with a beryl buckle on the right shoulder and draped a like sleeve to the left arm was stuff of lemon

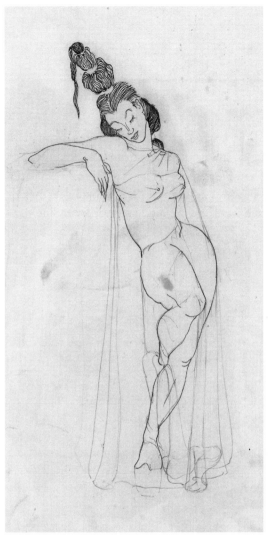

Drawing (date unknown).   Drawing (date unknown).

color. Over her shoulders she threw, like a cloak, a veil of palest yellow. Then, over her face, as was the custom among some peoples, she arranged a yash-mak of transparent cream tint, leaving only her eyes above it. Finally, over her head, so it fell to the floor all around her, she draped a vaporous scarf of whitest white, through which all the other scarves showed their separate and aggregate glamour. Salome was ready to dance.

The floor of the garden was paved with squares of onyx and crystal. Herod lay at a table at the apex; on his right hand was Vitellius, proctor of Rome, and on his left was an Asmonean priest. From where they feasted, at the very center of the crescent formed by the tables, they could see over the city to the sea. Every-one was drunken with revelry and wine and talking loudly. But Vitellius was curious. On every hand this night he had heard of Herod's captive prophet. So, though the dance by the Tetrarch's niece had been announced, he expressed a desire to see this Holy man. And Iokanaan had been brought to stand beside him. Tolmai leaned forward to whisper.

"'Tis said he is cousin to the poet, Jesus."

And Iokanaan spoke, saying, "Beware the wrath of God. For Jesus is His son."

Herod tried to quiet them, for he feared the speech of the prophet, but Iokanaan continued, saying, "For He is the King of Kings, come to deliver us from bondage."

And Tolmai spoke again. "'Tis this Jesus whom Pilate fears."

And Vitellius, remembering Tiberius, asked, "Why has not this pretender been put down?"

But before Herod could answer, Iokanaan spoke, saying, "Render unto Cae-sar that which is Caesar's. Jesus is the lamb of God."

A Pharisee spoke saying, "The man of Galilee is a mountebank."

But Tolmai answered, "He is but a poet. A teacher."

The Asmonean priest interrupted, "Yet one who some claim is a Holy Man, the King of Jews, a priest and a scribe. But there must be evil at his command and greater powers than even the astronomers or the learned men know—else how can he read without ever learning? He speaks all the languages heard."

And Tolmai agreed, saying, "My son Nathaniel sayeth that the poet speak-eth Greek and Latin and Hebrew and Persian. Yet he is but a carpenter from Nazareth, that lowly city on a hill."

With his Roman hand, Vitellius waved this controversy aside, saying, "But I wish to be amused. Prophesy for me, holy man!"

And Iokanaan spoke, saying, "The thong shall break, and the bundle of rods

Drawing, Salome Dancing before Herod (date unknown).

scatter, and the hatchet turn upon itself, that the Kingdom of God be everywhere."

Next, addressing Herod, he continued, "Thou art iniquitous, but thou lovest me, so mercy shall be eventually thine. Thy house shall perish, and in nine years thou thyself shalt die. Thy brother's wife, with whom thou art an adulterer, shall live in sin and die in pain. Thy daughter, thy niece, shall kill the thing she loves, and also shall this Salome—"

There was a crash of cymbals, and from behind a blue drape Salome appeared. The flute and the drum played a slow song as she glided to the center of the floor. Another crash of the cymbals, and she threw away her thin, white veil, and it fell, scented with spikenard, into Vitellius's lap. Again she sensuously glided around the crescent of tables, her eyes black and highlighted as she shed her creamy yashmak, and it floated to the feet of the Asmonean priest. Now the drum beat with a languid fury, but the priest was seeing her dance through the perfume of her body and myrrh, for he had buried his face in the delicate veil. Her pale yellow cloak she threw to the Pharisee, that he might smell the heady scent of tube-roses. The lemon-yellow sleeve scented with spices fell to Tolmai. The music became more ecstatic, her movements more acrobatic and sexual, as though she were at once a contortionist and a courtesan. Into the group of Sadducees she threw her scented orange scarf. Into Herod's rapt and incestuous face she tossed the vermilion stuff that covered her breasts. Then, through the red glow cast by the moon, she saw Narcissus standing there.

Her breasts hardened. Her lips grew soft, and her hips more seductively sexual as she twirled into a final passion-spasm and threw to the prophet the blood-red veil. It was scented with lotus.

The Tetrarch, with quickened breath, promised her her any desire. But Salome stood shamed and still, for now she recognized Iokanaan. And, turning to hide her nakedness and fleeing the banquet hall, she answered over her trembling shoulder, "My mother will ask my reward."

And the voice of Herodias followed her faintly, saying, "Give me the head of Iokanaan."

The moon was still red, and Salome was still warm with shame as she ran through her father's garden to meet her lover, the shepherd. The moon tinted the white tunic she clasped about her and caused lights to flash from the twin rubies on her fingers. Her hair and lashes still glittered with gold.

And she came upon him there, lying silent on the hill. She tipped nearer to him, keeping her head still and straight so the bells in her ears were silent. He was so beautiful as he slept, the backs of his white legs flushed rose by the strange moon. His cheek was a like soft color. And she could see his lids closed lightly and imagined the magic that the red moon would work with his gray eyes. He lay with one hand under his face, and there, crushed by his cheek, was the lotus flower in his relaxed hand. She kissed lightly the hollow behind his knee, then stood away and spoke.

"Am I not beautiful, Narcissus?"

When that did not awaken him—

"But not near as beautiful as thou." She sat beside him. "I am so hungered for thee, Narcissus, that thy beauty haunts me and I see thee everywhere." She was running soft fingers through his silvery hair. "And in sleep thou art beauty also. My father's feast boasted none such. Yet my love for thee so haunts me that I saw thee standing lover-like and lovely there."

She lay beside him and, gently, so as not to awaken him, drew his arm over her, and softly threw a leg over his and pressed close. But softly.

"Ah, Narcissus! Thy face and form are such great beauty they ache in me, and I burst with love for thee. See! 'Tis even I, Salome, thy Sa-la-ma, who courts thee as I would have thee court me. That I might wake and find thy beauty unexpected near, even as I am now to thee. Even as I feel thy lips soft on mine, drawing through pleasure from me my breath. Even as I am about to do with thee.

"But look! Wouldst thou tremble so from the very desire that thy lips would soon find mine? 'Tis the way with me. Now thou feelest through thy dreams, my breath upon thy cheeks. Thy lips are so beautiful, Narcissus; it is a pity I cannot kiss them and see them together."

The bells in her ears tinkled as she kissed him. But Narcissus was dead.

TREE WITH KERIOTH-FRUIT

"But didst thou ever see such beauty? 'Tis a sad beauty, and like to be that borne by a nebulous god." John was lying on the sand and luxuriating in the sun. Simon beside him was comparing with his artist's eyes the gold of John's hair with the brown of his own.

"And thou, John? Hast thou not seen thine own beauty? Or is it that thou art so enamored of the Baptist's word that thou seekest proof?"

"But such pleasant proof, Simon. The stranger has a poet's eyes and a pathetic beauty at the nape of his neck—'tis like a child's, or a poet's."

"They are much the same—"

"And poets are prophets—"

"And—" Simon mocked, "prophets are of God."

John was putting on his robe. "But true, Simon. Thou didst see the way in which the Baptist did look on him. Come, Simon! Perhaps he will pass by again. Perhaps he will speak."

"One would think thou wert enamored of this stranger. He is not patrician— that one can see that by his garb and his humble gait."

They were nearing their meeting place with the Baptist now, and John answered, "Thou knowest, Simon, that I have never indulged in the Greek refinement. 'Tis not according to the laws of Moses, nor truly to my desire. But the stranger does fascinate me. I am sure he speaks a poet's tongue."

"Perhaps the Baptist can find him the Son of God, and prove to skeptics that Jehovah—"

John lay a hand on his arm. "Softly! There is the Baptist."

Iokanaan, the Baptist, was sitting with Andrew beside the shallow river. As they approached to speak, the golden John touched Simon. "Look! Here he comes by again—the stranger."

Iokanaan had also seen him, and he had repeated as he passed his reference of the day before: "Behold, the Lamb of God—who taketh away the sins of the people!"

The poet passed by and continued on his way. The Baptist looked after him, then spoke to John and bade him follow. So John—John and Andrew—they followed. John with a pleasant tremor vibrating his young knees and excitement painting his face with even greater beauty.

The poet felt them behind him and turned. All of his breath gasped from him, for never had he seen such beauty as was John's—such abstract yet personal beauty. It excited him strangely and left him embarrassed for words. Him, the poet through whom all things became living words. In his embarrassment he halted and asked, "What seek ye?"

He trembled as he waited, for he feared that his curtness had halted them. But his voice was one of great beauty—the greater because it was full of the seductiveness poets use unknowingly to entice the very response they fear to rebuff.

Then John answered, "Rabbi, where stayest thou?"

The question was an answer so direct and beautiful that the poet was again lifted into the rare air he breathed and answered simply, "Come and see."

And the three went to the poet's home. And stayed.

Simon remained behind with the Baptist and watched them go out of sight. And Simon was sulky after the way of artists and jealous of the poet's color. The next day John returned, and Simon still was sulky. John tried to coax him into good humor.

"Didst thou find thy poet amusing?" Simon asked as they walked toward the sands.

"I found the poet a poet. And so, I think, did Andrew. His speech is more learned and hidden than even that of the Baptist—and, Simon, thou wouldst enjoy thyself."

"Listening to him speak?"

"And speaking likewise. Andrew spake, and Jesus listened. That is his name —Jesus. And I told him of thee. Thou must come and know this man."

"Perhaps—if it would amuse thee."

And John led Simon to the poet's abode, and the poet greeted him, saying: "Thou art Simon, son of Jona. Thou art Simon, son of the dove. Thou shalt be called Cephas. Hereafter thou shalt be Peter and be as the rock in which the dove hides."

And *they* talked. Simon, called Peter, who was a simple man, breathed to John, "He liveth completely in the physical beauty he hath inherited from his father's fathers — the sons of David." And Peter was impetuous in his affection.

It was in such a way, repeated many times, that the living group grew around its shining nucleus. Andrew brought his two friends, James the son of Zebedee and Philip whose name was Greek. And they also remained, for this Jesus spoke a poet's tongue, and every word was poetry.

Philip, with his gold Greek curls a tight halo around his face, sought Nathaniel, whom he loved. Nathaniel was lying under a fig tree with the Crishma spread before him. And Philip came with great excitement and flung himself down beside Nathaniel.

"We have found him, Nathaniel. We have found Him of whom Moses and the prophets did write."

But the patrician Nathaniel listened little to what Philip spoke, for he was jealous of one who could cause such a glow and bring such a light into Philip's blue eyes. But Philip was unaware and continued as he fingered Nathaniel's necklace.

" — and whom thinkest thou? A Herod prince? An Asmonean priest? A light of scholarly Hillel? A passionate Emir, follower of Gamela? No!" Philip paused impressively before declaring, "Jesus of Nazareth, son of Joseph."

But Nathaniel had turned his purple eyes away and was again studying the office of daily prayer. Only his black, scented locks and the white nape of his neck met Philip's gaze. When he spoke, his voice was hard and impersonal, devoid of its usual caress.

"Nazareth? Does the name not come from Nazora?"

"Come, Nathaniel, and see this man." Philip's voice was coaxing — and vain, for he was flattered by Nathaniel's jealousy. But Nathaniel continued to speak as if reciting a lesson from the Crishma.

"Nazora — the definition of which is, 'despicable, mean.'"

Again Philip interrupted him, saying, "Come and see!"

But Nathaniel continued the study of his prayers as though Philip were not there, saying only, "Nazareth, that obscure and ill-reputed town, on its barren hill. Can anything good come therefrom?"

Philip left. For Philip also was proud. Nathaniel watched him go with violet eyes grown almost black. But the next day he was there under the fig tree again. And the next day Philip, under the pretext of a talk with Jesus, led Jesus past the tree. Jesus saw Nathaniel with the offices of prayer spread before him even as Philip called out to him and, seeing on Nathaniel the sign of the great, spoke to Philip, saying, "The sign of God is on him."

And Jesus spoke also to Nathaniel, saying, "Behold! A true Israelite, in whom guile is not."

Nathaniel, looking up, spoke imperiously. "Whence dost thou recognize me?"

As Nathaniel rose and approached, Jesus answered, "Before Philip called thee, whilst thou wert under the fig tree, I saw thee."

Nathaniel recognized that Jesus did speak with a poet's tongue. And when Nathaniel spoke, his words surprised Philip, for Nathaniel said, "Rabbi, thou art the son of God. Thou art the King of Israel—"

And Jesus called him Bar Tolmai.

They were six now, and Jesus. Six now who listened to his word and repeated his sayings. Then one day Iokanaan baptized the poet and taught him God. And Jesus with his poet's tongue coined the golden rule and, with his belief in legends and the impossible, willed miracles to happen.

It was at the Passover in Tell-hum that Jesus first spoke words that brought the world to heel. For Jesus was devout and sorrowed to see the temple of God defiled; he beat with rushes the merchants and their flocks until the temple was cleansed of them. Nor did they, who were many, resort to violence against the fury of the handsome youth who said, "Make not my Father's house a place of merchandise!"

But later, learned men—priests and Pharisees and scribes—did approach him and in anger and in wonder say, "Give us some sign that thou speakest thus."

And Jesus knew the way of their minds, for he answered, "Destroy this temple, and in three days I will raise it up."

When the disciples told the story, they described that town and named it ever after Capernaum, His own city.

Time spun events. Iokanaan wandered into Machaerus, where Antipas of the House of Herod—Antipas, whose father had successfully brought about the death of Antipater and the flight of Agrippa—was Tetrarch and for many years had been at war. Iokanaan spread word of the new Messiah and so aroused the people that the Tetrarch was filled with fear and had Iokanaan entombed.

And now Jesus was a man inspired—a poet, mad with weighty declamations, who was preparing for martyrdom with majestic gestures. For his power had grown, and his divine madness had inspired the six who loved him and had gained him even more adherents—Matthew the publican, James son of

Alphaeus, Thomas who had at first doubted, Thaddeus, Simon the Canaanite, and Judas, man of Kerioth.

Judas became the disciple who was closest, because he loved Jesus. For Judas had heard of the miracles of Jesus, listened to his word repeated, apprehended the beginning of this fantasy, and realized its possible end—Judas was a student and knew how a landslide could grow from the journey of one polished pebble. And Judas knew the laws of Moses and the prophecies and the people's need for impetus to keep alive the religion of their fathers.

Judas had been slightly scornful of this rash poet whose inspired speech was bringing the world down around him. But Judas also knew that poets die giving birth to beauty and was envious, for *he* would have liked to have been a poet. Then Judas saw Jesus, surrounded by his eleven disciples. And Judas loved him and followed.

And Jesus was glad and always had Judas near Him. For they were as twins, so alike in thought and desire were they. And in appearance also, for the exact curve of Jesus's eyebrow shaded with deeper brown the darker eyes of Judas, so like Jesus's amber ones. The same chiseled lips sternly drew on Judas's face a replica of Jesus's soft love. For Judas *was* Jesus sculptured on a larger scale and painted more sensuous and passionate. And *always* Judas stood by Jesus as though to protect him. And was jealous of the affection bestowed on John. For John was the beloved whom Jesus loved as a mother loves her first-born child. But Judas, Jesus knew.

John the beloved was indeed as a child; Jesus could speak with him and on him round his poet phrases. But Judas was a man; Jesus leaned on him. Through Judas, Jesus could understand the forces he had loosed and, with prophetic poet's eyes, saw also his own end. He read in each happening the event ahead—the event which love blurred for Judas.

When there was discord in the little band over some word of Jesus which was opposite to some former one he had spoken, it was Jesus's way to say: "I have spoken, and it is so." And John's to say: "He has spoken, and it is even so." But Judas would say: "He has said this the one time, and it is so. And that the other time, and *it* is so. Both are so, even though different." And he would explain, and all would be well. For Judas made true Jesus's every saying through understanding. As a parent reads a child's first speech. As a believer explains a prophet. As a man explains a poet. It was a duty of love.

Jesus's fame grew, for he had the way with illnesses that humble people have and was gentle in his speech and strong in his beliefs. His quiet tongue could pierce the coma of death inspired by weariness and pain—soothe the invalid and smooth away the fears until the will to live was resurrected. All this Jesus could do with a look, a sound and a caress, so ineluctable was his will and so inspired his being and speech.

No one ever died in his presence, for he was the symbol of life to all who looked upon him. Only Judas knew that the symbol of life was death. And Judas feared, for to him also was Jesus life.

Jesus's power so grew that his belief grew also. For Jesus was a Jew, and Jews had but one God. But it was as a poet that Jesus said, "I am the Son of God."

Matthew, with his publican mind, heard it as the speech of man and spread word that deliverance was at hand. John, because he loved Jesus, knew that Jesus *was* God, and the disciples spread that word. Jesus spread his poetry; it became the word of God. Only Judas was silent—dark in his silence and strong beneath the light touch of Jesus. Judas loved him so much that he could not betray him. For Judas loved the man, but understood his meaning and knew that the symbol and the man were one.

Then Nathaniel told of the Baptist's death. For Nathaniel was the son of Tolmai, who had seen Salome dance and Herodias receive the dripping head while Antipas wept. Tolmai had been to the feast in Machaerus, as had other patricians, Pharisees and Sadducees. And Tolmai warned his son to be done with this Jesus—this Jesus whom Iokanaan had named and whose powers had grown so much that Vitellius found him inconvenient, this Jesus whom the Pharisees called a mountebank and wished ill.

All this Bar Tolmai told the disciples as they sat breaking bread and drinking wine. Peter tried to dissuade Jesus. John was fearful. And they all were excited, save only Jesus, who said: "I preach only brotherly love. I do no wrong." And Judas, who said nothing, but whose eyes were dark with tears.

That same night there was brought, to bewilder Jesus, a whore that he might judge. Above the screams and jeers he spoke, while Judas held his breath: "Let he who is without sin cast the first stone." And again his poet's tongue had served him.

After, when they were alone, Judas spoke and said: "Wherefore goest this thing, that thy courage alloweth thee to be mild? Who art thou?"

And Jesus answered saying, "The son of man."

To which Judas said, "If only thou wert in flesh as aristocratic as in spirit. For surely thou knowest a mob comes to heel when it is beat. Thy humbleness is majesty too great for them to know."

Whereat Jesus smiled and said: "I once, in a temper, played miscreant. Then I was a child; now I know my temper."

But Judas was worried and continued, saying, "And they fled before thee. Is it not so? And believed what thou didst say. But now—"

And Jesus raised his hand and said, "I do as I preach, that they may believe. For verily I say unto thee, Judas: Knowledge is greater than belief."

"But thou thyself preachest different, Jesus. Thou sayest, 'Believe and thou shalt dwell in the house of the Lord forever.'"

And Jesus asked: "Is that not one way of saying that belief leads to knowledge?" He quoted: "Believe and thou shalt know heaven," and after a pause continued, "For as I have said, Judas: I am no more a child, and now I *know*. I only speak so others may learn to know. First they must believe."

And Judas lay awake and wept. For he knew.

Event piled on event, and the poet was thirty-two. He had gathered around him his twelve friends for what was to be their last supper. And John was on the one side, and Judas was on the other. Times were filled with danger now, for the prophet had submerged the poet, and sentiment was high against the thirteen. But it was greatest against Jesus, whom the people called Christ. He was in hiding.

While breaking bread Jesus stayed his hand and said, with that certainty and sadness of his poet's tongue, "One of you present will betray me." And he was thinking of John, perhaps, who loved him and believed no harm *could* befall him, and so believing might boast a bit. Or Andrew, whose honeyed tongue was guided by the beauty of one word next to another. Or perhaps Peter, who was impetuous in his affection. Or James, who was a martyr born. Or Philip and Bar Tolmai, who when together were blind to else. Or Thomas, who doubted, or Matthew, who was still withal a publican. Or James son of Alphaeus or Lebbaeus or Simon.

And his hand, as always in trouble, rested on Judas's shoulder. And Judas shuddered, for he knew that Christ believed his own word. Knew that they all believed his word. Knew that his word was all ways true. And Judas knew that none of them would betray their teacher, and that Jesus would have spoken false. Knew that after that one false word, there would be ever doubt in their eleven souls. Knew that their belief had become a part of Jesus, that it colored and molded the greatness of his inspired speech and sweetened his soul. Then Judas knew the great thing he would do.

When Judas kissed the cheeks of Jesus for thirty pieces of silver, he proved his love for Jesus. In that minute, Jesus saw that each coin was proof that the betrayal had been bought so that the poet's word would be true. And Jesus wept also that *he* had betrayed *Judas*. For he felt he had done so through Judas's love for him and desire to see him be the Christ he called himself. And Jesus said to Judas, "Thou shalt sit on my right hand in the Kingdom of Heaven."

But Judas was shamed, and did not know that Jesus knew his soul. He was in torment that Jesus believed as did the others. And when Jesus stood before the Pontius Pilate, pale and regal, Judas on the edge of the crowd was pale and regal too.

Over Judas's face raced the same fatigue and pain and sorrow that painted Jesus's brow beneath the weighty cross. Then they crucified him—Jesus, the poet of man. And for three days and nights Judas's heart lived in a too-small space. For three days he could not weep, so great was his grief. Nor could he sob, so heavy the miasma of his pain. On the third night there was a storm. Judas went forth and climbed a hill and battled with the storm, screaming, "If thou art God, then stoop and ease thy son Jesus . . ."

And James, at the foot of the cross, said, "If thou be the Son of God, come down from the cross. If thou art the son of God, forgive."

And Jesus on his cross said, "Father, why hast thou forsaken me?"

Judas beat his breasts and tore his hair and whispered, "Thou knowest, Jesus, that had I saved thy life, thou wouldst be even more dead. Even as now in death thou livest to torment me."

At last Judas came to the brink of a cliff. He leaned against an olive tree and wept the long-desired tears. His soul grew quiet.

As Jesus on the Hill of the Skull murmured, "Forgive them, they know not what they do," Judas drew the cord from around his waist and hanged himself from the olive tree. And whispered with the poet's tongue he finally had been given:

"I did but love thee."

HARLEM

ON HARLEM

Nugent wrote "On Harlem" for the Federal Writers' Project in the late thirties. Although Harlem's glamor had begun to fade, the events of the twenties were still lively, recent memories. The drawings of dancing Harlemites that accompany "On Harlem" were originally published in 1928 to illustrate Wallace Thurman's Dance Magazine article on jazz dance, "Harlem's Place in the Sun."[1]

With the end of the war came the reaction. The entire country was caught in a boom of prosperity, spending, and license. The passing of the Eighteenth Amendment brought with it an entire topsy-turvy, exciting and incredible series of new industries, entertainments and pleasures. In New York, the postwar reaction reached exaggerated and glamorous heights. Money was easily acquired and freely spent. Saloons closed in fanfares of maudlin guzzling, only to be reborn as speakeasies. Greenwich Village blossomed into a mad bohemia that outdid any of those on the continent. Harlem flowered into a unique amusement center, and Broadway extended itself into the many side-streets.

Love cults, theatre groups and radical movements flourished in the "Village." That section of the city became the Mecca of practically every "strug-

gling" artist, pseudo-artist and hanger-on in the country. At Hubert's Cafeteria on Sheridan Square, the great, near-great and nonentities of the underworld, the stage, art, literature and society rubbed elbows as they ate cheap food. In the middle of all this hectic activity, fantastic characters came to life and frequently produced worthwhile works. Washington Square, McDougal Street, West Fourth Street, Waverly Place and McDougal Alley housed and entertained these hordes. Eugene O'Neill was becoming known, as were the Provincetown Players, who had a theatre in a barn on McDougal Street. Floyd Dell, Theodore Dreiser and Claude McKay actually found time to write, despite (or because of) their thousand other activities. The period was studded with the brilliant names of people and movements which have since become household words. *Liberator,* and later, *New Masses* came into being. The haute monde descended from Fifth and Madison Avenues, as did the equally expensive but not quite so social ladies from Park Avenue, to visit The Pepper Pot, The Pirate's Den, The Poet's Inn, Romany Marie's, The Garret, and the Mad Hatter.

The 1920s were ushered in with fantastic fanfare. Excess was the order of the day. Aleister Crowley's devil-worship cult flourished. Mable Dodge held democratic open-house, mixing laborers, debutantes, samurai, coolies, miners, communists, literary poseurs, shimmy-dancers, poets, waitresses, and mandarins with heedless dexterity. She even went so far as to introduce Negroes. The Theatre Guild was beginning to show signs of competent precocity and moved uptown to the Garrick theatre to ease its growing pains. John Barrymore went forth to wider recognition. The labor movement gained momentum. Bootlegging became the first industry of the land. Capital gormandized itself to the point of acute indigestion. Gang wars and labor strikes tessellated the headlines. Loeb and Leopold murdered the Frank boy. Mike Gold harangued for Communism in Union Square. Carl Van Vechten wrote about the Gramercy Park set and discovered the "exotic" Negro people and Langston Hughes. Countee Cullen became famous. The K.K.K. threatened Paul Robeson because a white woman kissed his black hand in the play, *All God's Chillun Got Wings,* at the Sheridan Square Theatre. Southern whites wrote about Negroes. Northern dilettantes discovered that Negroes possessed cultural as well as tap-dancing ability. Picasso found inspiration at the source—Africa. Harlem was discovered. A Negro movement started, publicized by Van Vechten, Muriel Draper, Heywood Broun and Joel Spingarn. Professor Locke edited *The New Negro.* Phillis Wheatley and Charles Chesnutt were rediscovered. Gin guzzling became even more the order of the day.

Negroes found their own interest in themselves reviving, encouraged as it was by the white trailblazers. Radical news pamphlets and magazines devoted to "the race" struggled into greater visibility. Being black (or even slightly colored) began to be fashionable and a means of livelihood.

Boom and prosperity swept over Harlem, magically heightening its already remarkable capacity for enjoyment and entertainment. Money flowed in and out of pockets as easily as laughter escaped lips. The air was alive with the beat of drums and the trill of clarinets, the clinking of never-emptied glasses and the rumble of luxurious cars rolling from fashionable avenues to stop before the more lively and colorful of the after-hour Harlem places of amusement.

Hundreds of honky-tonks and cabarets sprang up. The ever-growing crowds spilled into the thousands of speakeasies and gin-mills, which were already multiplying like mushrooms. Dim red or blue light glowed from the windows of apartments that seemed to rock with the shuffle of feet, as house-rent parties spewed their patrons into the adjacent hallways and side streets. Everywhere there was good feeling and impromptu jazz spirit.

Marcus Garvey exhorted the black peoples of the earth to join forces and take their place in the sun. Hubert Harrison deserted his superlative collection of erotic literature, second to none in New York, to translate his ideas about culture and the superiority of the black man into the Harlem idiom through which to harangue the man in the street from a soap box on any convenient corner. Sepia society gave lavish balls and dansants at the more properly exclusive halls in Harlem, demanding strict formal attire and guarantee of social eligibility. Paul Robeson's glorious voice was discovered hiding in the magnificent body which had carried him into the immortal ranks of the All American Team. The Negro was finding his place in the theatre, literature, music, sports and the arts. Or perhaps it was being found for him.

Ann Pennington, then with Ziegfeld's Follies, introduced the Charleston, the Black Bottom and the Mess Around—all dances which she had seen performed spontaneously while touring and fraternizing in Harlem. When the labor world wept in such impressive silence in Union Square at the murders of Sacco and Vanzetti, Negroes were conspicuous among the mourners. White comrades graciously gave their seats to Negro comrades at Labor Temple meetings. Claude McKay went to Soviet Russia. Julia Peterkin broadmindedly wrote about dear old plantation Negroes and scalawags. James Ford became a perennial candidate for the vice-presidency of the United States on the communist ticket. Paul Green dramatized black tragedy and had real live Negroes perform it. The Negro musical shows, *Shuffle Along* and *Runnin' Wild,* gave a world now warned and prepared a galaxy of tinted stars, including Florence Mills, Josephine Baker, Noble Sissle, and Miller and Lyles.

There was no "class" magazine which did not have contributions by or about Negroes. No poetry reading, literary gathering, cocktail partly, underworld group, gang war, creditable business, labor organization, art gallery, religious society, physical culture sect, love cult, or Yogi philosophy school was complete without having been graced by the inclusion of some member of this now strangely prevalent minority group. There was no pie in the city in which there was not a Negro thumb. The Negro in New York had come into his somewhat precarious and nebulous own.

To make a round of the cabarets and the honky-tonks that studded Harlem would have taken months. There was Small's on Fifth Avenue near 135th Street. Down a steep flight of stairs in a dimly lit cellar, a dozen or so tables surrounded a tiny dance floor on one side of which was the band—a five piece aggregation that played without the benefit of written music. None of the musicians could read music, nor did there seem to be any need for such superfluous knowledge. Other lights extinguished, a spotlight focused on a rotating mirror-chandelier which cast its million semi-bright reflections over the minute dance floor, and the band would just play. Jam session. Perhaps the clarinet would voice an unexpected, catchy riff, and pleased with the sound of it, would repeat the riff with variations. The saxophone might softly join in, feeling for harmony to the tune, and the drums would take up the improvised beat. Then the pianist would experiment with treble counterpoints, accenting the rhythm with a two-chord, gut-bucket bass and the thump of a rhythmic foot, while the bass fiddle would add its weird rhythm and monotone harmony. The patrons would be carried onto the floor on the almost physical wave of sensual sound, until there was no room left in which to move. There they would stand, belly to belly, pressed tightly one couple against the other, and shuffle their feet— "dancing on a dime." Shoulders, hips, entire bodies gyrated through all the ecstatic movements of more intimate congress as the dancers gave themselves

 up to the rhythm of the band and the tune which seemed to pulsate in their loins and hips, so subtle a part of the dim glow and sensual atmosphere had it become. The "Bump" and the "Mess Around," descriptive of themselves, were the only possible means of movement. The effect was hypnotic. The erotic and sensual undertones were the entirety. There was no vulgarity in the particularly sensual and practically sexual orgy taking place on the dance floor, in the loud laughter, or even in the lewd jests bantered about so casually in the dimly-lighted cellar. Everything was completely animal and for-the-moment.

Through all this the dancing waiters threaded their incredible way. Twirling trays high above the heads of everyone, balancing them precariously on one or two fingers, dancing between couples where paper could not have been passed, each waiter brought up his tray with a flourish and an intricate flurry of dance steps before some tiny table. Raw gin in a small pitcher and peppery ginger ale disappeared from the tray to reappear magically on the table.

The music would end. The lights would go on. A general noise would arise as the couples awakened from their trance-like gyrations to find their tables and order more gin and light more cigarettes to fill with yet more smoke the low-ceilinged cellar already so blue with fog. Then the lights would dim to extinction again, and a single circle of crimson or blue would grow to focus upon an entertainer. It might be Myra Johnson standing nonchalant and intimate, resting one elbow on the rail before the bandstand. She would stand in utter perfection, dressed with that incredible instinct for expensive simplicity which becomes second nature to the professional manikin, her soft brown skin cool and velvety in the thick hot air. An evanescent, intangible quality of personality would surround her like an aura, quieting even the noisiest and most drunken of the patrons. Then she would sing—perhaps some popular current song, perhaps a number received in exchange for sandwiches and a drink of gin from some derelict unknown. Aloof, yet completely intimate, she'd sing a double entendre version, going from table to table, squeezing between the closely-placed chairs, until the last measure of the song found her back before the bandstand, hands filled with silver and paper money, which she would drop into a kettle, there to be divided, along with the tips of the others, with the others. There would be thunderous applause and the band would begin another dance number, the floor would again become crowded with couples, the waiters would resume dancing about filling orders, and there would be an interlude before the performance of the next entertainer.

Black Bohemia had not only discovered and become habitués of such places, but had introduced them to their paler bohemian brethren. Vachel Lindsay, fresh from the triumph of his poem, "The Congo"; Muriel Draper, whose son Paul was even then absorbing Negro feeling for the dance though living in the "Village"; Mabel Dodge, bringing in tow some famous writer or her American Indian husband; Dudley Murphy, whose startling *Ballet Mechanique* was in gestation; and Carl Van Vechten, already familiar with and unofficial publicity agent pro tem for the New Negro, were all shown the glories of his Nigger Heaven through the kind auspices of the "Niggeratti," that small group of young Negroes who had been swept to the front on the crest of the wave of newly discovered Negro art and intellect. They were a smart-alecky group, some of whom were eventually to vindicate the expectations which had, unasked, arisen about them. This group was the semi-official guide to Hot Harlem; it was they who saw to it that the white patrons, spendthrifts, dilettantes and seekers-after-truth knew Harlem. And this whole white army was familiar with the hole in the floor of the dimly-lit entrance hall to LeRoy's, where Louise, who once boasted that she would kill any man who two-timed her or any woman who bit her in the back (and made good both brags), entertained.

Their white complexions even made it possible for them to attend the famous Cotton Club at 142nd Street and Lenox Avenue, which, while boasting that it was the very essence of Harlem, drew a rigid color line to keep that essence pure. The obvious Negroes who were allowed to darken the doors of this "typical Harlem hot-spot" could be counted on the fingers of one hand. There was a great black doorman posted to keep the tabulation in the lower brackets and to "spot" those whose light skins might make them so brash as to attempt to invade this holy of holies. The club was famous for its "Creole" (high yeller) chorus. So very famous had this chorus become, in fact, and so lucrative a source of income for the pale-tinted chorines, that a white girl was once inspired enough to "pass" successfully and gain admission to the chorus. This "lily-white" sepia night spot was under the "protection" of gangsters—the same crew that, with high-handed methods and in no uncertain way, had wiped out a competing establishment, the elegant Plantation Club, the day before its scheduled opening.

The Plantation had planned to open in two stories and the basement of a house on 126th Street near the corner of Lenox Avenue, which had been elaborately decorated with thousands of dollars worth of mirrors and a miraculously matched and polished hardwood dance floor parqueted in intricate design by accomplished artists. A superlative show had been rehearsed and costumed. Negro performers, having little or no fear of gangster threats, had blithely continued rehearsing. But the night before the opening, when the cast appeared for rehearsal, the place was in shambles. The mirrors were shattered, the glass-like floor hacked to splinters, the expensive and spectacular costumes burned with acids. The owners of the club were adequately discouraged.

The owners of Club Alabam had also been discouraged, but not for the same reason. Indeed, there seemed to have been no good reason for the failure of the club to become a successful venture. It had been beautifully decorated with Negro scenes—jungle, plantation, cabin, Harlem, etc.—by Aaron Douglas. It was spacious and successfully cooled; it boasted an excellent cuisine, an excellent line of liquors from the proper bootleggers, and a fine group of entertainers. Yet it failed to capture the public fancy.

The influx of visitors and tourists from downtown sent prices soaring, so that more and more Negroes had to find other forms of entertainment.

For the mass of Negroes in Harlem were economically insecure. Whole communities had to live in one apartment, taking turns at using the beds, kitchen and bath. Even such a division of expenses did not seem to lessen the difficulty of meeting the ever-growing demands of the landlords, who continued to raise the rents higher and higher. Mostly employed as porters, laborers, houseworkers, and elevator operators, Harlemites found their salaries far from adequate. Their love of rich and plentiful food did little to help. So they had hit upon the simple device of combining a way to make a few much-needed extra dollars with the opportunity to have a good time: they gave house-rent parties. For the reasonable stipulation of twenty-five cents admission, one could enjoy a pianist, red lights, a pot of chitterlings or pigs' feet, and a jug of corn licker; there could be revelry until daybreak, with the added attraction of less worry about facing the landlord.

House-rent parties, playing the numbers, and religion became the only pleasures of the many who could not afford to go to the Italian-owned speakeasies and gang-owned nightclubs. The new gambling game, numbers, with its great appeal—the seeming opportunity to make sixty dollars with ten cents—sprang into immediate and understandable popularity, enriching a small group of exploiters. Holstein, Brunder, and Pompey (owner of the Cuban Giants Negro baseball team) were the foremost "bankers" of this unlawful lottery, which was to become a bone of contention between the big underworld outfits of New York. They were the first great numbers "Kings," "Barons" and "Czars." Hoodlums like "Bub" Hewlitt, who had been convicted thirty-three times before finally serving a sentence, had things very much their own way, serving as

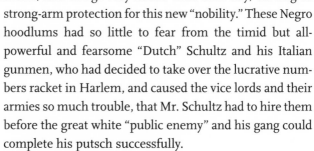 strong-arm protection for this new "nobility." These Negro hoodlums had so little to fear from the timid but all-powerful and fearsome "Dutch" Schultz and his Italian gunmen, who had decided to take over the lucrative numbers racket in Harlem, and caused the vice lords and their armies so much trouble, that Mr. Schultz had to hire them before the great white "public enemy" and his gang could complete his putsch successfully.

All this while, Harlem's entertainment value and contributions were growing. Countee Cullen, Langston Hughes, Claude McKay, Dr. Bud Fisher and Zora Hurston were becoming poets and authors whom one must read. Ethel Waters, Florence Mills, Duke Ellington, Cab Calloway, Hall Johnson, Rex Ingram, Canada Lee, Harry Wills, and Rose McClendon were all being introduced to the greater public through motion pictures, theatres, sports, radio and the concert stage.

This was the heyday of Harlem, when the Negro was still being discovered. When clubs and speakeasies were still the source from which and in which most Negro talent could be found. When 133rd Street was known as "Beale Street" after the Memphis street of that name made famous by W. C. Handy, the "Daddy of the Blues." New dives with fantastic, self-descriptive names sprang up until almost every doorway in the block between Seventh and Lenox Avenues had its sliding peephole and password. Small's had expanded, moved to Seventh Avenue, and was even more popular, if less colorful, than before. In its place on Fifth Avenue the Sugar Cane now held sway, as complete as had been Small's while it was there. Happy Rhone's Black and White had given way to the Capitol. There were clubs to suit every taste and pocketbook. There was the Clam House, where Gladys Bentley—a heavy, bulbous, colored female with the invert's preference for wearing male attire—sang dirty songs in a husky tuneless voice all night long as she played the piano. Pod's and Jerry's, 136, the Nest, the Mad House, and many others—each operated without detracting in the least from its neighbors.

Baron Wilkens's emporium, to which the more experimental of the white females came to traffic with the more advanced black pimps and "sweetbacks," was still operating, taking full advantage of the Nordic's fashionable trek to Harlem. The red-light district—from 110th to 115th Streets—had expanded and now extended up Lenox Avenue to above 125th Street, sending through the side streets tentative fingers which frequently curled to embrace Seventh and Fifth Avenues.

And Harlem indulged in its religious orgies with as great a gusto as its other emotional and artistic outlets. The spectacular Reverend Becton, with his fifty-odd exquisitely-tailored suits and his handmade shoes, shirts, and ties, held unbelievably profitable revivals at Reverend Cullen's church on Seventh Avenue. Theatrically he would stride up onto the altar dais, which his presence transformed into a stage, and begin his performance. His orchestra of attractive young men, who were slightly on the effeminate side, would accompany the congregation as they sang jazzy versions of the Baptist hymns Becton would start. An attendant would stand at rigid attention behind him, ready to hand him a spotless hand-drawn handkerchief with which to wipe away the heavenly sweat that dewed his brow when the word of God proved particularly heavy. The washer-women and day workers would gaze at his tall handsome figure and become so overcome with the "light" that they would pour out their hundreds of painfully earned nickels and dimes into the collection plates. The nickels and dimes swelled into a fortune, furnishing Becton's home with sybaritic white velvets, great sensuous divans, and massive gold crucifixes. He dwelt in holy (regal) splendor until an aggregation of Philadelphia racketeers, weary of seeing him pocket the wealth that had been theirs until this man of God had revealed the beauties of religion to the masses, riddled his elegant body with bullets.

Stephanie St. Claire held sway in a palatial home near Mount Morris Park, holding seances and becoming (as a sideline, of course) one of the powers in the numbers racket. The Barefoot Prophet was a familiar sight with his giant six-foot-six frame, dispensing luck, the right number, and the word of God for whatever pittance one might give him. Elder Thorne shouted and jazzed her way into the upper-income group, converting hundreds to the barbaric way of God, until God gave some enterprising radio network the insight to recognize her international entertainment possibilities; radio so popularized her that in later years she became the featured attraction at one of the Harlem nightclubs that had moved down into the Broadway sector.

There was Prophet Costonic, who enthralled his cult followers by preaching the word of God and a garbled version of the Christian Science doctrine, accompanied by a formulary of hocus-pocus strangely resembling devil-worship. And all the while Father Divine was becoming God. He was not so quietly building up *his* religion. "Peace" was its byword. "It's wonderful," was his contention. "Peace! It's truly wonderful!" Negroes and whites, rich and poor flocked to him, spreading his word countrywide, buying hundreds of thousands of dollars worth of "Heavens" (as any property of his became known), finally establishing one "Heaven" in the heart of social Newport and another at Krum Elbow in the neighborhood of presidential Hyde Park.

Harlem continued its hectic, money-spending, impossible way, creating colorful character after colorful character. It offered Julian, "the Black Ace," who flew and fell over Harlem, unwittingly preparing for the day when Italy would war with Ethiopia and he would fly and fight for his black brothers before becoming an Italian pilot and citizen in a fit of pique. Harlem continued to eat at Craig's and to discuss music and art at Eddie's while giving its pennies to Sewing-Machine Bertha, who could buy and sell most of her benefactors. It continued to produce Chappie Gardiners to hoax a willing world masquerading as Ethiopian princesses when they were in reality houseworkers from the Bronx. Or Catarina Jarbera, who traveled the path of song from the blues to opera. The cabaret and the church continued to be the points between which the Negro was held taut, through which he grew and in which he forgot for the moment his great economic problems.

For it was still no easy matter to pay an executive's rent with a porter's salary, and the high cost of food had not dimmed the Negroes' instinct to eat well and copiously. Garvey's economic house of cards had collapsed after his imprisonment and deportation. The numbers offered a million-to-one chance to win a six-to-one gain. Bathtub gin and rot-gut corn, which had been no competition for the cheap drink to be had in the speakeasies, was even less attractive when prohibition was repealed. Sufi preached racial hatred and black Nazism and grew rich before he was killed in a plane crash, although his white secretary somehow managed to survive it. His death left Mme. St. Claire a not-too-despondent widow. The Negro continued to turn to the church and cabaret—and Communism.

THE DARK TOWER

"The Dark Tower" was Countee Cullen's regular column in Opportunity, *which he turned over to Nugent as a "guest conductor" for the October 1927 issue.*[2]

Lest one meandering columnist should bear down too severely on the patience of *Opportunity*'s subscribers, the "Tower" for this month has been turned over to a guest conductor who will accomplish the double kindness of presenting our readers with a new personal angle on things, while at the same time permitting the usual wielder of this baton to limber up his fingers after a pleasant period of summer inactivity. . . . Introducing Mr. Richard Bruce, artist, poet and for October 1927, impresario of "The Dark Tower."—Countee Cullen

I have just looked over the proofs of *Caroling Dusk,* an anthology of verse by Negro poets, edited by Countee Cullen. It is going to be a beautiful book, with a

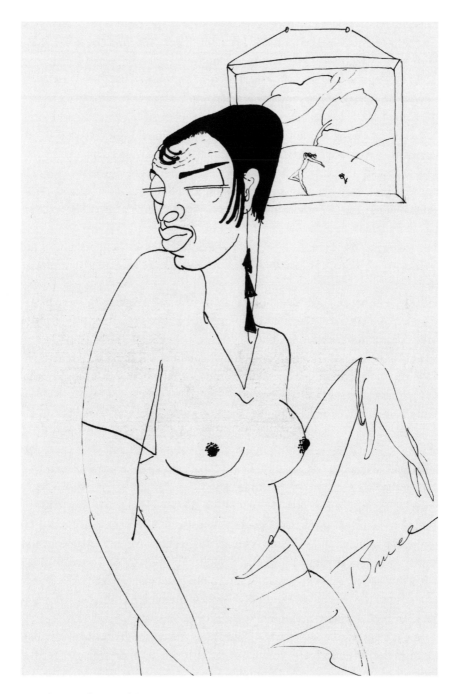

Drawing, Harlem Sophisticate (circa 1930).

jacket by Aaron Douglas. Nearly all the Negro poets are represented: Langston Hughes, Georgia Douglas Johnson, Arna Bontemps, Angelina Grimké, Claude McKay, Paul Laurence Dunbar, Alice Dunbar Nelson and W. E. B. Du Bois being among the best known. Albert Rice is represented by a few very lovely things. Mr. Rice is new to most of us. A very interesting feature is introduced in the autobiographical sketches. Each artist has written his own except in three instances, in two of which the poet is dead and in the third too young. I shall get the first copy off the press. . . .

And in connection with the proofs: I had taken them down to a friend's house to look over and discuss. It was in the middle of our discussion that she reminded me that there would be a demonstration such as I had never seen before in Union Square. So off we went to Union Square. We reached a vantage point just opposite *The Daily Worker's Bulletin*. As we took our places the bulletin read: "Japanese Workers Flood Streets Before U. S. Embassy Buildings." There was dead silence. Only a tenseness that we had first noticed. People talking in rather hushed tones. In Italian, Jewish and English. In French, Armenian, and Russian. Greenwich Village was well represented by made-to-order suits and workingmen's shoes, patched suits and silk socks, sandals and smocks and long hair, cigarette holders and notebooks. And Little Italy by tight-fitting suits and patent-leather shoes. Corduroy trousers and well-shaven faces. Rough blue shirts and black hair. And Russia by working clothes and florid faces. Haunted eyes and red hands. There was an overtone of hushed laughter and joking. But the merriment was a trifle forced and artificial and only tended to make the tense undercurrent more palpable. Strong individual and personal emotions vied with party emotions. A sense of helplessness and anxiety mixed with indignation seemed to pervade the crowd. People speaking in hushed tones. Smoking furtive cigarettes as though talking and smoking were forbidden. Whispered commonplaces spoken absently as all eyes shifted from time to time toward the bulletin board. An enormous crowd trying to appear individual and careless. Or grouped and defiant. Whispering. And we continued our conversation—in whispers. Speaking of the psychology of having each poet contribute his biographical sketch of— The bulletin board again: "Fifteen Minutes To Live." The voices renewed their farce.

Mounted police kept a passage clear in the street, and patrolmen kept one clear on the sidewalks. The crowd divided. Part of it on the right, under the bulletin board. Then a line of mounted police. A clear street. More mounted police. A crowd, patrolmen, and a clear space; then patrolmen and the crowd, filling the park and spilling out into Broadway and Seventeenth and Fourteenth

Streets. Right in front of us a tall, dark boy with tangled hair was offering silent prayer. A little blond girl with him kept her eyes glued to the board. There were excited movements in the office window next to the one displaying the bulletin. The window was thrown open. All sound ceased. The window swung to again. "Ten Minutes to Live." And the hum and buzz of the strained voices renewed. The false laughter and furtive smoking. Our conversation. Shifting. The bulletin again. "Sacco and Vanzetti Bravely Await Death." The crowd breathed again and shifted. It was becoming restless, and a constant patrol by mounted police and patrolmen was necessary. The bulletin. "Witnesses to the Execution Begin to Arrive." The sound of shifting feet and nervous laughter became an accompaniment to the appearance on the bulletin. "They Enter the Death Room." Another bulletin. I could not see it. There was perfect silence. Then a scream. And another. And another. In front of me a young man was tearing his clothes and giving voice to wordless cries. Someone screamed—*Assassini*. The word was put into his mouth. *Assassini. Assassini.* It was taken up by individuals. Tears and sobs and shouts. And cries of *assassini*. But the greater number was silent and motionless. The bulletin announcing Vanzetti's death was an anticlimax. Immediately the police attempted to disperse the crowds. Mounted police. Police in armored motorcycles. Patrolmen. And from the center of the park a woman's voice began the "Internationale." We were carried on the crest of the crowd. Down Fourteenth Street, singing, shouting, weeping, gesticulating. And police. At Second Avenue another attempt was made to disperse the crowds. Mounted police charged on the sidewalk. People scattered. We went down Second Avenue. At Twelfth Street a crowd suddenly overtook us. A charge of police in armored motorcycles scattered them. We ran behind the green lattice that protects the sidewalk tables at the "Royal." At the table were gathered most of the Jewish intelligentsia. So we sat and sipped iced coffee and discussed the evening.

The next day was dark and rainy. Harlem was in gala attire. All the street lights were lighted. And thousands of red, green, and yellow lights were strung across the streets. Banners and signs and flags. Elks' heads and purple- and white-garbed people mingling in the already overcrowded streets. Someone shouted "They're coming!" All traffic was stopped; mounted police kept the streets clear. With a blare of horns and drums, the parade struck Seventh Avenue. People were hanging out of every window. Crowded every available foot of sidewalk and street. A white-dressed band passed by. Pandemonium of cheers and personal greetings and shouts. A lady drum major strutted by clad in royal purple satin and yellow. Shod with golden slippers. As resplendent as Caius or Solomon. Banners, floats, pandemonium. And laughter. All beneath a heavy sky, jeweled with string upon string of red, yellow, and green electric lights. No rain could wash away the purple or smiles or gold or laughter. And then night. Seventh Avenue resplendent. Beautiful. The electric lights given back again by the glassy streets. Laughter and gaiety. Vendors and hawkers. Corn puddin'; Virginia ham; corn bread; feasts for sale; and festivity. On and on into the night. Dark clothes and gala ties alternated with white clothes and purple ties. Dresses. Red, white, yellow, and orange. Kaleidoscopic. And plumes, and feast, and joy. And all around, signs of welcome. Four days and nights in carnival attire.

I have just finished *Copper Sun* by Countee Cullen. It is very charmingly illustrated by Charles Cullen. Mr. Cullen's latest book of poems continues to fulfill his promise. It is replete with apt and beautiful imagery. One verse particularly stays with me as a perfect example of the possibilities for beauty and rhythm given a poet:

> I who employ a poet's tongue
> Would tell you how
> You are a golden damson hung
> Upon a silver bough.

It would be difficult to find four more beautiful lines. And those are merely an introduction to the poem itself.

Langston Hughes has returned to New York after having been south all summer. He has a number of very interesting tales to tell about the flood area and New Orleans. Strange tales about visiting voodoo gatherings where a "conjer" woman put a protective charm upon Miss Zora Hurston and himself. And waters so calm and peaceful that one could hardly believe it was flood tide were it not for the houses jutting up like strange and melancholy water flowers. Were it not for the miles and miles of mud and ooze. Some of it hard and cracked like a bas-relief map—some of it soft and rich, giving off colors of the rainbow under the sun. Were it not for the refugee camps, cluttered with bedding and pans and chairs and trinkets salvaged from the waters. Were it not for the thousands of congregated men and women and children. The laborers fortifying levees. The patrol of soldiers and the bustle to acclimate oneself to one's surroundings. Strange sights and weird streets in New Orleans. The vaults with their tier upon tier of tiny doors. Some ornamented, some plain. And Baton Rouge, partly built on stilts. Out into the waters and swamps. And the flowers and steps growing right out of the water. And after all that, New York again. Mr. Hughes should have much material for a number of new poems.

The Theatre Guild has been rehearsing for *Porgy* by Du Bose Heyward, which opens on the third of October. Frank Wilson plays the name part, and the cast of principals includes Evelyn Ellis and Rose McClendon. The play is very good, so far as I can see from rehearsals, Frank Wilson making an excellent cripple and Miss Ellis an excellent Bess. As for Miss McClendon, her part as Robbins's wife gives her wide range for her powers. The atmosphere bits are done by local Negroes, among whom you are certain to recognize a number of friends.

GENTLEMAN JIGGER (excerpts)

Gentleman Jigger *is an unpublished novel on which Nugent was working at the same time Wallace Thurman was writing* Infants of the Spring. *Like* Infants, *Gentleman Jigger is a roman à clef. Parts of the two novels contain slightly different versions of the very same incidents. The fact that Thurman's novel was published, while Nugent's was not, does not mean that Nugent imitated Thurman. Indeed, in interviews and in one chapter of* Gentleman Jigger *(which is not included here), Nugent alleged the opposite: that Thurman copied from him.*

The surviving manuscript of Gentleman Jigger *is of no help in resolving the issue. I have found only one manuscript fragment in Nugent's papers that tracks* Infants *verbatim—the letter that Paul Arbian sent to Gabriel D'Annunzio, which is quoted in* Infant's *last chapter. If Nugent's allegation is true, Thurman may have revised* Infants *after Nugent confronted him, or Nugent might simply have discarded those portions of* Gentleman Jigger *included in* Infants.

Leaving the issue of plagiarism aside, the interesting fact is that Infants *and* Gentleman Jigger *narrate actual events from two slightly different points of view. Reading the two in tandem provides a uniquely three-dimensional picture of life at Niggeratti Manor.*

The chapter titles are not Nugent's; they were devised for purposes of identification.

SALT LAKE SAGA

"Salt Lake Saga" is a fictionalized, tongue-in-cheek account of Wallace Thurman's family background. Although omitted from the later typescripts of Gentleman Jigger, *it is included here because of its intrinsic interest. In this text Emma Pearlman is Thurman's grandmother, Emma Gladden Jackson; her daughter, Hagar, is Thurman's mother, Beulah Jackson Guinn.[1] Henry Raymond Pellman is (Henry) Wallace Thurman himself. Anthony Brewer is Langston Hughes. Burton Barclay is Countee Cullen.*

Some facts have been changed to suit Nugent's narrative purposes. For example, Thurman's grandmother was born in Missouri and his mother in Colorado. The family did not move to Salt Lake City until after 1890, so the fictional family's in-

volvement with Brigham Young and Salt Lake City's earlier history is pure invention. Nonetheless, much of Nugent's narrative parallels reality: Thurman's grandmother was indeed a leading member of the Calvary Baptist Church in Salt Lake City. Her parents were not saloonkeepers, but she herself was, apparently, a bootlegger. Thurman's mother did in fact have several husbands, and evidence gathered by Thurman's biographer, Eleonore van Notten, strongly suggests that she was a "good-time gal" who sometimes exchanged her sexual favors for money. Thus, Nugent's suggestion that Thurman was introduced to alcohol and same-sex practices by one of his mother's husbands is not entirely outside the realm of possibility, and this story may be of some help in understanding Thurman's complex psychological makeup.

Somewhere in the caravan of Brigham Young was a very discontented wife assisting in that pilgrimage to Salt Lake City. Not that she resented the idea of being one of four wives. Not exactly. But (as she put it) she objected to his . . . well, her husband's choice of wives. To be exact, it was the nigger she disliked. Not that she disliked Negroes. She just disliked sharing her social position with this particular one. The woman wasn't a decent nigger. She was not dark enough to be decent. So Adeline Baldstock deserted her husband, his mixed wives and Brigham Young and married a young Jew named Isaac Pearlman.

Isaac Pearlman was the sole result of the misalliance of Jacob Pearlman, a Jew who had opened a clothing (overalls, shoes, picks, candy, peanuts, dice, fruit, and wagon wheels) store in aristocratic Charleston. Expecting to be ostracized by the "good" families and to be hooted at by the "poor white trash," and having lacked the foresight to arm himself against ostracism with a wife, he looked with seeing and covetous eyes upon Emma. It was a sad mistake to make, for Emma was the comely mulatto slave, mistress and cousin of Mister Gerald Cotman (white) of one of the "first" families there. Emma and Jacob decided it would be safer to have their child in some place slightly removed from the aristocratic city of their romance, so they fled. And continued to flee until the birth of Isaac called halt to their flight in St. Louis.

There Isaac was taught to count and fornicate by the ever provident religion of his fathers. By the time he was sixteen, he was proficient at both and dissatisfied with the limitations of his environs and the prejudices abounding there. So he decided to widen his scope. He went to Salt Lake City.

Salt Lake City was, in fact, neither city, town, nor anything of certainty. Then came Mormonism, and with it prosperity, along with three or four Negro families. Isaac opened a saloon and went to bed with Adeline. He had no intention of cutting off his most lucrative source of income (pimping) by marrying her, but he counted without *her*. Their first child was Emma, named for the beauteous mulatto grandparent in St. Louis. The child's brown complexion would have startled Adeline (to say the least) if she had not been warned by certain statements of her husband that all was not well. She would have left him if his technique for concocting children had not been so attractive. However, the gentleman's Jewish antecedents placated her pride, his admitted ability as a lover satisfied and excited her physically, and then, of course, she did feel duty-bound to provide little yelling Emma with the loving diaper-changing hands of a mother. Being a great one for "society," she became colored and dictator of the group of four Negro families in Salt Lake. She helped found the Zion Baptist Church No. 1 and became first psalm-singing deaconess. And little Emma grew up in church and daddy's barroom, a young social leader.

By the age of seventeen, Emma the second's knowledge of a growing city, the barroom and the Baptist church had led her to believe emphatically in Mormonism. Not that she had the courage of her convictions, for by this time she was too definitely a debutante to dare voice her opinion that it was certainly much easier physically to be one of four wives than mistress of four men. But her Jewish blood, with its superstition that money can buy release, persuaded her to enlarge with her promise her father's barroom clientele and her mother's Baptist congregation. But life had taught her one thing, and that was that a promise is more intriguing than its fulfillment. So at the age of twenty-five she married Walter Hitchkock.

Walt was the owner of the rival saloon in Salt Lake. He was impotent. Emma was a faithful wife, giving herself (and then only because she was a woman and Walt *was* impotent) to Seth Howard. Seth was a handsome blond Negro, scion of four or five excellent black and white families scattered over the south—a poetic ne'er-do-well who had drifted into Salt Lake in hopes of being lost and alone, intending to pick up the crumbs of this population too busy to notice him. Not that he considered Emma a crumb, but he was ever a gentleman and willing to oblige, and Emma wanted a baby. Walt discovered his wife's duplicity and drank himself to death in record time. Emma, at twenty-eight, was a widow. Seth, being an artist and having the soul of a poet, married Walt's heiress. He was a perfect genius at fashioning children.

Salt Lake had by this time become a city almost. Certain families had grouped together and formed an aristocracy. Emma and her Seth were at the crest of this group. After all, Seth was handsome and did have a way with him. And they did have money. They owned the only two saloons in town. (Isaac and Adeline had sold out to Seth and gone to St. Louis to live on their capital. They died before their capital did—Adeline of overeating, Isaac of protracted amours.)

Emma was very successful with her children. They all died save Hagar. By the time Hagar was born, Salt Lake possessed a theatre, a bank and a cemetery. Seth sold his name in the saloons and became a porter to the theatre and the bank (that occupation was more respectable). The money from the sales he invested in securities. They lived beautifully on his porter wages and the dividends.

Hagar grew up wildly. At sixteen she was a raving beauty of light brown complexion, silky hair and Nordic features. She ran off to Los Angeles with a black buck nigger with no name. "Henry," he called himself. And knowing that one must have two names before one marries, she provided him with one from her family. She and Henry Pellman were married in Los Angeles. She promptly had a child and lost her husband. He apparently had become impatient during her brief confinement and absconded with the little money she had in the bank (put there for her by Seth and Emma) and a brown girl who danced in the honky-tonk. Hagar recovered from both childbirth and marriage. Philosophically, she decided that it had served her right for marrying so black and wrong. She secured a divorce and started home to mother. On the way she met Malcolm Preston. Malcolm was twenty-four, yellow, soft-voiced and a porter. He intrigued Hagar, so she left little Henry with Emma and went to search for love once more. This time with Malcolm.

Little Henry grew; he learned to call Emma "Ma Leany" and to say his prayers before he saw his mother again. Everyone called her "Hagar," so he did likewise. Hagar and her beautiful husband came to stay with Ma Leany. Things were hard with Malcolm just then. Henry liked him. Malcolm would take the little black boy out, buy him candy, tell him stories about everything and kiss him good night. He liked Hagar too. Hagar would rush him in and out of stores while she bought this or that and give him ice cream or candy or put him in the theatre till she came for him.

One day a big black nigger came to the house to see Hagar, and Henry heard them fussing. He went out and got Malcolm. Malcolm came and he talked. They all talked. Then the big black man said "Goddamn" and picked little Henry up and ran. It was great fun—Hagar and Malcolm running and yelling, chasing Henry and the big black nigger, who fled in a buggy behind real horses.

Henry lived with his father for five weeks. Then he became tired of crackers and milk and ran away. A policeman took him back to Ma Leany. He returned with a slight taste for liquor. Big black Henry had usually put a little whiskey in his crackers and milk to insure a good night's rest. But a disappointment awaited little Henry at home. Hagar and Malcolm had left—Hagar to have a child and a divorce, and Malcolm to court a girl he had gone to school with in Philadelphia. In Los Angeles, Hagar achieved both child and divorce. She left Little Malcolm (it was a boy) with a friend when her money ran low, and she started on her second trip homeward.

For a few years she remained with Ma Leany, Seth and little Henry. Henry was eleven when Hagar met Weston. Weston was an insurance man. Hagar used to take Henry with her when she called on Weston. They would sit and drink and talk and smoke. Then Hagar and Weston would talk silly love talk while Henry smoked and drank highballs. It kept him out of mischief. He also read, but that was more dangerous. One could get so many indecent ideas from books. Henry did. By the time Hagar had left Salt Lake with her third husband (for Chicago this time) Henry had learned that his mission in life was to rape little girls. He did. And possessing imagination, he experimented with little boys. Both were disappointing, so he asked Hagar to send for him. He went to Chicago and lived with Hagar and her new husband. Weston had been replaced by Frank Standly. Henry admired his mother's taste. She chose better and better each time. Frank was really quite beautiful. And friendly and oversexed. He drank well and often, and had priceless rows with Hagar. Before Hagar tired of him, he successfully attempted to seduce Henry, leaving an everlasting impression. Never again by man or woman would Henry be so thoroughly captivated.

Hagar ran off to Reno in an automobile with a lawyer to divorce Frank. She was tired of his ability in argumentation. Henry consoled Frank until Frank met a little girl, with whom he ran away. Henry went back to Ma Leany. He stayed quietly in Salt Lake until ready to enter college. Then he wrote Hagar in Los Angeles that he wanted to go to University of Sunny California. So he got to see her lawyer husband. He also met his young half brother, whom his mother had rescued from a stable, respectable home. Henry's half brother later vindicated his relationship by a term at San Quentin.

Henry entered Sunny California and discovered that he was black. He discovered also that that fact made him more acceptable to the whites than to the few Negroes there. He went through college with flying colors and a faculty for being helpless, effectively cloaking his really stupendous ability to take care of himself at the expense of everyone else. He had his appendix and sentiment removed in one grand operation. The nurse refused to baby him. In a fit of temper he threw himself down on the school steps and broke the stitches of his operation, discovering in this way the advantage of being so slight of stature that the slightest mishap called forth the sympathy and love of all creatures better adapted by nature to protect their fellow man than he was.

After college Henry returned to his mother and Los Angeles. (She was sans husband just then.) He worked for a while in the post office, became a devotee of H. L. Mencken, and decided to start a magazine, meanwhile concluding that Hagar was a nymphomaniac, and that he was, too. The magazine—*The Visioner,* filled with Mencken-like articles by Henry Raymond Pellman—was fairly successful. Henry heard of Anthony Brewer and Burton Barclay, and, being an opportunist of the first water, smelled the Negro renaissance and came to New York. He became editor of *The Mirror,* a black tabloid that failed after a few attempts. But not before he had met Anthony and Burton. He then became assistant editor of *The Porter,* a magazine with offices on Seventh Avenue in Harlem. He was one of America's most promising Negro upstarts. And a full-fledged Negro, too. So Black! So handsome! So small and so brilliant! He had come at last to Harlem.

MEETING RAYMOND

Nugent (Stuartt Brennan) presents in this chapter a fictional version of his meeting with Wallace Thurman (Raymond "Rusty" Pellman). Others mentioned include Langston Hughes (Tony), Carl Van Vechten (Serge Von Vertner), Countee Cullen (Burton Barclay), Jessie Redmon Fauset (Molly Restag), and W. E. B. Du Bois (Dr. LaFrance). Nugent has recounted the story in several formal interviews; this version is almost the same as those, so there is little doubt that it is quite literally true. It is, however, a story that is not at all flattering to Nugent. Why did he persist in repeating it?

The most likely explanation is that Nugent's encounter with Thurman was an epiphany of sorts. It was the occasion for confrontation with the skin-color prejudice that infected "blue-veined" Washington society in general and Nugent in particular. This prejudice contradicted Nugent's concept of himself as a rebel against convention and Washington society; it was also totally alien to his persona in later years. Here, then, is the story of how he began to transcend it.

Tony was taking Stuartt to the Y.W.C.A. for lunch and was going to introduce him to Raymond Pellman. Stuartt had already met Serge Von Vertner, the

Livingston of this Empire-State Africa. He had met the incredible Serge and Burton Barclay in the same breath at the awarding of the *Epoch* prizes one night in Harlem. Stuartt had met a number of people that evening—a number of real live artists and authors and "celebrities." There had been Molly Restag, who had written a novel about "the better class" of Negroes—not a very good book, Stuartt had thought, since it dealt so closely with a segment with which he was altogether too familiar. And Dr. LaFrance, a pompous, important-looking, yellow Negro with an impressive Van Dyke beard, who had contributed to America some of the finest and driest prose of present-day literature.

But mostly Stuartt remembered Burton Barclay and wondered how such lyric poetry could emanate from that round and rubicund figure, made more ridiculous-seeming by the sweeping tails of the evening clothes he had worn to grace his reception of the first prize. He had looked like a little brown pig. And Serge Von Vertner, the big white discoverer of High-Harlem, who wrote perfect, neurotic, precious books spiced with the gayest sophisticisms, and who stared with undressing blue eyes from a red face deceivingly moronic. Stuartt had been very disappointed by his first glimpse of Parnassus.

But there was still Henry Raymond Pellman, who, to Stuartt's way of thinking, waded waist-high above the other Negroes. He was the sepia intellect par excellence. Pellman did not have to live up to the promise of sonnets of brown-and-white loves, nor was he compelled to mouth into the void of American democracy the voiceless cry of protest against the wrongs done to Negroes. Anthony was taking Stuartt to meet him now.

When they entered the Y.W.C.A., the sight and smell of so much food was almost an inspiration to Stuartt. He was always at his best around food. He was a gourmand as well as a gourmet, appreciating quantity as well as quality. He liked the lazy feeling, the slightly overstuffed sensation, the Sybarite's pleasure in the indulgence of too many delicacies. He was intrigued by the lavish display of biscuits and corn bread, by the savory steam from the soups. It was just as Stuartt was succumbing to the invitation of the food that Tony pointed to a table and said:

"There is Raymond Pellman."

It was a distinctly unpleasant shock—so unpleasant that Stuartt lost all desire for food. Silent and empty-handed, he followed Tony to Pellman's table. So this was the brilliant Raymond Pellman—the Negro from whom he had expected so much. This little black man with the charming smile and the sneering nose, sparkling, shifting eyes and an unpleasant laugh.

Stuartt decided that Pellman was not to be trusted. He was too black. Stuartt had been taught by precept not to trust black people—that they were evil. And Stuartt was the totality of his chauvinistic upbringing.

Pellman greeted them politely and as peers, conversing with scintillating brilliance and authority. None of his terms were vague. He was certain of his knowledge. So certain that it was an affront. There was something a little indecent about anyone so black being so certain. Stuartt felt decidedly uncomfortable in his presence. So, after a polite ten minutes of torture, he took his leave.

Stuartt walked down Seventh Avenue, oblivious to the magic of spring and Negroes. The rhythm of his heels syncopated the bitterness that stained his thoughts. So that was Raymond Pellman—that insignificant little black man. Stuartt's pride was hurt somehow. He remembered bright bits of Pellman's conversation, and tried to be objective about his feelings. After all, Pellman was one of the most charming persons he had ever met. Yet Stuartt could not accept him. He wondered were the lack lay.

Suddenly, with a rush that swamped and humiliated him, soiling him as it did with nasty knowledge, Stuartt realized that his entire dislike was based on color. It nauseated him that he should allow anything as trivial as he had tried to make himself believe he knew color to be to stand in the way of an interesting relationship. Not even a close relationship, necessarily. Stuartt felt revulsion at his own retrograde thinking. He had believed his revolt against the inanities of his caste to be honest and deep rooted—real. Apparently it was not.

The more he thought of the magnitude of the injustice he was doing Pellman, the more disgusted he became with himself. It was a situation which, had he been confronted by it in something he was reading, would have left him only one reaction to the character in his own position—a great disgust and a complete lack of sympathy. After more than an hour of walking and moralizing, he came to the conclusion that the only gentlemanly thing to do was to go to Pellman and apologize for his thoughts. And Stuartt was a gentleman, as befitted his caste. So Stuartt turned back and walked up Seventh Avenue to the offices of The Porter, the magazine Pellman edited. Hesitating only a moment, he mounted the stairs and in a few minutes was ushered into an inside office.

Pellman had been a little annoyed and more than a little philosophical when Stuartt's name had been announced. He was beginning to get used to having young aspirants taking up time he could use to so much better advantage, although perhaps this bright-complexioned friend of Tony's had a little more on the ball than the many others who usurped his time so continually. Tony had an instinct for selecting as companions youngsters who had something. Then too, he had been rather impressed with Stuartt. Although he had said nothing and sat there aloof and almost condescendingly aristocratic, Pellman had been aware of Stuartt's great soft eyes that seemed so intelligent and arrogant. His instinctive distrust of light-complexioned Negroes was something Pellman was trying to overcome. He couldn't help but realize that there were always two sides to any prejudice; that while experience had proven to him that he was usually right about light Negroes, it was a qualified truth. Maybe this was one of the exceptional times. He donned his most editorial mien, softened it graciously with a border of friendliness due one whom he had met through Tony, and had Stuartt sent in.

For a split second they surveyed each other, during which their emotions and thoughts raced. Pellman was thinking what he could do with the many advantages he saw indigenous in Stuartt's color, bearing and aristocratic mien. Stuartt was thinking that this was perhaps the most difficult thing he had ever had to do. Yet Stuartt felt safe, in the way slave owners felt safe facing the chattel they may perhaps have mistreated. He felt big and small and embarrassed. It was a difficult thing he had to say, had to make understood, but Stuartt was graceful and a gentleman, and finally it was said. A muddled though sincere apology.

Throughout Stuartt's stumbling apology, Raymond Pellman was silent. He recognized the sincerity, but he was furious at the assurance he saw in Stuartt that his apology would, of course, be accepted. It was as Pellman had always known such things actually were. He did nothing to help Stuartt through his welter of embarrassment; he sat with an empty smile frozen and forgotten on his face, aware that Stuartt could not see behind it, wishing he could and glad he couldn't. He was assailed by doubts. Could the two of them be friends — have real trust? He was nagged by the knowledge that perhaps he, Raymond Pellman, might be considered a mean and bitter black if he did not accept this offer, or perhaps a Good Man Friday if he did. Yet trust was important, if he actually believed — as he thought he did — that the only way in which to have any acceptance in this empty democracy was to have all Negroes recognize each other, and for them to be one and proud — as proud of themselves with their differences within the race as of their similarities to the group that had loaned so much paleness to sections of the minority group to which both he and Stuartt belonged. When Stuartt had finished, Pellman smiled boyishly and charmingly and extended his black hand.

Stuartt was more naive, after the manner of those who have always held themselves aloof through some belief in their own superiority. He was oblivious to any possible turmoil that might have traversed Pellman. It never occurred to him that Pellman might not be able to forgive him for having, even for a while, objected to his blackness. Stuartt was too honest a snob to feel such psychological nuances. They just did not exist. After all, Stuartt had condescended to accept Pellman—oh, quite equally.

So began their friendship—for such it became. They made arrangements to meet each other frequently. Even after Stuartt left his home in Harlem at the invitation of a friend-and-landlord who had become tired of supporting an indigent artist and went to live on Ninety-ninth Street, they continued to see each other nearly every day. Pellman called him "the vagabond poet," and Stuartt called him "Rusty." It was a friendship.

Stuartt found living down on Ninety-ninth Street thrilling, to say the least. Ninety-ninth Street, between Central Park and Columbus Avenue, was a district the police patrolled in pairs. Stuartt lived with a young West Indian (a further defiance of social convention—after all, America for Americans). He was black, too—a black, young West Indian who wanted to be an artist. Naturally he thought that contact with a person like Stuartt would in some way be of help to him—a belief with which Stuartt concurred. His name was Evan. He paid the expenses and Stuartt supplied the atmosphere. Stuartt had found another landlord-friend.

At first Stuartt made notes on everything he saw and heard. That was the way writers functioned. The various black thugs in the block not only accepted Stuartt, but also could be depended upon to protect him when necessary. Stuartt was a good listener and would sit through hours of recital of their adventures. He believed everything, or seemed to, and wasn't at all adverse to allowing them to hide the objects of their petty thefts in "his" domicile until they could feel safe about disposing of them. Naturally they thought the place was Stuartt's.

So at first he took notes on everything and was going to use them sometime to write a great book. He felt very much like Villon. But his fingers itched to draw or paint some of them, and soon he had a mounting pile of impressions, portraits, caricatures and sketches. The notes began to be forgotten.

RENT PARTY

In this chapter, several additional characters are introduced who, like all the characters in Gentleman Jigger *and* Infants of the Spring, *correspond to real people. Sterling is Service Bell, the singer. Dr. Parke is Alain Locke. Leo is the artist Rex Gorleigh. Although depicted here in an unflattering light, Gorleigh eventually established a solid reputation as an artist; his work was included in Locke's* The Negro in Art *(1940) and exhibited in an important Negro art retrospective in Albany in 1947.*

For some reason Negro art wasn't doing so well. Neither Rusty nor Stuartt had capitalized on it for over two weeks now, and consequently they were two weeks in arrears with the rent. Or rather, Rusty was.

They were sitting around and pondering. Sterling came up to help them ponder. He brought a quart of gin with him—a quart of gin miraculously salvaged from some past party. And so they sat and sipped and smoked and pondered. It was Stuartt who slipped his way into clairvoyance.

"I think I have the idea," he offered with a hand-behind-the-back tone.

"What is it?" Rusty sounded exasperated and impatient. Sterling sounded excited. They both waited. Stuartt sipped luxuriously again from his gin and ginger ale.

"We'll throw a party." He paused, waiting for their exasperated disappointment. When they refused to oblige, he continued. "A party like all the dicty niggers would like to go to, but are afraid to. Like all the o-fays would like to go to but are barred from." Stuartt took another languid sip. "In short, we'll give a house-rent party."

By the end of the next week, all preparations had been made. Everyone they knew had been phoned or written. Leo had offered his room. All the furniture had been lined up around the walls; the light bulbs had been changed and now were blue. On a table in the alcove were piled sandwiches and a ten-gallon crock of gin, ginger ale and grapefruit juice. The back room, belonging to Rusty and Stuartt, had been cleared completely. Music was to be furnished by the wheezy portable victrola. One of the neophytes who worshiped Stuartt would wind it and keep it playing.

Sterling floated around in his paisley dressing gown. Leo beamed from behind the table in the alcove. Rusty strutted about, inspecting and glowing as though it were all his own handiwork. And Stuartt was curled up on the lounge in the front room reading and tasting the punch, as though a blue light were the only kind under which one should look at the Beardsley illustrations for the

Lysistrata. Pete, a new addition to the fold, was posted at the door to collect the admissions. He was the official bouncer, turtle-neck sweater and all.

It was eleven thirty before the guests began to arrive. The first were several groups who "made" all the rent parties so that, in mingling, they could distribute cards announcing the dates of their own (more legitimate and authentic) house-rent parties. From then on the flow was continuous. Slightly colored debutantes of sepia society. Dr. Parke with a group of miscegenated intellectuals. Serge Von Vertner with his neurotic group culled from Gramercy Park, the theatre, Paris, London, and Cairo. Groups from the village. From Park and Fifth Avenues. An Italian princess who had been born in Virginia beside an English peeress with whom she had not spoken since they had had a battle both verbal and physical over a much-to-be-desired part in a Broadway miracle play. Producers, number-runners, chorus-girls, gangsters, schoolboys, sailors, motion-picture stars, prizefighters, athletes, bartenders, dope-peddlers, parents, schoolteachers, authors, gigolos, artists, whores, pickpockets, millionaires, reporters, communists, laborers. All colors from white through to black.

They gossiped and grouped in cliques. Gin was passed. They danced.

A big, black thug teaching a pink and gold actress to "bump" and "mess-around." More drinks. The Italian Princess exchanging beauty secrets with a nut-brown cabaret performer. Gin. The back room a mass of swaying colors and sexes. The English peeress held spellbound by the lanky intrigue of a yellow number-king's body movements. A pretty young convent-raised girl the shade of maple-sugar accepting fashion hints from a boy in a Paquin evening gown. Dr. Parke learning the intricacies of dictator-government from an attractive young Italian gangster. More gin. Sterling plying a producer with gin and talk and hopes. Bum wandering around getting drunk and looking silly like a storybook college lad on a "binge." More gin. A fight in the center of the dance floor. Pete put them out. A stage star almost perfect in face and figure expounding the advantages of being discreetly sadistic when enacting a love scene before an audience. Stuartt in a corner seated on the floor explaining with graceful gestures the importance of Picasso between majestic commands for more gin. A young, black roustabout advising a detective to play 267 ("that's where we are") for fifty cents ("that's what it cost to get in").

At about four-thirty A.M., there was an interruption by the police. Someone had complained about the noise and that there were white and colored people coming in and going out of the house at all hours. It was decided that Stuartt would handle them. And Stuartt did. He plied them with liquor, re-establishing his acquaintance with two whom he recognized as having almost arrested him one morning for sleeping in a hallway. They joined the party.

By five-thirty there were people lying all over the house in various stages of drunkenness. Leo was washing the glasses and effervescing to Rusty, slumped in a chair. Every now and again the pacing and mumbling of the "pig-woman" could be heard—a few words filtering down from above, past the amorous pairs on the stairway. "Sin and destruction—sin and destruction! God's in his heaven. No good can come from it—" Her lamentations wafted over the head of the Italian Princess asleep with her head in a sepia pimp's lap; over the lengthy kiss of the convent-raised girl and a gigolo; over the snores and slobberings of Bum, whose sprawling legs very effectively pinioned a mahogany million-airess.

Stuartt was taking a bath. In the back room there were still a few desultory dancers moving every part of their bodies save their feet. A policeman with a spilling drink in one hand was imploring Stuartt through the bathroom door to let him in—he had to "go," and he'd wash Stuartt's back.

Suddenly Rusty jumped up. "Stuartt!" he shouted peremptorily.

Stuartt grunted above the splashing of the water and the importuning of the policeman.

"Get 'em out of here. All of them. Get them out!" Rusty's voice was almost hysterical.

Stuartt continued to splash. "Okay. I'll get rid of them."

"For Christ's sake hurry! I can't stand any more." Stuartt could hear Rusty pacing the floor nervously.

"All right—all right. Don't have a baby! I'll be through in a minute."

Twenty minutes later they were counting the spoils. Rent paid for the two weeks gone and two weeks to come and some left over for dinners. They all went to Tabb's for breakfast—Stuartt, Rusty, Anthony and Bum. Leo stayed behind to clean up. It was Sunday morning.

At the table they were each writing poems, in a sort of contest while waiting for their food. Anthony read what he had written—

> Weary, weary—
> Wish that I was dead
> Weary, weary—
> Gin clouds in my head
> Stayed up all night

Drinkin' gin
Mixed with wrong and right and sin
Weary, weary—
Wish that I was dead
Weary, weary—
Gin clouds in my head . . .

And Rusty read his:

Cacophonous night breaks in fragments on the street
Recalling a bleeding dawn that is flung
Like a dirty dead dog, stewing in the heat:
We are peacocks playing in odorous dung.

And Stuartt read his parody on *his* own work:

Pheasant feathers, pearls and pears—
(Who cares what a princess wears?)
Ruby goblets, crystal plate—
(Who cares what the princess ate?)
Spend your sorrows, save your tears—
(Who cares what a princess fears?)
Mauve flamingos, pallid doves—
(Who cares whom a princess loves?)
Not the loveless lovers taking
(Loveless love so body-slaking—)
Peacock feathers proud with pleasure
Overflow in painted leisure—

They had their breakfast and on their way home passed the devout on their
way to church. Over the remains of the gin concoction, they post-mortemed
the party.

With the gain from the house rent party and the amount that Leo could contribute, they moved downstairs to larger quarters. Leo was beginning to be influenced by the *deux enfants terrible*, Rusty and Stuartt. He had decided that he
was an artist and, since he was, that he would devote all his time to art. Art
with a capital "A." He gave up his job. Stuartt did not work, nor did Rusty, so
why should he?

His determination was quite commendable, but he overlooked the inconvenient fact that he was neither Rusty nor Stuartt. He had neither the ability to create a desire in people to be of material assistance, as had Rusty, nor the easy-going personality that refused to be insulted (and made it pay), as had Stuartt. Leo felt perpetually indebted to everyone for everything. He bored everyone with too many thanks. He lacked the amusing chatter with which Stuartt re-paid those who contributed to his well-being. Leo had an inferiority complex that would not allow him to receive graciously.

Leo's inferiority complex was not of the vindictive and shrewd sort, as was Rusty's. He lacked the perception to see irony in making those whom he really considered superior to himself feel in duty bound to support a dependent. In short, Leo was another of those persons who are more taken with the glamour of being known as an artist than with the work entailed in actually being one. And he made the mistake of thinking that the haphazard life that Rusty and Stuartt lived was glamorous. He did not realize that it was as much a profes-sion as any other form of prostitution. So he moved to the lower, larger, and more expensive apartment to be with his gods, thereby helping to lessen—considerably—the expenses of his two exemplars.

He was domestic enough to take delight in keeping the place clean and pleasant-looking, in cooking the meals, and in being general factotum. His training (he had been a gentleman's gentleman) stood him in good stead, for he had in reality only changed employers. No doubt he appreciated his most recent employers all the more because he paid them.

In between times he drew bad pictures and wrote bad poetry. At least that was the evaluation put on his output by the omnipotent Rusty and Stuartt. It was an evaluation arrived at without either of them ever bothering to really notice any of his work, so certain were they that he was, at best, mediocre.

But Leo was content that his works should lie by the side of the masters. He was content to mix and serve (and frequently supply) cocktails so he could mingle freely with the illustrious names he had before merely heard bandied so nonchalantly about by these two who now shared an apartment and their lives with him. To be able to say that he lived with Stuartt and Rusty, to men-tion off-hand that Tony, you know, Anthony Brewer and Burton Barclay (the poets) were by and had stayed for impromptu dinner amply repaid him for the hours he had spent sweating over the preparations for the meal. He began to say things—things that he himself found shocking—because they seemed to be in the tenor of the things he heard them say. He learned to drink, but ne-glected to learn the secret of never getting drunk. Anyhow, Stuartt never got drunk and always saw to it that everyone was taken care of.

Being an excellently trained menial, Leo was happy in his capacity. Life continued merrily at two-sixty-seven.

NEGRO ART

Howard, whose art is the subject of this dinner conversation, is Aaron Douglas. The negative assessment that Nugent presents here of Douglas's work is unjustified; in his murals, especially, Douglas moved far beyond his German teacher, Winold Reiss, in the subtlety of his designs and the sophistication of his palette. Interestingly enough, however, he did, as Nugent predicts here, reach a point (after he joined the Fisk faculty) beyond which his art did not develop further.

Leslie, another character in this chapter, is Leland Petit, who was the organist at Grace Episcopal Church (on Broadway at Tenth Street). A prim and delicate man — and a homosexual — Petit was ideologically committed to integration and spent a great deal of time in Harlem putting his ideals into practice. He appears not only as a character in Gentleman Jigger *and* Infants of the Spring *but also as Mark Thornton, the title character in Blair Niles's novel* Strange Brother.

The final portion of this chapter, which is devoted to a discussion of homosexuality, parallels very closely a similar conversation in Thurman's Infants of the Spring.² *As written, the passages are not identical or even nearly so; it appears that these were two separately written accounts of the same (apparently quite memorable) event. The conversation was present in Nugent's early manuscript but omitted from the later typescript. Perhaps the typescript was prepared after* Infants of the Spring *was published, and Nugent wished to avoid the issue of who was borrowing from whom.*

It always amused Stuartt to dine at De Vore's with white friends. There were many features, and many facets to each feature, of this amusement. Somehow it never seemed to Stuartt that any of it touched him, although he was immersed in it all. It was like swimming in ever-changing waters, temperatures rising and falling, running swift or slow. Only he seemed well-oiled, and the waters rolled off him; his passage through them was eased and helped. He never really got wet at all.

There was something about this walking-on-the-waters attitude of Stuartt's that annoyed Rusty exceedingly. And fascinated him just as greatly. But between them, since they were friends, they were always ready, both of them or either of them, to notice every little nuance and incidental gesture of the other diners, and they would hug it close, exchanging little looks that fenced everyone else out, and would giggle or lift an eyebrow. This secret and impolite malice would make any palefaces at their table self-conscious beneath the imagined focus of the glances of the other diners in this not-too-familiar land, and the slightly tense atmosphere so unintentionally and deliberately created at their table would tickle the senses of both Rusty and Stuartt even further, and they would titter even more. Tenseness and self-consciousness would deepen, causing their enjoyment to heighten, and it would snowball—situation growing out of nonexistent situation until Rusty and Stuartt were hilarious. It was all so impossible to explain to anyone else. That very impossibility would become a part of the almost hysterical amusement that gripped them. Rusty and Stuartt could seldom be serious dining at De Vore's. But today seemed about to be an exception.

They had finished their soup, and the conversation had turned to painting and sculpture. Rusty was holding forth on Negro art. Everyone was hanging onto Rusty's words. He had long ago convinced them that he was the logical source of all information Negroid. He was the leader of the Niggeratti, and the Niggeratti led the New Negro. But except for Rusty, they were all rather apathetic leaders. Rusty was the only one of them who had the initiative to push things to the fore—anything, everything—and shade them with black. He was the superb showman—the black Barnum, the opportunist par excellence. He was also vain and had decided that the group was to be recognized as important, and that he was to be recognized as the most important of the group. He was.

"It is a thing I think should be more greatly developed." Rusty always spoke in a manner that could be quoted and had no fear of clichés or trite expressions. "After all, we are Negroes, and as such we are entitled to draw on the culture of Africa—to borrow its forms as we have borrowed our forebears' pigmentation. Africa and the best there is in it should be inspiration in every sense of the word and every use of its meaning. Yet how many Negro artists have the courage to admit that they think African art is beautiful?"

"Or *do* think it beautiful—or for that matter, even consider it art?" Stuartt interjected in his parenthetical way.

And Rusty continued, as he almost always did when Stuartt punctuated any remark or thought he was expounding, just as though there had been no other spoken word. "How many are proud of the fact that these things were executed by their forefathers?"

"He calls this art, 'Things!'" Stuartt was ready at that breath with further interjection. "'Executed—'"

"Only one person that I know of," Rusty answered his own question. "Howard. Howard has taken the essence of African art and converted it into modern form. So in consequence, his drawings of Negroes, with thick lips and pointed elbows, are not liked by Negroes. Good Lord!"

Stuartt again stopped eating long enough to mildly ask, "Howard? What does Howard know about African Art?"

Sterling froze at this heresy. His reprimand stood solid and stiff in the transparency of his disapproval. "You are not going to contend that Howard's art is Nordic, are you Stuartt?"

"Don't mind Stuartt, Sterling. He just likes to needle." Rusty turned to Stuartt and continued, "What *is* Howard's stuff then? I suppose that with your usual destructive sort of criticism that precludes the possibility of anything constructive, you are about to contend that his stuff isn't even good."

"But he couldn't say that." Leslie's pink face was serious. "Howard's work is beautiful and—I agree with you, Rusty—essentially African."

"But 'stuff'—merely 'stuff,' as Rusty so succinctly denoted it." Stuartt was bland again, but there was a stubbornness in his attitude like a steel stay in a velvet corset. "You are all a little silly. And there is really nothing I can say at all. A fellow artist's work, workers of the world forgive me, is one thing I do *not* like to talk about. I don't particularly relish having the old 'professional jealousy' cliché thrown in my face. At least not at mealtime, when I am already busy digesting. Much more pleasant things, too." He took another forkful of food with all the careful precision of a dancer knowing that the next graceful step hinges upon the present graceful gesture.

"And after I said what I thought, should I be so rash, no matter how much I might belittle my own art, I would only be called insincere. No. Go on, my philistines, believing in Howard if you like—believing in this lacquered and distorted caricature of him and his works. Listen to the great god Rusty expound on a subject about which be knows nothing at all with all the dogmatic emphasis of ignorance."

Stuartt gestured another graceful forkful into his mouth, as though to silence his lips.

"Maybe you could enlighten us, then." Rusty waited a moment and, as there was no answer from the seemingly unperturbed Stuartt, continued, "Since Mr. Brennan refuses to lift the pall of our ignorance—"

"Well, what *do* you know about African art?" Stuartt's voice was still soft but now more urgent. "Nothing. Or you wouldn't say so pompously and glibly, 'African art.' One doesn't say 'German art' or 'Italian art' unless it is understood what is meant by such general classification. One might classify art into schools based on time and masters and then into locales. But in most art the feeling that pervades and influences one country is usually felt in other countries strongly enough to produce great similarities. And—"

"Don't *you* be silly, Stuartt. One says 'Greek art,' 'Roman art' or 'Egyptian art' and presupposes that dates have been supplied in routine education. So—'African art!'" Rusty paused triumphant.

"I guess in a way that's fair enough," Stuartt admitted wryly. "But in another way you take semantic advantage. And psychological advantage. You know I can never be coherent about things that are really vital to me. I'm as much like people as people even, and I don't function on all intellectual fours when I'm emotional, either. Art is vital to me. I have not only *thought* about it, I *feel* about it as well. Silly of me, but too true. And you *don't* know a damned thing about African art. Emotionally, psychologically, intellectually, categorically or any god-damned way at all, except in that everlasting dilettante way that's so fashionable these days."

"Such violence!" Sterling sipped his tea with a delicacy that parodied broadly Stuartt's recent gesticular sarcasm. It seemed to spur Stuartt on, even as it brought his voice under closer control. He seemed to be directing his onslaught at Rusty, though.

"You couldn't tell a Gabun piece from an Ivory Coast or a Sudan or a Congo or a Benin. In fact, I doubt if you knew there were great enough differentiations in African art to allow for any classification."

"African art?" Rusty inserted a little maliciously.

"If," Stuartt went right on, "I were to show you a Gabun, you would probably say 'Egyptian,' if you liked it. Or 'trash' if you didn't. But you'd not appreciate its design. To explain—or I suppose what I really mean is to *accent* for you— the symmetry of the pattern of small repeated lines of highly conventionalized planes and masses about the nose as center would be futile. To point out the beauty of the concentric triangles of mouth, chin, eyes, ears, nose, headdress— the deft in-out-up-down swelling lines and surfaces which make the piece all one smooth perpetual rhythm—would be a waste of time."

Stuartt paused for breath. Or perhaps he paused because he felt a little silly, as one usually does when lost in explaining beauty. No one said anything for a few screamingly loud silent moments. None of them, except Rusty, had ever heard Stuartt speak really seriously before, and even Rusty was absorbed. This would come in handy someday. He recognized it for other than textbook authority. It was the actual authority of artistic and emotional appreciation.

Stuartt felt as if he were dangling in the air. He began to retrace his way back across the tightrope of speaking as he felt to the firmer platform of saying what words could say and still be dismissed.

"Or take a Gabun full figure, embodying the perfection of rhythmic concentration on individual anatomical parts, restrained only by the artist's desire to execute a living whole and his recognition that design is implicit in everything, but that each thing has its own individual design. Repetitions of soft bulbous protuberances carried out in curve of forehead, breasts, trunk, torso, legs. The intense concentration to dissociate the body into units all blending into a perfect design as a whole. I suppose you'll tell me that I couldn't differentiate either. That I, neither, could name this or that. Well, perhaps I couldn't. Nor even vocalize about what I felt. But *I do feel the differences*." Stuartt wet his lips with a sip of his iced tea, then with kindly maliciousness said, "Remember these things, Rusty, if ever *The Bookman* wants an article on Negro art."

Rusty ignored the thrust for the horse-play it was.

"But how does all this discourse concern anything I have been saying about Howard?" he asked.

Stuartt sighed a mock sigh, but he was rather sincerely impatient also. "After all, the discourse itself should have explained its reference. Just because Howard's figures have pointed joints and bulbous foreheads—"

"But if those are the essence of African art and the essence also of Howard's, then what—?" Leslie looked around the table, unable to quite finish phrasing his question.

"Yes. What then?" Sterling gave Leslie a moral boost.

"Why, are you all completely stupid or blind? Howard is just a sponge. He has absorbed a technique invented, or discovered, as you will, by his teacher. He promptly adopts it, adapts it, and perfects it, and it becomes 'Howard's Art.'" Howard is his teacher. Fortunately, his teacher is an artist, so the copy isn't quite a counterfeit. And it is his *teacher* who is influenced by African art—African art and Picasso, who is likewise influenced.

"But isn't that just what all other artists do?" Rusty's voice was so sincerely full of question as to seem timid.

"Not *artists*," Stuartt said quite patly. "That's my very contention. Soon Howard will have exhausted his style. Then what? If he is an artist, a creative artist, he will have derived enough to grow further. That's it—he could grow instead of reaching an end. The artist is continually evolving from what he has created in the past. He is a sieve through which all things pass, and only the finest remains to be used and then sieved again. The artist is continually advancing until, in later pieces, one cannot see the tiniest trace or similarity to his earlier work. But Howard won't. He'll reach a standstill."

"Oh, stop being highbrow and talk sense." Sue was tired of being silent.

"Right, Sue," responded Stuartt.

"Say, isn't that a handsome man!" Stuartt pointed to a couple who had just come in.

"I don't think so, particularly," Bill answered.

"But you, after all, are not as aware of sex appeal in males as I am. It annoys you. It amuses me. You see, you are afraid. I am not."

"And why aren't you afraid, Stuartt?" Leslie was baiting Stuartt again. "Are you so certain of your charm—your influence with women—?"

"Yes, I am," Stuartt interrupted.

"Or," Leslie continued, "are you attracted by men?"

"Yes again." It was Stuartt's delight to play with words. Leslie was so serious.

"Then you are queer?" It was almost an assertion.

"Queer?" Stuartt thought a moment, lit a cigarette, and inhaled a puff before answering. "I don't *think* I'm very different from you or Rusty or Bill. But maybe I don't understand you. What do you mean by 'queer?'"

"I mean: do you like men?"

"Yes, don't you? And women, too. And I'm very fond of eats. Does that make me queer?"

Leslie was not to be shaken off. "Have you ever had a woman in love with you?"

"Yes."

"A man?"

"Yes." Stuartt was totally unperturbed.

Leslie was flushed and triumphant. At last he had cornered Stuartt. "Which did you prefer?"

Stuartt flicked his ashes into a cup. The others waited. Had Leslie really cornered the always-victorious Stuartt?

Then Stuartt answered mildly in an earnest voice. Only Rusty noticed the laughter in his eyes.

"Well you see, Leslie, I don't quite know. I enjoyed both immensely. But then, I've never been in love myself."

Leslie was silenced. During the general laughter, someone suggested that they leave. So out they went. On back up Seventh Avenue. Everyone was in excellent spirits. They stopped in a speakeasy and had a few drinks. As they were coming out, they met Rusty's "find," as Stuartt called him. He was a pickpocket.

Many times, upon discovering that they were hungry, he had gone out into the subway to return an hour later with several wallets.

They all went towards 267. Stuartt and Bill left to catch a train to East Orange.

STUARTT GETS A JOB

Bum, a character in this chapter, is Harold Jan "Bunny" Steffanson, Wallace Thurman's lover. He was a nephew of Vihjalmur Steffanson, the Arctic explorer.

Stuartt continued to grow in his part as court jester. He liked the privileges with which such a position abounded, and his ability to amuse and intrigue grew. But even so, there were times when there was just no one on hand to pay his share of the rent or buy him dinner. This was one such time. So Stuartt got a job.

"I've got a job."

Stuartt made the announcement just as though it were an everyday occurrence, not the most startling thing he could possibly say. He said it with a master's eye to the effect he was certain it would have, for no one had ever known him to work. None of these people. That had been his secret, his reputation. Like any smart entrepreneur, he knew the value of surprise. Hence he announced his job.

"A job?" Rusty gasped. "Not work? Not you!"

"What the hell?" was Bum's succinct summation.

"It's very simple. A job. Work. I think it ought to be fun." Stuartt seemed very calm about the whole thing. He began mixing drinks and passing them around. The expressions of surprise and disbelief on their faces amply repaid him for the bother he knew it would be to get up in the mornings for a while. Bum was still looking at him in amazement.

"Christ in a handbasket. If that doesn't deserve a binge, I don't know the makings. What time did you start?"

"Eleven tomorrow morning," Stuartt said offhandedly. "Now what about that drink? I could use one as an ante-anesthetic."

"At once." Bum grinned. "Come on, Rusty."

"Well, I never!" Rusty giggled.

In another moment they were on their way. First stop was the corner speak. Rusty ordered gin rickeys, Stuartt his usual pink Tom Collins. Bum looked superior as the drink was placed before Stuartt.

"Why the hell don't you order a man's drink for a change?" he asked.

"They cost too much; I drink too much, and I'm tired of putting you and Rusty to bed after each and every session." Stuartt sipped his drink. "You can't make me drunk anyhow," he continued, "So why be extravagant?"

Bum snorted and called to the bartender, "Give the kid a whiskey and soda!"

"Bourbon," Stuartt murmured.

Rusty extended his glass. "Here's how."

"Skoal!" acknowledged Bum.

"Ditto," Stuartt said and drank the pink drink down. He chased it with the whiskey and soda. Then they were out on the street again. It was going to be their regular binge route, so without a word as to where, they went on to the Sugar Cane.

The Sugar Cane was the cream of the honky-tonks. It was a tiny cellar with several tiny tables strewn around a tiny spot cleared for dancing. The five-piece orchestra played by ear and in such a wise arrived at the strangest and most intriguing of rhythms and tunes. A score of dancing waiters threaded their way in a fascinating and bewildering manner through the tables and the dancing couples, performing all sorts of intricate tap-steps, balancing all the while their trays laden with ginger ale bottles and great cups of raw gin. There were also several weirdly attractive entertainers who sang salacious songs sotto voce. The establishment was frequented mostly by denizens of the sepia underworld. Hardly an evening passed that there was not some exhibition of the intrigues that kept the place alive. Anything was liable to happen there and usually did. Every Saturday night there was a shooting, or at least a fight that turned into a free-for-all. It was just the sort of place to become the rendezvous of neurotic intellectuals who persist in having a cause and seek artistic excuse for the satiation of their craving for the unusual. The Sugar Cane was doomed. It was too perfectly what it was.

Stuartt and Rusty were so well-known there that the waiters and entertainers all called them by name. That pleased them greatly; it made them feel as if they were of the cognoscenti. It gave them the same feeling experienced by some insignificant artist when George, headwaiter at the Algonquin, conducted them to a "best table." Stuartt and Rusty were so well received because they always brought someone who spent extravagantly. They were helping to doom the place. Tonight, the someone was Bum.

They sat for a couple of hours listening to "Louise" sing the salacious verses of "Shake That Thing," drinking gin and dancing with girls picked at random. The element of danger connected with picking girls there at random pleased them. One never knew when one was encroaching on some bought-and-paid-for private preserve.

About two o'clock they left and went to their favorite speakeasy. They were just leaving there when it happened. They saw two Chinese fighting and joined the rapidly forming crowd to watch. Here was something new! It was just the fitting end to their evening—an oriental fistic exhibition.

The fighters swung wildly and ineffectively, hit and miss. The crowd was very amused. The sing-song voices of the combatant Chinese were strident and excited, hence all the more amusing. Rusty, Stuartt and Bum stood on the sidelines and cheered—first one of them, then the other—indiscriminately. The fight was at its height when a short, stocky man who looked like the stock Irishman in all Irish jokes came forth and, stepping between the Chinese, held them apart while he tried to find out what it was all about. He could make neither heads nor tails of their excited gabbing. Apparently becoming provoked at their struggles to get at each other, he lost his temper and hit one of them in the face. It was a swift, brutal blow—a sudden downward chop that tore the skin on the Chinese's face and floored him. The man then calmly wiped his knuckles on his handkerchief, straightened his coat, cast a belligerent and rather sneering glance at the crowd, and prepared to move off.

It was then that the surprising thing happened. A figure stepped from the group and struck the man full in the face, duplicating perfectly the blow that had floored the Chinese. And with the same result. Then, calmly, not waiting even to see the effect of his blow, the new combatant turned and walked off. In silent amazement Rusty and Bum followed him. They were nearly half a block away before anyone broke the silence. Then Rusty gave vent to a nervous giggle.

"Well, I never," he almost simpered. Stuartt continued in silence. Bum looked at him curiously.

"What made you do it?" he asked.

"God-damned white bastard. What did he have to do with it? They weren't white." Stuartt's tone was as violent as his words, although the voice was so low as to be almost a whisper. They walked on in silence and turned into their house. As he opened the door, Stuartt could be heard to mutter again. "God-damned white bastard. So God-a-mighty superior and cocksure."

Rusty and Bum were too amazed for speech. Neither of them had ever thought it possible that Stuartt would take offense at anything, particularly anything as hackneyed as the race question. And that he should hit anyone—that was *too* fantastic. They were seated, and Stuartt had mixed and passed them drinks, before Bum spoke again. Bum sounded a little tentative.

"That was a swell blow though, Stuartt. I didn't think you could do it. It was perfect."

"Neither did I." Stuartt had taken a book and was seated on the floor under the lamp. He didn't look as though he had done anything to cause wonder. He had opened his book to its marked place and seemed engrossed and oblivious. Rusty and Bum continued to discuss the happening.

"He just walked up to him and knocked him down. Didn't even turn to see what happened to him. I never." Rusty was excited in his own particular way.

Stuartt spoke without looking up from his book. "Only one of two things could happen to him. Either he'd fall or he wouldn't." Then he turned a page.

Bum was puzzled by aspects more profound. He was having his entire theory of relationships brought into a focus he'd never touched on or thought of. He became suddenly aware that he was white and that Rusty and Stuartt were not, and that this was Harlem, and that he was the lone one, and it made him feel very different—like Livingston must have felt when he remembered. Complications *could* arise from this difference, and it was just a little uncomfortable.

"Yep," he answered Rusty automatically. "I had never imagined Stuartt striking anyone either. But what seems to me to be even more important is that it was a white man."

Holy Mother, he thought, it makes things sound just like I don't mean for them to sound, but what the hell can you say? And mean what you mean?

"It sort of changes the aspect some," he added a little lamely.

"You're not going to try to make a race thing of it, are you Bum?" Rusty looked at him with amusement. "Leave that to Leslie when he hears about it."

"Well, can you make anything else out of it? If the man hadn't been white, well—"

"There would be no question of color, I suppose," Rusty snorted. "You're being sophomoric."

"If the man had not been white," Bum continued, ignoring Rusty with the familiarity of an old friend, "I doubt if Stuartt would have hit him."

"Right, Bum." Stuartt spoke, and they were both startled as if they had forgotten he was there. Bum pounced on the admission.

"See," he said to Rusty. "It boils down to just—"

"To just a lot of crap, my sweet." Stuartt sounded honeyed and relaxed. "Syllogisms are only syllogisms. And black is not always a reason for difference from white. Be adult." He turned back to his book. But Bum was not allowing any such superior evasion.

"But it was in this case?" He made it sound as much like a statement as a question.

"Also," Stuartt admitted. He put his book down and addressed Bum with the sort of patience one uses with stupid children. "You're all wet Bum. It's merely that I have a sense of fitness, and that sense was outraged."

"And you make a habit of going around fighting everybody who outrages your sense of fitness? Shit!" Bum got up and mixed himself another drink.

Stuartt handed him his glass, and as Bum returned it refilled, answered mildly, "It has never been so completely outraged before."

"Fine," agreed Bum with an edge of sarcasm. "Fine. And why was it so sensitive tonight?"

Stuartt grinned at him. "Maybe liquor. You can blame Harlem gin for anything. Maybe just plain decency. Then again, maybe artistic temperament. Maybe all three."

"H. Mahogany Christ, Stuartt! Talk like you had a gut. I suppose it would have been the same if it had been me." Bum felt himself making more of this than he knew Stuartt was, but he couldn't help himself. It was all too damned personal and uncomfortable.

"Maybe," Stuartt admitted. "All depends. Timing is so important. You would have timed it better, I'm sure. Then, what the hell. It wouldn't have meant the same thing."

"But I'd still be white." Bum's voice rose on the statement.

"You'd still be white," Stuartt agreed. "Nothing could be whiter."

"Then talk sense." Bum looked instinctively to Rusty to come to his assistance.

Stuartt smiled at them and spoke to Rusty. "Let me carry the black man's burden this round." Then to Bum. "O.K. Because it was a white man, it becomes a Race question. Chinese and Negroes and a lone white man (you don't count right now). Because I hit the white man, it is a race question. No wonder Mr. Mason and Mr. Dixon got away with that line of theirs."

He held up a silencing hand that stopped Bum's retort. "So all right, it's a race question. Well, let's make an analogous example. Suppose you were in another group of people, mixed not too greatly, and you were all watching a fight between, say, two Eskimos. And a man suddenly stepped in and knocked one of them down. Just because his fighting ability was great. Would you take offense then?"

Bum answered instantly and hotly. "That all depends. What color is the guy?"

"Uh-huh." Stuartt nodded sadly. "That's the rub. That is why it has to be a race question to you. All right, let's say he's colored."

"I think I'd knock him down if I could. But then, I've never laid claim to the non-possession of race feeling. You have. You do."

Stuartt just looked at Bum for a few moments. Kindly and infinitely down on him. "Defense rests, your high-and-mightiness. You can't see it any way but as a race issue. Allow me the pleasure of being capable of enjoying emotions more personal and less narrow." Stuartt looked at him mischievously before adding, "It's really all right, Bum. Some of my best friends are whites." Stuartt turned back to his book. As far as he was concerned, the incident seemed closed.

"But you must see, Stuartt, it *is* basically a race problem," Rusty spoke up. "Bum is right. I hadn't thought of it that way, but what else is there to think?"

"And there you have it, in black and white," Stuartt murmured and continued blandly with his reading. He did not even look up when there was a knock on the door.

It was Leslie, with a young colored man. Greetings were exchanged. Stuartt disturbed himself long enough to mix them all new drinks before returning to the floor and his book. Rusty and Bum told Leslie about the episode; both were very curious to see how it would affect him. Leslie was pleased. He acted as though it meant to him that there was still hope for Stuartt. He might still become an asset to his race. Leslie's views kept talk alive and argument rolling. It grew so loud that Stuartt was forced to look up in the middle of a sentence being dramatically emphasized by the colored boy.

". . . has been weighing on me with the weight of twelve centuries removed. No. I'm not supposed to have weights. I am supposed to laugh. That big black laugh—"

Rusty giggled and looked at Stuartt, who whispered, "Sounds like a blurb for a Paul Green book, maybe." But the young man paid no attention to them. He was worked up to a state that allowed no outside interference.

"Despite being a mixture of many bloods, the proportionate one drop of Negro blood must predominate."

He didn't even hear Stuartt's murmur, "Naturally."

"Well, I'm sorry. I'm very sorry that I can't put you all at your nice interracial ease by denying a conflict that *does* exist. Yes, I suppose you are surprised, but what can I do? With a mother who is a mixture of Scotch, French, German and North American Indian? With a father who is Negro and Spanish and Irish and Negro?"

He was nearly weeping in his excitement. Everyone sat silent. There was nothing to do. Rusty made the first move. Then Stuartt got up and gathered the glasses. He was passing them out again before he spoke in his vaguely cynical and amused voice.

"You must be from Washington, D.C. I know how you feel, but why be so Hamlet about it?" Stuartt's smile broadened a little. "My mixture is as bad as yours. So I brag that I'm on top of the sepia social ladder."

"Hell! It's all right for you to brag. You're yella. You don't feel things as much as I do—"

"And you're black and only blacks can feel," Stuartt interrupted with sarcastic annoyance. "So Rusty has been telling me."

But the lad went on, oblivious to Stuartt's comment. "You can't, or you wouldn't be such a parasite. You'd have to let it out sometime. There are no compensations. None. Even the word 'none' can't express enough."

They were all silent again. Stuartt looked as though he was bored. Bum and Leslie were embarrassed by this unexpected intimacy. They were embarrassed for Rusty and Stuartt and further embarrassed that they were embarrassed at all. And Rusty was embarrassed. Ashamed that they should have been allowed such an insight. That such privity should have been forced on them. And it all played hell with the carefully balanced relationships he tried so hard to keep afloat. Bum and Leslie would likely class them all with this crying black oaf now. His voice betrayed him as he spoke.

"Well, why weep about it? Does that help any?" He was trying to be diplomatic, spreading oil on the waters. Oil that Stuartt promptly proceeded to inflame.

"And why not weep? He has every right. I'd much sooner put stock in his sincerity, since he chooses neither time nor place nor a nice, neatly-selected audience. After a certain amount of thinking—just living—one does explode." Stuartt grinned at himself a little as he stopped for breath. He had not meant to be trapped into mounting a soapbox. But he went on, nevertheless, and seriously too, for him.

"You, Rusty, say 'I'll prove to them that I'm an author, not just a Negro writer.' That's crying. I get sarcastic and say nasty things about my relatives both white and black. And after all, I am representative of a certain class of Negro in America. But not just Negro. No, I won't allow that, even when I'm being my broadest. That's crying. So I say nasty things about Whites. Or about how like sheep Negroes are. I vent my spleen on conditions. I establish a reputation for being an unfeeling cynic. That's crying. What's the matter with us is that we have all got an inferiority complex, and we've got it so bad we're afraid to admit it." Stuartt bowed elaborately to them and made ready to sit on the floor again.

"You're crazy." Rusty was still trying to gather the battered remains of his little kingdom. "If you weren't excited, you wouldn't talk like that—"

"And the truth is usually told in such moments of excitement, when we don't stop to think 'what the hell' about it." Stuartt's remark was as bored-sounding as he still looked. "Now that we've had the unusual pleasure of having white-folks help us wash our dirty clothes, let's drink and forget it. Of course we won't, but we'll all pretend to. It's so much easier, and we have such a good time being progressive. So let's drink to a bunch of four-flushers. That takes us all in, regardless of color."

They emptied their glasses. Stuartt turned to the by-now embarrassed young man again. "At least we have something to be thankful for. We should all be glad I'm such a mongrel, because I'm certain that only a weird collection of bloods like mine could produce such a beautiful and polyglot cocktail. I think I'll call it 'Quadroon.'"

Stuartt kept his elevator job two weeks. Then the strain became too much. He hated the routine hours, so he threw up the job and spent his $32.50 salary by blowing the gang to a good time. They did all the cabarets and speakeasies. The next day he could again luxuriate in the fact that he had no money, no job, and no responsibilities.

ORINI

The later sections of Gentleman Jigger *have no parallel in* Infants of the Spring; *Nugent devotes them to tales of his involvement with gangsters. Nugent was fascinated with Italian men (see "You See, I Am A Homosexual"). His fascination extended to the criminal element. There is no reason to suppose that this section of* Gentleman Jigger *is any less faithful to reality than those devoted to life in Niggeratti Manor.*

Stuartt was very excited, and it enhanced his appearance. This was the "underworld" he'd been reading about in the newspapers—this beautifully appointed cabaret with its tasteful and expensive floor show and its evening-dressed clientele. He wondered how many of the socially prominent guests present were aware that their neighbors at the next table might be some infamous "Public Enemy No.—" and his bodyguards. He felt buoyant with that sense of unreality that was becoming so customary with him since he had discovered that Frank was the "Artichoke King" the New York newspapers headlined so frequently.

He glanced across the table to where Frank was sitting, and as usual he found it difficult to reconcile this curly-haired Greek, who looked so much younger than his thirty-three years—this young man who had such soft brown eyes and such a willful childish mouth—with the notorious character the newspapers accused of instigating so many brutalities. Stuartt felt a glow of reflected glory at being with a man who was such a "big shot" that Orini himself was coming to transact a deal with him.

Frank glanced up from his glass of White Rock and smiled into Stuartt's eyes. "Havin' a good time, kid?"

"You bet." Stuartt wanted to touch Frank. He reached across the table and touched Frank's fingers. "Yep, you're real, Frank. Sometimes it's hard to believe."

Frank smiled back at him in that rather possessive and assured manner that always excited and slightly annoyed Stuartt. It was like taking too much for granted and always made Stuartt wish something would happen to make Frank less sure. He would never make the mistake of showing his likes too well again. He was learning.

Frank had a beautiful body and was an excellent model. It was his vanity that made him so. Stuartt was glad he had nearly finished the nude portrait of Frank—the one in oils which he called "Habeas Corpus." There was only a little detail left to do now on the background, and then it would be ready for exhibition. Stuartt was certain that it was a good piece of work and would cause comment. That's what intrigued him more than satisfaction at having done a fine work: the comment, the stir—the seeing and hearing his name—the sensation of being sensational. For "Habeas Corpus" *was* sensational. It was bound to cause all sorts of prolonged comment and discussion, partly because of Stuartt's treatment, partly because of his execution, which was sure and mastered, although iconoclastic, and partly because of the fact that Frank was the model. For Frank exuded the sex beauties—the awareness of them and the love of them—that seemed so characteristic of his ilk. Because Frank's sex beauties were radiant and *his*, because they intoxicated others, because he sensed that intoxication and became intoxicated in turn, a portrait of him was not to be ignored. And if interest in the painting did begin to lag, there was always the possible stimulus of revealing the identity of the model.

Yes, Stuartt was well pleased with the way in which he was ordering his life. And here he was in Chicago, in this gay and dangerous night club ("dangerous" was Stuartt's most romantic adjective) with Frank, who was so obviously proud of Stuartt. With Frank, the exhibitionist, who was showing him off, so certain that he could depend on Stuartt to back his attitude of possessiveness. And truthfully, Stuartt was sensational. His excitement and his own ambiguous exhibitionistic quantities lighted him as though from within. He knew that women were looking at him desirously, that men were vaguely aware of and jealous of the friendship and dependence he showed with Frank. ·

Stuartt knew also that his actual relationship to Frank was not evident. His attitude was too much that of the idolizing young friend. It seemed to manifest so exactly that perfect sort of friendship which most men subconsciously romanticize about but seldom enjoy. Stuartt was the walking, talking, living incarnation of the romantic portrait men and women paint to fill some void in their imaginings.

Needless to say, Stuartt could not precisely identify this emotion he so universally aroused, but he was aware enough of its manifestations, without knowing their cause, to take unconscious advantage of it whenever it suited him. At the moment he was quite content to sit, the center of attraction, and share his feeling of well-being with Frank, who no longer excited him physically, but toward whom he felt affectionate and with whom he felt comfortable. The pride with which Frank exhibited him flattered Stuartt, and he gave himself up completely to the voluptuous excitement of his surroundings.

Frank interrupted his reverie. "Here he comes now, with the blonde." Stuartt stood to be introduced. So this was Orini—"Sweetheart Orini." Stuartt went through the graceful politenesses of meeting Miss Day and Orini and sat down.

"Everybody calls me Bebe." Miss Day had a deep, husky voice that was most attractive. She wore clothes like only women in the cinema do. An extravagant chinchilla wrap slid gracefully from her fabulously white and beautiful shoulders. Smoke-gray chiffon molded her perfect figure and fell in billowy fullness from her sheathed hips to the floor. Silver slippers were barely visible through the nebulous, smoky hemline. A silver chain, with one pendant black pearl, and black pearl earrings were her only jewels. She ordered champagne. Stuartt was fascinated.

"Order up kid—they're on me." Orini was speaking, and Stuartt was antagonized by his peremptory tone.

"Yes Stuartt, order up." Stuartt was surprised at the placating, almost coaxing quality he detected in Frank's voice—surprised, then a little angry. He glanced at Orini, who was waiting for him to order. Stuartt made his stare as offensively impersonal as he could. This man antagonized him as nothing or no one had ever done before, sitting there like a dictator—his handsome black eyes hard, his thin lips impatient—unaware of Stuartt as a person. Stuartt finished the whiskey and soda in his glass, then, looking past Orini, spoke to the waiter.

"Nothing for me, thank you." Stuartt turned back to his contemplation of the dance floor.

For a moment Orini looked at him, then spoke to Frank. "Order whatever your buddy's been drinking for him." Orini turned back to Stuartt. "We always drink one drink for friendship," he explained, as though the matter was closed. Frank ordered—double whiskey and soda.

Stuartt began to be unaccountably angry. It was with difficulty that he kept his voice steady and his smile impersonal and pleasant as he countermanded the order by saying to the waiter, "Really, don't bother—I'll have nothing. I may have a drink later at the bar." Immediately he was sorry for his ill manners.

Orini was looking at him, a curious smile in the corners of his lips, his black eyes steady and fixed in their regard of him. After a few seconds they flickered, and he spoke in that same rich but impersonal voice. "Okay, Sweetheart." He turned to Frank.

Stuartt paid no attention to their conversation or to Miss Day. For some reason he felt mortified. He couldn't account for this instant anxious antagonism. Orini inspired him to be insulting. He heard Orini's voice.

"Bebe, have a dance with the playmate there. We gotta talk."

Stuartt knew that the girl had gotten to her feet. For a moment he thought he would refuse—that he would say he didn't dance—and wondered what would happen. But when he turned to speak, he saw Miss Day and her expression. She was nervous. Well, so was he. Then he realized how great would be her embarrassment. So he rose and led her to the floor.

As they wound their way through the tables, she spoke. "Say baby, you certainly got your nerve. Orini's sore."

Stuartt was casual—much more casual than he felt—as he answered, "Nerve's all I have. Let's tango."

She grinned up at him. "Okay."

Stuartt requested a tango. As the orchestra played an introductory bar, the majority of couples left the floor. Stuartt swung his partner into the sensuous rhythms and slow intricacies of the dance. She was an excellent partner. Soon Stuartt had the exciting sensation of being on a stage—dancing as exhibition couples dance. His sense of the theatrical was heightened by his realization of the theatrical possibilities of his partner and himself together. She was dressed perfectly, exactly as girls are dressed when doing exhibition dances. He wore tails. He was glad he had worn them, even if it had been because he never had worn them before, and he had thought they would attract attention.

Together they were being sensational. Stuartt was injecting all sorts of Harlem dance hall movements into the soft Latin steps. When the music ended and Stuartt bowed slightly to her, they became aware that they had been dancing alone by the applause which burst forth.

"Gee baby, you sure can dance!" Bebe was ecstatic and sparkling as Stuartt led her back to the table through the lane of applauding people.

"Anyone could dance with you, Miss Day."

"'Bebe,' baby, 'Bebe.' Don't be so formal."

They were nearly off the dance floor now. The applause still strong when the orchestra struck up "The Merry Widow" waltz.

"Shall we?" Stuartt asked. He was very excited—intoxicated by the applause. Perhaps more so than she, who saw a more romantic angle. It was romantic to float away to the strains of a marvelous band and the applause of many people, in the arms of the one of the handsomest men she had ever seen. And one who seemed so solicitous, so different from the men she knew, so soft-spoken—a gentleman. One who was not afraid even of Orini.

"Okay baby." Bebe's voice almost choked with excitement and the romantic possibilities of the moment. So they swung gracefully onto the floor, both conscious of the effect they created as they blended, glided, and dipped in unison, smiling into each other's faces. All lights were extinguished, and a soft amber spotlight followed them as they danced, apparently oblivious to everyone and everything but each other. When it was over, they were each silent as he lead her to their table, neither apparently noticing the applause that followed them. Stuartt stood until she was seated, and then he met Orini's gaze. For a moment he returned the gaze. Then, turning to Bebe, he spoke.

"You'll pardon me please? I'm going to the bar—"

Stuartt was a little ashamed of himself, yet proud. And provoked that he had allowed the annoyance he felt in Orini's presence to make itself so manifest. He ordered a whisky and soda and stared at the ornate bar, sipping and reflecting. He was making a fool of himself. There was only one consolation, and that was that no one would realize why—no one with the possible exception of Frank. But then, Frank had never seen him exhibit such a mood before. He'd never had such a mood. No, no one would realize. They'd just know, maybe, that Orini antagonized him and that he showed it. They would just take it to be that sort of instantaneous dislike that on occasion springs up so spontaneously and without reason.

They would not know that he resented Orini's deft manner, his careless, masterful gestures, his impersonal eyes, his caressing, sarcastic voice and the excitement all these things aroused in him. It angered Stuartt that after the few glances he had offered Orini, he was able to reconstruct in such detail Orini's every physical aspect. His sleek black hair with the one uncowed wave in it, causing a dark lock to fall to his eyebrow whenever he nodded or leaned forward. His compact figure, so slender, yet showing hard contours beneath his dark gray "sharkskin" suit, the same way an Indian's body is so pronounced through his clothing. His too-lavish attire—gray silk shirt, maroon tie, collar pin showing a small black pearl on either side. The fine linen handkerchiefs he used, the suggestion of perfume, the too-highly-polished shoes, the Turkish cigarettes in a case so slender, so simple, that it vulgarly proclaimed itself to be platinum. Nor could Stuartt forgive Orini his slim, still fingers and the tremendous sensation they aroused. It must be his "defense" to dislike this man.

In any event, it was evident enough that he need not see more of Orini during his short stay in Chicago. Because Stuartt was quite certain that this man was unobtainable, which was a sensation that he had not had for so long that it was novel. Novel, disconcerting and unpleasant. He had grown quite used to having everyone looking at him desirously. And this man didn't. This man who was the first at whom *he* had looked desirously.

Stuartt glanced into the mirror behind the bar. He smiled wryly. He was remembering Ray, his first encounter with the "underworld." Orini was all that Ray only promised, and Ray had excited him. Stuartt ordered another drink.

"They're on me, bartender—"

The voice came from a young man with a hard face, who was flanked by four other men who rather aggressively seemed to proclaim that they were his bodyguards. It was very obvious and very exhibitionistic, and at any other time Stuartt would have been interested in knowing them. They were the sort of symbol of crime that intrigued him. But just now he preferred to continue his own trend of thought uninterrupted. His glance in the mirror took them in and dismissed them quite unintentionally as he slipped deeper into his own peculiar frame of mind. He absently reached into his pocket and flipped a coin on the bar.

"I said they're on me, handsome."

Stuartt neither turned nor answered. For a moment his mind was a blank— then he resented the voice even more, because he realized how unwittingly he had made a situation. His feelings were a combination of fright, embarrassment and anger at the person who had caused the first two.

"I'm talking to *you*!!"

There was a silence at the bar that made Stuartt know that he'd have to meet the situation. Suddenly he felt reckless and spectacular. He turned to face the belligerent, and after looking him over slowly from head to foot, uttered one word.

"Impossible."

A look of surprised anger crossed the face of his antagonist, and he started forward as if to strike Stuartt, then hesitated and drew up. Rocking back on his heels with his thumbs in his vest pocket, he took full advantage of the dramatic silence before he spoke in a cold, hard voice and asked through a tight-lipped smile, "What do you mean, wise guy?"

Stuartt knew that all he had to do was laugh and pass it off as a joke, and he'd have nothing to be afraid of. His stomach was quivering. When he opened his mouth, it was with surprise that he heard his own voice, soft and insulting, answering, "I don't *know* you, handsome."

He turned his back and reached for his drink as though the entire incident were but an annoyance he had dismissed. Any second he anticipated a blow or a shot or one of the other fantastic things that *can* happen, like in a movie. Then he heard another voice saying, "It's OK, Luigi. He's particular because he's a friend of mine."

Stuartt wanted to turn. To see what was happening. Instead he sipped his drink and wondered that his hand was steady. Then he heard the voice again.

"Have a drink now, Sweetheart?"

Stuartt recognized Orini. "Sure. Help yourself. They're paid for," Stuartt answered, and, tossing a silver dollar on the bar, sauntered back toward his table.

He had just reached the edge of the dance floor when he felt a hand on his arm. It was Orini, who asked, "You don't like me, do you Sweetheart?"

Stuartt looked at him for an instant, savoring him completely before answering. "Why do you say that? Have I been impolite?"

Orini didn't answer. He just continued to embarrass Stuartt with his fixed gaze. Stuartt, as was his custom, resorted to speech when he felt uncomfortable.

"I would hate to be too impolite to a friend of Frank's."

There was still no word from Orini. Stuartt felt his resentment mounting again. "But of course, I'd find it difficult to be too impolite." Stuartt made his way back to their table.

Orini following silently. For a while the four of them were silent. Orini was the first to speak. He turned to Frank. "How long have you known your playmate?"

Frank smiled expansively as he answered. "Oh, he's okay. I known the kid 'bout a year and a half now."

"So you bring him to Chi with you? Just for a good time?"

"Yeah," Frank answered, and Stuartt was certain that Frank did not detect any hidden motive in Orini's words. He interrupted.

"You see, Orini, we are friends. I don't suppose I could make you understand how deep our friendship is. But when I learned that Frank had to come to Chicago, I wanted to come too. I'd never been here before—so I came."

"Yeah, I can see that—"

"I came to see the gay places I'd heard so much about—to go to the museum, to do lots of things. Oh, I expected a lot from Chicago. I expected fun places . . . things . . . people . . . gambling . . ."

"And now you seen 'em. So what?" The conversation was between Stuartt and Orini exclusively now. It was pregnant with an underlying emotion of dislike, of which Frank and Bebe seemed oblivious.

"So what? If you'll pardon the vulgarity, 'So blah.' Nothing comes up to my expectations—the places, the things, or the people. I prefer New York."

"So you don't like the people?" Orini's voice was impersonal.

Stuartt turned to Bebe. "Miss Day understands, I'm sure, that present company is excepted."

"So Chicago is all washed up for you."

"I don't know yet. I haven't gambled yet, you see."

"Well, we'll arrange that now. We'll go to my place. Waiter!"

Orini signed the check and spoke while doing so. "Frank, you take Bebe home, then meet Stuartt and me at my place." He gave the waiter a sizeable tip. Frank was helping Bebe into her wrap.

"Here's the key." Orini laughed slightly. "We don't use passwords or invites. Everybody's got their own key. You and Bebe grab a cab."

Stuartt was lounging back in his chair. He drew out his key ring. "Take the car, Frank, since Mr. Orini is taking me."

"Be seein' ya, then." Frank had his hand on Miss Day's elbow. She turned.

"Goodbye, Stuartt. Hope I see ya again. Good night, Sweetheart." She allowed Orini to kiss her.

"Nite Babe," and they were gone. Orini turned to Stuartt. "Lets get goin'."

Stuartt rose and followed Orini. As he passed the bar, he stopped. Taking out a flask, he asked the bartender to fill it with whiskey and water.

"You can get stuff where we're goin'," Orini said.

Stuartt only smiled as he paid. Putting the flask in his pocket, he answered, "Thanks, it's all right. It's a thermos flask."

During the drive they were silent. They drove into the driveway of a lakeshore estate and stopped before a little side door. Orini let himself in with a latch-key. "Okay, Sweetheart," he said, and Stuartt followed. A man took their things. Orini led the way up a flight of stairs into an elegantly furnished apartment.

"Have a chair."

Stuartt sank into a pneumatic easy chair. When he looked up, Orini was standing, his back against the door, with a strangely expressionless face, contemplating Stuartt. "Make yourself at home, Orini. The place is yours—"

"Yeah, I know." But Orini said no more.

Stuartt began to feel uneasy. "You seem to be forgetting your manners. Would it be too much to ask for a glass?" he asked.

Still Orini didn't move. He only nodded his head. "You'll find drinks in the cabinet there."

Stuartt rose and went in the direction indicated, selected a glass, and returned to his seat. He poured a drink from his flask, carefully screwing on the cover, lit a cigarette with exaggerated nonchalance, and inhaled deeply before reaching for his glass and taking a tentative sip. He was very frightened, for he knew that he had goaded Orini into taking some sort of reciprocal step and realized his own helplessness, and impotence, placed as he was in Orini's apartment, isolated from assistance of any kind. He was determined, however, not to let Orini know that he was disturbed.

"So you don't like me, Sweetheart?" Orini's voice was soft.

Stuartt glanced up casually. "I hadn't thought about it seriously, Orini," he answered.

"Well, think about it now, baby. Think while you're still able."

"'Still able?' You talk like a murder mystery, Orini."

"Yeah, sweetheart, while you're still able. While your pretty face is still pretty."

Stuartt felt himself sink with an almost physical slump into that fatalistic state which seemed to pervade him in times of stress.

"Oh, then you have been observant enough to notice my appearance." It sounded trite to Stuartt, but he was pleased to find that his voice was still unconcerned and vaguely insulting. Orini remained silent, so Stuartt continued. "Why don't I like you, Orini? Well there are many reasons why, if I thought about it, I might not like you—"

"Yeah? Well name 'em, Sweetheart! I'm in a hurry."

"They're not so important that they can't wait—"

"I said, name 'em!" Orini's voice was uncomfortably colorless. "Name 'em if you got the guts—cause in a few minutes, I'm going to get to work and—"

"That's the first sign of manhood I've seen you evidence so far, Orini—this sudden desire to fight. Surely you don't intend to ruin your manicure by trying to beat me yourself. You might muss up your pretty hair." Stuartt was panicky. He knew there was no escaping the beating he was in for and thought he might as well bluff—keep up his semblance of fearlessness and contempt.

Orini had reached the end of his patience. He stepped from the door.

"Okay, Sweetheart—"

Stuartt had a moment of nausea now that the inevitable moment had arrived. He reached for his glass and sipped, then, looking at Orini with every appearance of casualness, spoke again in his soft cool voice. "'Sweetheart.' . . . They tell me you say 'Sweetheart' when you're very angry, Orini—when you're going to see that someone is, as your kind so quaintly say, 'put on the spot'—"

Orini was still advancing. He was only a few feet away now. Stuartt puffed on his cigarette. "But I thought you always got others to do your work for you." Orini was standing directly in front of and over him now, so close that his legs touched Stuartt's knees.

"Well, Sweetheart, you want to talk a little first?"

Stuartt allowed his gaze to track up Orini's legs, slowly past the slender waist and the dapper shoulders to his lips. Stuartt was vaguely amused to discover that even in this moment of fear, he was excited by what he saw—excited by the feel of Orini's legs against his knee. He half smiled at himself as he spoke.

"All right, handsome. I'll tell you why I don't like you." Stuartt dropped his eyes to Orini's legs against his. "But have a seat. You excite me standing so near."

Orini threw one leg over the table at the side of the chair. Stuartt leaned back into the far corner of the chair away from Orini. He wanted to watch him.

"There are several reasons. You are overdressed—too pressed and shined, too elegant for good taste. And I *have* good taste. You think that because you are Orini, everyone should jump to do what you like. And everyone does—except me. You could kill me before I would jump like that." Stuartt's voice was still conversational and casual. "You're so damn good-looking that you think all women will fall for you and all men will be jealous of you. Well, I'm good-looking too. I'm also a gentleman. I can't boast that I've ever killed anyone or put them 'on the spot'—but then, I don't need a bodyguard to fight my battles for me either. Orini, you wouldn't be a bad fellow if you weren't so conceited, but as it is—well, I would never even have *tried* to be polite if it hadn't been for Frank."

Orini's face was imperturbable. "So Frank told you to be nice—"

"No, Frank didn't. But I know what it would mean to him. You see, Orini, as I told you before, I like Frank. I'm his friend, and there's nothing I wouldn't do for a friend. But you wouldn't understand that. You're too selfish and conceited to have any *friends*. You couldn't like anyone but yourself, like Frank can—"

"So Frank likes you, and you're nice to me because you are Frank's friend?"

"Yes."

"You wouldn'a paid no attention to me if Frank hadn't wanted you to—"

"That's right."

"I oughta smack your goddam' face, you little—"

"I'm surprised that you haven't. There's nothing to stop you. We are alone—and will continue to be alone be unless you begin to get the worst of it."

"What kinda lousy punk you think I am? I'm gonna smack the hell outa you with one hand behind me—"

"I'm sure you are, Sweetheart." Stuartt reproduced Orini's way of saying "Sweetheart" perfectly. "I'm sure you are. I'm going to let you."

"Let me? Well, I like—" Orini was so angry he stood up and leaned toward Stuartt.

"Well, I'd rather be beaten by you alone than by everyone who'd come running if you yelled—"

Orini slapped him a sudden blow in the face. Stuartt didn't move. He could feel the print of Orini's hand growing red and angry on his cheek.

"You goddam lousy punk. Get up!" Orini slapped him again.

Still Stuartt made no move.

"And have you take it out on Frank? No. I like Frank too much."

Orini was standing over him, contemptuous.

"You lousy coward—"

"Locked in *your* rooms Orini? Try it some time in *my* rooms."

"Shit!"

"Yes, I guess you would. But remember Orini, I've got to think of Frank—"

"What the hell has Frank got to do with it?"

"I'm Frank's friend. I can't forget that, and neither would you. I don't know what you might do to Frank."

"Your 'Frank' alibi's gettin' damn weak. You're yella."

"I suppose *you* would think so. You've never had a friend. No one has ever liked you like I do Frank."

"Anyone would think you and Frank was lovin' each other—"

"All the more reason for doing whatever I can for him."

Orini relaxed with a suddenness that seemed to halt Stuartt in mid-sentence. A nasty smile twitched his lips. "Oh, I *see*," he said, with an upward inflection. "I always thought Frank was a queer."

Stuartt was frantic when he heard Orini's remark. He could see Frank suffering the jibes of all gangland—losing respect, losing his prestige. None of them would want to have a queer for a leader. Stuartt felt helpless and inadequate. And at the same time, cool. He had to re-establish Frank in the respect of this man some way. He didn't know how. He began to talk, fighting for time to think.

"Well, Frank found me less expensive than a woman, I suppose—and less liable to talk. A woman got him his only sentence. She got jealous. Well, people like me—when we like someone—well, we don't do anything to hurt them." Stuartt hoped Orini didn't know anything about it.

"So Frank fell for a queer." Orini laughed slightly.

"Is there anything so funny about that? Every man wants someone around who he knows is crazy about him."

"And you're crazy about Frank."

"No, I'm not—but he thinks I am. And I like him too much—"

"Then what the hell—?"

"'What the hell,' what? You wouldn't understand, Orini."

"Damn right I don't."

"You see, I like Frank better than any man I know, but I'm not crazy about him. I don't guess I can love anybody."

"And the boys don't know. That's rich."

"Didn't know till now. I suppose you'll broadcast it. Well, try and make anyone believe it. Frank has a girl, and I have a girl—but we don't let them get too tied up with us. And the girls are satisfied with their men. Even you, Orini, couldn't get *my* girl from me—although *I'd* be willing . . ."

"You don't like girls?"

"Yes, but I like men more. I have Frank. It keeps me off the streets."

Orini had seated himself to enjoy this new experience. But Stuartt knew that he was in greater physical danger than before. He also felt that he was succeeding in re-establishing Frank. He was on more familiar ground now—if he could only keep Orini interested . . .

"I'd tell you if I thought you could understand."

Orini was silent. Stuartt continued, "Well, Frank was the best looking man I'd ever known. I met him through a friend of mine. No one but Frank—now you—knows I'm queer. And I thought I'd like to do a picture of him. So I asked him if he'd pose, and he did—for a nude I wanted to do. Well, seeing him there so handsome and naked, I would get excited, but naturally I never said anything—until one day, he said he'd thought all artists were queer, and I said they weren't and asked him if he'd thought that I was. He said he had thought so when I asked him to pose, but he didn't now. He said, in fact, that I was one of the most regular fellows he'd ever met, only I spoke different and had different ways, but he supposed that was because all artists are nuts.

"So we talked, and I found out that he liked me a lot—that he could trust me. Then I said, 'Suppose I *was* queer—what then?' Well, he was embarrassed and said there wasn't any use supposing. Then I told him that I was. Well, that's that. For a while after the first time, he tried to find some similarity between me and what he thought queers were like—and found out that he liked me just the same. And about that time his girl squealed on him, and he got into trouble. I helped, so he only got five days for disorderly conduct—"

"How'd you do that?" Orini interrupted.

"Lied," Stuartt answered. "So—well, we tied up together."

"He live with you?"

"No. He has the keys to my place."

They were both silent for a few moments. Then Stuartt continued. "So you see, Frank trusts me. I can't afford to get him into trouble with you—he's been too nice to me. So I tried to be polite—"

"Well, what's so wrong with me that it hurts to be polite?"

"I've told you, Orini."

"You sure? You sure it ain't because you kinda thought you'd like to—well, have a good time with me, and I didn't latch on—"

"Don't be silly, Orini. I don't go for other men when I have one. And Frank's all right with me."

"You couldn't go me for one night, even?" Orini was laughing at him now.

"Not for one night, even—even if I *wasn't* with Frank."

"Oh, no?"

"No."

"Suppose I was to say I was curious to know how you and Frank act when you're alone?"

"I'd say, 'I'm sorry, Orini, I don't know what you mean.'"

"Suppose I said I was gonna *make* you show me?"

"I'd say, 'You couldn't.'"

"Not even by—" Orini's face became expressionless again, "well, by saying I'd forget to tell the boys about Frank—"

"Orini!" Stuartt got to his feet in fine semblance of concern. For he was no longer worried. He knew now that he could handle Orini, and that Orini would never tell if he was intimate with *him*. "You wouldn't be such a rat!"

"*No?*" Orini asked it with rising voice.

"Yes, I guess you would." Stuartt sank back into his chair, a picture of perturbation. "I guess I'd even do that, if you'd lay off Frank." He looked up. "But what guarantee have I that you will—"

"You have to take my word."

Stuartt seemed helpless as he answered, "I suppose I'll have to trust you."

"I'll let that crack pass." Orini spoke with an edge on his voice. "What about it?"

Stuartt appeared to think a few moments. "Okay."

Orini reached for the phone. In a moment he spoke. "When Mr. Adrenopopolis comes, tell 'im his buddy left—alone—and if he wants me, I'm out."

Stuartt had lit another cigarette and was pouring two drinks. Orini was sitting low in his chair, legs thrust before him full length.

"Well?"

Stuartt brought him a drink and thought of Ray as he spoke. "'Well' what?"

"Well now, for an example," Orini answered, "we'll see what it is that makes Frank think you're so good."

Stuartt didn't reply. He was excited—as excited as he had been that first evening with Ray. He walked back to his chair and sat silently.

After a few moments, Orini spoke again. "Well, when do we start?"

Stuartt was at loss for words. "What are you expecting, Orini?"

Orini drank from his glass, then smiled. "Christ, you look bashful."

"I am." Stuartt was truthful when he admitted it.

"Then let's pretend I'm Frank. That ought to please you. I'm Frank and this is the first night you laid your racket."

Stuartt was amused and relieved. "Okay, Orini. First you take off your coat and vest and hang them on the back of a chair."

Orini followed Stuartt's instructions, a slight smile playing in the corners of his mouth. When he was settled back in his chair, Stuartt rose, went to it, and extracted the wallet from the inside pocket of the coat. This he opened and took out a sheaf of bills, replacing a five-dollar note and putting the wallet back.

"What the hell?" Orini half rose with an exclamation.

"It's all right, Sweetheart. I did the same to Frank the first night, and he asked 'What the hell?' too."

Orini hesitated a moment, watching Stuartt put the money into his own folder. Then he relaxed and smiled faintly.

"You've never known a boy before, Orini?" Stuartt had gone to the bathroom and was running a bath.

"Hell no!" Orini stated emphatically.

"You're a strange Italian, then. You have a treat in store." Stuartt had come to stand beside him where he sat.

Orini looked up with a near approach to a grin on his face. "Women have been okay with *me*, baby."

Stuartt smiled. "I'll change that. Come on, Sweetheart, take your bath."

Orini got to his feet and, with a slight swagger, began to disrobe, dropping his clothes wherever he happened to be at the time of removal. "You know, fella, I'm beginning to see what makes people look at you the second time on the street," he said.

Stuartt was silent, enjoying to the full Orini's movements, his voice, and his body, which was becoming more and more visible as he shed first trousers, then shirt, with nonchalance. Orini's words were smothered for a moment as he drew his undershirt over his head.

"Guess they sorta get an idea of this sorta thing when they look at you."

Stuartt watched the hollow of Orini's stomach, his raised chest and the muscles of his arms rippling gently under his tannish skin as he asked, "Did *you*?" and only half heard Orini as he answered, "Naw, not exactly. I didn't know you was a fag just looking at you. That never crossed my mind, but you *did* make me look another time—an' I ain't never looked twice at no man for nothing."

Stuartt only half heard, because he was excited by Orini's body—as something to paint. Already he could see it as an anachronism in a picture—an intriguing anachronism. He'd do Orini undressing, his feline nudity contrasting beautifully with the background of an ultra-modern room with silver walls and red chairs, his tan torso—that strange yellow-brown shade of white contrasting with his black trousers and socks as he bent over to unlace his shoes—seeming browner against the silver and drawing colour from the vermilion chair. With his complex ability to think, apparently, of several things at once, Stuartt was simultaneously annoyed that he could be composing a painting in his mind's eye while his senses were being excited as they never had before by the very same body, while at the same time he was able to keep his end of the conversation alive. For he was answering, "I don't like the word 'fag,' Orini. I'm not a 'fag,' you know. I hate painted, screaming sissies."

Orini laughed. "Okay kid." He started for the bathroom, stopping to drink the remainder of his highball. Again Stuartt found himself thinking of Orini as a subject for a painting and was excited sensually by Orini's body. If only he could get motion like that in his picture. The nape of Orini's neck was strangely pathetic, like a small child's. Yes, silver was the background for the picture. Orini would very likely like to be cuddled. Orini would be his best picture, better even than Frank.

Orini was entering the bathroom now. He stopped and turned, striking an exaggerated, yet simple pose and looking at Stuartt with insulting arrogant eyes and a slightly contemptuous smile on his lips. "How is it, kid—okay?" he asked and with a laugh went on into the room. In another moment Stuartt heard him splashing in the tub.

Stuartt recognized the gesture as inspired by a certain mixture of embarrassment and vanity. It was more or less the same sort of vanity—the same sort of pride in his body, the same sort of awareness of his figure tapering like a long "V" from shoulders to narrow hips—that was Frank's and Ray's. Stuartt had noticed most the beautiful slimness of Orini's ankles and wrists. Stuartt should have known they would be exactly as they were. His hands, with their beautifully modeled fingers, had promised the exquisite symmetry that was Orini's.

Stuartt undressed and went to a chest of drawers, where he found, after rummaging a bit, pajamas. He put on a maroon suit. The heavy silk was like a caress to his skin. On the pocket of it was embroidered a large monogram, "MO."

"What's the 'M' for, Orini?" Stuartt raised his voice; Orini was still in the bathroom.

"Huh?" Orini poked his head around the door. His hair was all tousled, and his dark skin was glowing.

"The 'M' here on your clothes—what is it for?"

Orini grinned. "Oh, that's my first name—'Mario.' Bring me some pajamas, kid."

Stuartt selected a suit of rich, creamy white and took him only the trousers. "Mario," he repeated as he handed them to Orini. Orini took them, but Stuartt did not release them. His eyes were caressing Orini's head and shoulders, just as his voice had caressed the word, "Mario."

Orini looked up, attracted by the quality in Stuartt's voice as Stuartt repeated his name. "What's the matter?" he asked.

Orini's emphasis on the "what" and his dropping of the last syllable on "matter" was a lapse into the Italian English that ordinarily never showed in his speech, except to faintly colour his "R's" or to stress slightly the penult of words which in English are accented on the antepenult. Stuartt was embarrassed that Orini would look up and catch the admiration he knew must be manifest in his gaze. As Stuartt released his hold on the garment, his eyebrows lifted in the vaguely cynical manner habitual with him. Stuartt spoke casually and with a suspicion of mockery. "Your good looks surprise me, Sweetheart." The reproduction of Orini's way of saying "Sweetheart" was epic. "You actually look natural."

"Hell," was Orini's sole reply.

Stuartt watched him step into the pajama trousers. "I'd like to do a picture of you, too, Orini. You'll be almost as good as Frank."

Orini didn't answer. He strode past Stuartt to the liquor cabinet. Stuartt noticed that Orini wasn't slightly bow-legged as he had imagined. It was that he planted his feet so exactly straight as he walked that he produced a subtle illusion of bow-leggedness.

"How 'bout another?"

Stuartt followed him into the room and sank into the pneumatic chair. "Fine," he answered.

Orini mixed the drinks and came over to Stuartt, standing before and above him again. "Well?" he asked.

Stuartt sipped his drink. "You'll do. You look so much nicer without your hair plastered down. I could almost like you."

Orini grinned.

Stuartt stood for a moment beside the bed, looking down at Orini. Suddenly he was amused at the idea which flashed across his mind. He bent down and kissed Orini lightly on the corner of his lips. It awakened Orini; he stared dazedly about before seeing Stuartt standing a few feet away near the table. Orini grinned and yawned. "Hello kid. Goin' somewhere?"

Stuartt smiled back. "I hope so. I'm late now."

Orini grinned again and stretched prodigiously. "Sure baby. I'm gonna let you out—by 'n by—but sit down. Take it easy. Ain't you gonna be polite?" Stuartt sat down with a smile and lit a cigarette, but remained silent. Orini propped himself up on one elbow. "Come over here and sit." Stuartt came to sit on the edge of the bed. Orini seemed extremely pleased with himself. "I ain't the poison now like I was, eh kid?"

"No, Orini—but then, you never were quite poison."

Orini smiled. "I didn't think so. Not after all them pretty speeches you made last night." Stuartt made no answer, and Orini continued. "And we still got a little business yet."

Stuartt smiled. "You mean my beating?"

"Well, let's say a little 'exercise.' D'ya think I'd forgot."

"No. I just thought maybe you'd change your mind."

Orini still seemed pleasant and conversational, but Stuartt noticed that his eyes had regained that cruel, calculating glint he'd noticed the night before. Even his voice was threatening in that impersonally soft, even way Stuartt had come to recognize.

"Okay, Orini," Stuartt said.

"Call me Mario, Stuartt." Orini was mocking. "Like you did last night—remember?"

"Yes, I remember."

"I ain't so bad, huh. Maybe you kinda can't remember summa the things you was saying."

"Oh, I quite definitely meant some of them." Stuartt smiled.

"Go on, kid, tell me all about it. Tell me pretty. I might like it." Orini stretched luxuriously.

"You tell *me* Orini. Tell me how you enjoyed your novel experience. I'm *good*, you know.

Orini answered briefly. "Yeah, you're good, all right."

"But don't jump to conclusions, Orini. You're one of the handsomest people I've ever seen, and your hair is lovely. But you're still Orini to me."

Orini reached out suddenly in anger, but Stuartt was on his feet out of reach. "You lousy little punk."

"No, listen a moment, Orini," Stuartt remonstrated. "Remember, I won't be able to talk when you're through with me, so you say."

Orini quieted. "Okay, baby."

Stuartt took a long breath through his cigarette before continuing with aggravating calm. "You see, Orini, I didn't forget our bargain either. I've lived up to my half—and very well, too, you'll have to admit. But—"

"You tryin' to tell me it was all put on an—"

"Yes, Orini, that's what I'm inferring. It was my bargain and put on for your special—"

"Like Hell!"

"And now," Stuartt continued, "it's late, and you've had your fun, so I must leave."

Before Orini knew it, Stuartt was at the door and holding it open. He leapt out of bed, swearing. "You goddam little punk!"

With a laugh Stuartt blew him a kiss, slammed the door in his face and held it. He spoke softly through the door. "I wouldn't let everyone know I'd spent the night here, if I were you. They might not understand any more than Frank's boys would have, if I act up." He could hear Orini subside on the other side of the door. Stuartt smiled as he said softly, "Goodbye, Sweetheart. And I do think 'Mario' is a lovely name."

Stuartt was met at the door by a man who helped him into his coat. As he left, Stuartt heard the hall phone ring and knew that Orini had phoned down to have him stopped. For a moment he panicked. Then he ran down the long gravel drive to the road. He could hear footsteps crunching somewhere behind him. In another moment he was on the highway, running toward the next estate. By this time he didn't know whether he was being chased or not. He ran up the drive to the mansion and rang the bell, struggling for breath and calm. When the butler came to the door, it was a very debonair and self-contained looking young man who spoke. "I beg your pardon, but could I use your phone to call a taxi? I've—"

The butler was about the refuse, when a young girl came down the stairs. "What is it, Harrison?" she asked.

Stuartt spoke. "I'm sorry, Miss, but some friends of mine seemed to think it a huge joke to leave me stranded here at this time of day in this get-up, and I was just asking the use of the phone to call a cab."

The girl laughed. "Certainly, come right in. That will be all, Harrison." She turned back to Stuartt. "You certainly are not attired for this hour."

Stuartt smiled in return. "Thank you. Then if I may—"

She was taking him in rather thoroughly. "I'm driving in, and if you don't mind being seen in an open car dressed like that—" She left the sentence unfinished. "It's a roadster," she explained.

Stuartt was his most charming. "You're too kind. Thank you."

As they were driving she turned to him. "I'm Wayne Traveller."

"And I'm Stuartt Brennan," he replied. And so they conversed pleasantly until she stopped in front of his hotel. Stuartt stepped out, quite oblivious to the stares of the noonday passersby.

"You've been very kind, Miss Traveller. I hope sometime to be able to return the compliment and rescue you."

Miss Traveller laughed. "Maybe that can be arranged. Call me some time." And she drove off with a light wave of the hand.

HARLEM RENAISSANCE PERSONALITIES

These vignettes were composed when Nugent was working for the Federal Writers' Project in the late 1930s, with the exception of "On Carl Van Vechten," which has been transcribed from a 1983 taped interview.

ON GEORGETTE HARVEY

Only a few decades ago, St. Louis was a waterfront town with all of the color and high life that goes with the romantic memory of such places. America grows with such rapidity, and changes are so startlingly sudden when viewed through the gauge of the history of this still-new country, that our history achieves a de-formed and telescoped congruity. But during the "gay nineties" travel was still a hardy adventure, river traffic caused exciting towns to spread bawdy fingers back to caress the wealthy gentlefolk, and there were rough and colorful characters aplenty. John Henry was still too alive to have become legend, Frankie and Johnnie were creating a folk song with their love, and "slavery" was a word which St. Louis had not yet recognized as obsolete.

With such life all around her, and adventure being what it was, it is not surprising that the little girl with the coffee-brown complexion and the deep — very deep — contralto voice should begin to find singing in the church choir and the compliments of the elders and sisters of that church just a little tame. So Georgette Harvey went "bad." She became a theatrical performer. There was still an opprobrium attached to such activities which the more respectable folk were not hardy enough to abide. No respectable female would associate with show folks. They were all of loose morals. They walked home alone at night. They exhibited themselves for money. They showed their ankles (clad in silk at that), and they used rouge. They were all "fast." So it's easy to imagine the consternation which Georgette caused when she flouted her fairly respectable family and the horror-raised hands of her church by going on stage.

But Miss Harvey had definite ideas about the ways of the world, and in no time she had worked her sinful way to that Mecca of American theatre, New York. When she arrived, the Negro had reached new heights of popularity on

Georgette Harvey (circa 1929). The inscription reads, "To my Pal Bruce, From your Pal Georgette. 'Ah Dear'."

the stage. Marshall's was catering to a brown bohemian world, most of whose members were either then or later to become famous. Williams and Walker, Ada Overton, Abbie Mitchell, Jim Europe, and Ella Madison were among the host of celebrated personalities, and in her mind and determination, Georgette was already adding her own name to the list.

She organized a group of six girls, and they did a song and dance turn of sorts. Of very high sorts. She played Snow White in a dramatic production. She sang. Soon, of course, her exceptional voice was recognized. She and her five girls went abroad—to England, France, Germany, Belgium, and then back to America. Vaudeville had become an accepted form of entertainment here by then; she and her aggregation soon became known and in demand.

This aggregation she ruled with an iron and autocratic hand. She husbanded her girls, their energies, and their talents in more ways than one. She was the court of last resort for all their affairs—private, public, personal, legal and amatory. None of her girls ever got into trouble; she perspicaciously saw to it that they married in time to prevent that. Usually they married well. Such moral concern for her girls frequently disrupted her act, however: she was constantly having to discover newer and better talent. But she was well-fitted for such a task, and each succeeding voice replaced the preceding one with one still better. So by 1911 or thereabouts she was the leader of an exceptionally fine group of singers, each of whom, besides working perfectly in chorus with the rest, was a soloist of no little merit. It was about this time that she returned to Europe.

This time she returned to even greater glories than before in the variety halls of England, Scotland, Ireland, the Scandinavian countries and all of the continent. As she visited each country, Georgette learned the language with that remarkable facility for tongues which some people (Negroes and parrots) possess. Finally they arrived in Russia. Czardom was at its apex. Diamonds, rubies and snow dripped romantically over everything. Sables clothed all the drozhky-driven aristocrats. There was a plethora of nobility. Every head that bowed to every other head in "Red Square" was a noble head. Palaces were not centrally heated but they were palaces—cavernous, empty, overstocked palaces with silver candelabra, crystal chandeliers, rivers of wine, tons of venison, endless banquets and gaudy guards, brilliant ladies and beribboned diplomats vying for attention and attraction against shining marble and heavy, dull damasks.

The many badly-clothed and ill-fed persons whom one always encountered in the streets in droves only tended to make this lavishness all the more exciting. Georgette Harvey and her troupe became favorites of the people who mattered. The other people—the many, many people—never saw them entertain; Georgette and her girls were far too expensive. They were for the carriage trade—rare and exotic delicacies to be savored only by the noble palate.

Georgette Harvey was an excellent businesswoman. She took full advantage of the exciting strangeness which her color and that of her troupe afforded this sybaritic elite. The troupe became the toast of the dance halls, and Georgette herself, with her florid gestures and generous physique, her stentorian tones and blustering personality, easily became the focal point of any scene or situation in which they happened to find themselves. And scenes and situations were many and varied. All accompanied by a jewel or precious bauble, a few thousand rubles discreetly offered, sable coats and ermine stoles casually donated, along with lavish dinners and extravagant displays at which they were the guests of moment.

Georgette was quite the curiosity. Her facile command of the rather difficult Russian language and her ability to speak to anyone in the tongue by which she was addressed became a never-ending, seven-day wonder. She commanded her little troupe in the same high-handed manner that a Captain used with his Cossacks. And with the same success. She swept on her overpowering way acquiring money, friends, jewels, furs, prestige and newspaper clippings—dragging her cortege in her successful wake.

Then "came the revolution." Everything was upset. There was massacring in the streets, the Romanoff family was decimated and the legend of Anastasia born, and the aristocrats were put to rout. Georgette gathered her jewels, clippings, furs and rubles and, herding her little troupe before her, bought, fought and schemed her way across turbulent Russia, dodging the Red Army, fleeing the White Army, adopting improbable disguises, protecting her girls, pushing her incredible way all the thousands of impossible miles to Siberia. There, after a short respite, her group now scattered, she made her lone way into Mongolia, then China, and finally into Japan. There she stayed long enough to leave speaking Japanese.

Upon her return to America, she again organized a quartet of girls. She had lost her White Russian wealth; in one way or another, one must live. She succeeded at that quite ably. When, in 1927, Rouben Mamoulian insisted upon her to play the part of Maria in the Theatre Guild's production of *Porgy*, she loyally insisted that her three girls also receive a place in the play. After her success in that opus she found herself much in demand for dramatic parts, and from that time on could and can be seen at almost any time on Broadway in some successful production, her latest having been as Mamba, in *Mamba's Daughters*, produced in 1938.

ON ROSE McCLENDON

Rose McClendon's rise to position of "First Lady" (Negro) of the American stage is, while extremely individual in detail, illustrative of the strange manner in which such heights were sometimes reached by Negroes. She was the wife of a chiropractor who was also a Pullman porter. Her social activities took up the greater part of her time, along with being a good wife, keeping a splendid home and preparing fine meals. She was an active worker with many organizations for Negroes—the NAACP, the Urban League, the Utopia House charities and the Hope Day Nursery. Because she spent so very much time putting on little plays with and for the children—plays which she frequently wrote as well as directed and costumed—she decided that she should learn something about the stage. So she enrolled at Sargent's School of Dramatic Art.

Her first part on any stage was with the Bramhall Players in a play called *Justice*. She had gotten the part because she had lost her way getting there and

Bust of Rose McClendon by Richmond Barthé (circa 1935). The inscription in the plaster reads, "To Bruce from Barthé."

was an hour or more late. It was a very hot day and she was angry, hot and disgusted. Before Mr. Davenport, who owned and directed the theatre, could say a word, she angrily burst into a tirade against him for being in such an inconvenient place, for picking such a hot day for the interview and for sending for her in the first place. She got the job.

Due to her excellent performance in that play, she was engaged to work with Charles Gilpin and Evelyn Ellis in *Roseanne*. All the while she was continuing her activities with the children and the church. When she was sent for to play a part in *Deep River* and was offered a certain salary, she refused to consider it, saying that her price was much more than that and naming an amount which seemed to her exorbitant. Arguments that she was unknown and really untried and that she could command no such salary fell on deaf ears. She merely countered by saying, "Well, you sent for me. I didn't ask for the part," and went back to her children's plays in Harlem. She got the part and the salary she had demanded.

So sensational was she that overnight she became the toast of Broadway and the intelligentsia. She went on to greater glory under Jasper Deeter in *In Abra-*

Rose McClendon (circa 1929). The inscription reads, "To Brucie Wucie Poo, from Rosie Posie Pow. Rose."

ham's Bosom and then *Porgy* for the Theatre Guild. Later she was to become the toast of the workers when she became active in the Theatre Union. Her personal Broadway successes continued even when the play in which she appeared did not last any great length of time. Such a play was *Never No More,* in which she played the part of the mother whose son was being lynched so realistically that the audiences were appalled. Brooks Atkinson of the New York Times characterized the performance as "one of the most harrowing scenes ever put on the stage."

Rose numbered among her friends the great from all walks and endeavors, and she continued to offer her services and assistance to groups and organizations as long as she was alive. She had become affiliated with the Group Theatre and other, even more radical aggregations. She remained the only glamorous Negro "star" lady of the dramatic stage up to her last illness, which caused her withdrawal from Langston Hughes's *Mulatto.* Even from her sick bed, she was vital enough to be interested in the proposed Negro branch of the Federal

Theatre, lending whatever aid she could, suggesting names and ways to John Houseman and Hallie Flanagan.

She died in 1936 at the age of 51.

ON THE DARK TOWER

After A'Lelia Walker, the "Mahogany Millionairess," had made her bid for space on the upper rungs of the sepia social ladder—a bid which had been cruelly rejected by the securely Familied "lily-whites" of Washington, Philadelphia, Boston and points South, East, and North—and after she had fatalistically decided to make the best (and a much more amusing best it was) of the less exclusive entertainment and sporting strata, she decided to become, as the wealthy of all other groups and races become, a patron of the arts. This would not be such a difficult thing to do. Artists are proverbially needy, and biologically they are a breed of "chiselers," looking perennially for bigger and better "freebies." Moreover, artists and their close associates had entree into the tiny closed circles which had refused the ambitious A'Lelia. Should she make herself their friend (and bountiful provider), it was more than conceivable that they might in turn leave the sacred doors a little ajar, or perhaps even go so far as to become active about casually sponsoring her among their friends in the restricted groups. For A'Lelia had not quite been able to accept her social failure.

But there was also, as part of the heiress's motive to be a patron, the sincere desire to help her friends who "did things." It was not enough that she have them to her house, invite them to parties, and wine and dine them. She saw that there was a real need for a place—a sufficiently sympathetic place—in which they could meet and discuss their plans and art, to which they could bring their friends, and at which they could eat for prices within their very limited reach. She had a naive fantasy of herself hovering in the background—a completely accepted and well-liked "angel."

The Dark Tower was named after a column in *Opportunity* magazine authored by Countee Cullen. Countee was one of her famous poet friends. She dedicated a floor of her mansion (the one on 136th Street in Harlem) to the enterprise. The large, elaborately floored room that overlooked the back garden she had redecorated simply. There had been much talk about those decorations, for of course the "patron saint" had held many conclaves with her protégés. Among them were several artists who were anxious to daub the great clean expanse of wall which tantalizingly presented itself. Aaron Douglas was the one who had the soundest ideas, but he never had the opportunity to prove them, although it was decided at one time that he and Richard Bruce would collaborate. (The latter really to be under Aaron's supervision.) That was another of the ideas concerning the prospective haven that just faded and died from malnutrition. Either A'Lelia was too busy with some party or some poker game (she was very fond of poker) to find time at that moment to put her stamp of approval on it, or the artists could not manage to be all at the same place at the same time (because of similarly important distractions). Or if by some miracle a complete gathering *was* contrived, someone would produce a quart of gin like some immaculate conception, or a few dollars, which was an even greater miracle, and the serious meeting would evolve into the more serious business of having a good time. It was 1928, when Negroes were still being discovered and were busy proving that they were human, with, surprisingly enough, quite a few human characteristics; it was during the lush and lavish days of prohibition and the Negro Renaissance.

Every time the little group of consultants were gathered at A'Lelia's ("—and this time, we really must get something done—"), there would be much discussion getting nowhere, until one by one the various members of the aggregation would leave to go about their private (and much more important) matters. But out of this welter of ineffectuality finally emerged several salient points. Food was to be so reasonably priced that the artists could afford it. There were to be recognized members to whom reductions would be offered; others, both members and non-members, who could afford more would pay more. Those (artists) who had nothing at all, and there were quite a few, would be allowed to eat gratis. The place was to be completely informal—a quite homey, comfortable place to which they could bring their friends for a chat and a glass of lemonade, coffee or tea. Yet it was to have enough quiet dignity to impart weight to the poetry evenings and other gatherings which would, of course, take place there. From time to time there were to be hung on the walls of the room, with no ballyhoo, the pictures, etchings, and other works of the struggling artists. It was all to be quite Utopian; it was to fill a great gap by supplying a much-needed place for fraternizing. Plans hung uncertain fire, wavering in the winds of greater or lesser enthusiasms for quite some time.

Eventually the artists (and everyone else) received notice that the Tower was opening. This came as somewhat of a surprise to the members of the planning committee, who had thought that they were working with A'Lelia. Their last meeting had been just as vague as had any of the previous ones. Settlement of details great and small had been just as ephemeral and negative. Nonetheless, they had received their invitations to the "grand opening" from the energetic and impulsive A'Lelia.

Those engraved invitations should have warned them, but blithely and blindly they attended, one and all. The large house was lighted brilliantly. There was an air of formality which intimidated them as, singly and in pairs, they arrived. Bravely, however, they went up the flight of stairs to be greeted by the hostess and the hired man who would check their hats for a small (fifteen cent) fee. The great room and hall were a seething picture of well-dressed people. Everyone had worn evening clothes. One of the artists was nearly refused admission because he had come with an open collar and had worn no cravat, but fortunately someone already inside recognized him, and he was rescued.

The artists (singly and in pairs) pushed their bewildered way through the crush, looking about them for others of their own persuasion. The laughing, chattering, evening-clothed people were quite at home. Colored faces were at a premium; the place was filled to overflowing with whites from downtown, who had come up expecting this to be a new, hot nightclub. One by one the artists made their uncertain way toward the kitchen. At least they could eat. There was something leveling and comfortable about eating. Then they saw the menu. Coffee—ten cents; sandwiches—anywhere from twenty-five cents to fifty cents; lemonade—a quarter; and on and on. They left hungry.

It wasn't until later, on other days when they gathered their straggling courage, that they saw the decorations—the decorations, about which there had been so much and such extended talk. There was a poem by Langston Hughes and another by Countee Cullen painted on the cool cream walls. A'Lelia had had a sign painter in; the artists, her protégés, to whom she had tried to give the work of decorating, had promised to be too expensive, and she was a businesswoman. But any of them would have done this little trifle of lettering for at least five dollars less than it had cost her, had they but known that this was the extent of her decorating aim.

There were small vermilion tables and chairs scattered about. Sari Price Patton supervised and pervaded the tea room (for such it really was) with stiff dignity that quite forbade the loose comfort for which the place was to have been born. The open-collared, tieless artist even wore a tie when he went. Prices remained out of the reach of most of the people for whom the establishment had been conceived and brought into being.

The New Negroes made one or two loyal attempts to try to support the place—the misplaced idea of the place—but they could not afford it. A'Lelia gave several soirees there, to which she invited all of white social New York, including visiting royalty and Rothschilds. Slowly but surely the place began to fail. Finally A'Lelia, in a rash of disgust (the artists had let her down, they didn't come and anyhow she was losing money on the joint), closed it, less than a year after its gala opening. Such was the brief life of the Dark Tower.

ON BLANCHE DUNN

One of the personalities of Harlem, a product of the twenties, is also perhaps one of the best dressed women in New York City. In 1926, when she was about fifteen or sixteen years old, just a wide-eyed little girl fresh from the West Indies, Blanche Dunn made her first impress upon Harlem. Her delightful brown complexion, the regal balance of her well-shaped head upon her slender neck and her personality made her much sought after. Among those whom she met in those early years was Wilda Gunn, a girl from Cleveland and a dress designer who took Blanche under her wing. It was under her tutelage that Blanche learned the secret of perfect dress.

Soon Blanche began to be included in every gathering. Harlem was just being discovered and exploited. Carl Van Vechten was forever drawing sepia surprises from his uptown hat with which to startle and please a naive and sensation-seeking downtown. All the Negro artists and artistes were at one time or another revealed by him to a panting public. Blanche was offered as an example of the exotic bits of beauty with which fabulous Harlem abounded. She found being a brown beauty among these pale sophisticates pleasant enough, even exciting. She easily picked up enough of the characteristic chatter of this polyglot group to be able to do a little harmless gold digging. All of the artists (and artistes) managed a "donation" here and there; Blanche did likewise. For she *was* an artiste—an artist at dress and social behavior. Her wardrobe began to acquire silver foxes and exotic jewelry. She was to be seen at all Broadway first nights, dressed as well and as expensively as any of the paler ladies who vied for such honors, wearing her color as others did their well-known names, and to the same end. It was a common thing to hear people say, "Oh, everyone was there," and reel off an imposing list of names, finishing usually with, "and that stunning colored girl—you know, the one who always goes to first nights."

She knew everyone, and when they came to Harlem, they all (everyone) looked for her. A party was not a party, a place not a place, without Blanche. Her popularity downtown opened doors for her in Harlem, and being on the right side of these Harlem doors opened yet more white doors to her. The snowball of her popularity grew, as did the number of her admirers, the greatness of their names, the extent of their expenditures, the lavishness of her wardrobe, and the distinction of her charm. There was always a table reserved for her at the "Hot Cha," one of the more popular speakeasies in Harlem, for the Italian management had in short order recognized the fact that most people wanted to see her around. But Blanche was in some ways still naive, and very probably did not realize that she was in reality being used as a "shill." She only knew that everyone was "so nice" to her, that her drinks were free and that she could just sit at her table, sipping, and sooner or later everyone who was anyone would come in, pay their respects, and pay her court.

This life which came so easily, pleasant and unfought for, became in reality her career. Her ability to accept the fact that the world was a pleasant place in which to live never diminished. And why should it? It was early in the depression that she was persuaded that a shopping trip to Paris and a pleasure tour of Europe might prove amusing; she returned to America after having proved to herself that such *was*, in fact, the case. Saratoga and the races beckoned, as did Atlantic City, the football games, and the Broadway first nights. She answered their call. It was all a part of life to her by this time (along with more trips to Europe) and still is, for Blanche is nothing if not vital, and she lives her life to the full quite calmly.

ON "GLORIA SWANSON" *(Real Name: Mr. Winston)*

When "Gloria Swanson" came to New York and became one of the most popular "hostesses" to be found in any of the nightclubs, he had already left behind a colorful career in Chicago. Mr. Winston, who had adopted the name of the glamorous Gloria Swanson as his own, had been a darling of the underworld and sporting element in the windy city. In 1928 he was hostess at the "Book Store," a speakeasy-nightclub which immediately grew in popularity once he became known as a permanent fixture there.

"Gloria" had been a perennial winner at the "drags" in Chicago. His net and sequin evening gowns were well-known, habitual and expected. As a matter of fact, there were very few persons who had ever seen him in male attire at all. Seldom coming on the street in the daytime, breakfasting when the rest of the world was dining, dining when the rest of the world was taking its final snooze before arising for the day, his public life was lived in evening gowns, his private life in boa-trimmed negligees. Prohibition was at its most success-fully unsuccessful, crime was at its peak, graft was the order of the day, and life was lived at a highly accelerated pace. Winston—plump, jolly, and bawdy, with a pleasant "whiskey" voice, his every gesture and mannerism more feminine than those of any female, his corsets pushing his plumpness into a swelling and well-modeled bosom, his chocolate-brown complexion beautiful, and his skin soft and well cared-for—was just the sort of playmate for the fast-living element.

He had the free, loud camaraderie that distinguished the famous Texas Gui-nan. Gangsters and hoodlums, pimps and gamblers, whores and entertainers showered him with feminine gee-gaws, spoke of him as "her," and quite en-thusiastically relegated him to the female's function of supplying good times and entertainment. He could also cook.

His "Book Store" was a rendezvous protected by the fact that his "protector" was a big shot—a well-known underworld figure. All went well until his "boy friend" had a fit of jealousy—a tantrum of violence during which he practically wrecked the joint. After that, all protection ceased. The police began raiding the place, but even that novelty began to wear thin, and soon it was no longer the same pleasure spot it had been before.

So "Gloria" came to New York, where he had little trouble in finding em-ployment in a popular cellar night spot on 134th Street in Harlem. There he reigned regally, entertaining with his "hail-fellow-well-met" freedom, so per-fect a woman that frequently clients came and left never suspecting his true sex. He sang bawdy parodies and danced a little, all very casually and quite impersonally, lifting modestly to just above the knee his perennial net and se-quins or his velvet-trimmed evening-gown skirts, displaying with professional coyness a length of silk-clad limb.

He had come to New York at a time when "male" and "female" imperson-ation was at a peak as night club entertainment. Jean Malin was the toast of the notorious gangster "Legs" Diamond's Club Abby; the Ubangi Club had a chorus of singing, dancing, be-ribboned and be-rouged "pansies," and Gladys Bentley, who dressed in male evening attire, sang and accompanied herself on the piano; the well-liked Jackie Mabley, one of Harlem's favorite black-faced co-mediennes, habitually wore men's street attire; the famous Hamilton Lodge "drag" balls were becoming more and more notorious; and gender was be-coming more and more conjectural. "Gloria Swanson"—with her loud, friendly expansiveness, her "boy friends," furs and evening gowns, her ever-ready wit, and lace-draped apartment—easily became and remained queen of them all.

Remained queen, that is, until Mayor La Guardia's police began to object to the sexes confusing the less sophisticated denizens of New York with such indiscriminate interchange of habiliment and behavior.

"Gloria's" admirers could not even recognize "her" in the masquerade forced upon him by this sudden tightening of the law. And masquerade of the most successful and impenetrable sort it most certainly was when "Gloria" wore male attire. Then, "never-raining-but-it-pours," the erstwhile glamorous "Gloria" became ill. The illness put an end to his attempt to readjust himself to the constriction forced upon his talents, and "she" was forced to withdraw from public life altogether.

ON ALEXANDER GUMBY

He came to New York when he was about nineteen years old. That was in the days when Bert Williams and George Walker were partners at making the Negro popular on the New York stage, thereby creating theatrical history during the fin de siècle. Alexander Gumby was dazzled by the glitter of life in the big city. Fresh from being a best butler in a most "first class" family in Philadelphia, he was anxious to fit into this new and better environment. He became a bellhop. Bellhopping was a most lucrative art, for art it most assuredly was to be able to satisfy at one and the same time one's employers and one's patrons and to be able to turn this most difficult procedure into coin. As the dollars mounted into tens of dollars, which they rapidly did, he put them away into the bank and spent money at Marshall's with both profligate hands. He breathed the same air as the famous of his race. He worshipped "Art-with-a-capital-A."

He wrote a song and had it published. It was even performed, from which time he felt himself to be a full-fledged member of this colorful aggregation. However, he decided that being a bellhop was not quite high class enough, so he became a butler again and went away to Riverdale to buttle at his best. This occupation, which he raised to the level of an art, did not prevent his constant excursions into the city proper to live the fast life of the bohemian group with which he now felt himself to be identified.

Gumby became a sport. Fancy clothes, a perennial walking stick, pale yellow kid gloves, and a diamond stick-pin helped make him the Beau Brummel of his particular little group. He was the member of this group who was most cognizant of and familiar with the various and sundry arts, artists, and their lives.

L. S. Alexander Gumby. The inscription reads, "To my most worthy Friend Bruce, NY Hospital, Dec 2nd 1953."

He had a hobby, as all gentlemen do — a hobby apart from the collecting of artists. He collected rare books. He had a flair for this activity that amounted practically to genius. His instincts were nearly infallible. He also collected newspaper clippings, which he kept in many file boxes. In his spare moments he mounted them carefully in scrapbooks of mammoth size and meticulous organization.

It was this secondary hobby which was to become a most important and interesting contribution on his part. He collected newspaper items on everything, on anything. There was nothing too small, there was nothing too large but that he would follow it through in every detail, until he had every scrap of information published about it. It was this amazing ability to garner every little news item about anything that he happened to fancy that was to make his scrapbook collection so invaluable.

At this time, however, Gumby was much too interested in establishing himself as a member of the group of doers to realize that this secondary hobby of his would ever be of importance. He continued to go to literary teas and social lawn parties, to patronize nightclubs where the theatrical great congregated, and to host soirees in his furnished apartment in lower Harlem at which he could exhibit his latest bibliophilic catch.

Gumby took the examination and became a postal clerk. This greater income allowed him more freedom in buying his eternal first editions, newspapers from which to clip articles, and, every now and then, a Chinese vase or cloisonné samovar. He took an enormous studio—it had really been a store—on Fifth Avenue between 131st and 132nd Streets. It was to be a salon. For months he prepared. Finally came the opening. It coincided with the advent of the New Negro.

Nineteen twenty-six was a most auspicious year. Gumby knew all of the New Negroes—or knew those who knew them, which amounted to the same thing. Sooner or later (usually sooner) they all visited his studio and were introduced to those others around him whom Gumby, with his social dictator's instinct, wished to impress. Countee Cullen, Claude McKay, Langston Hughes, Rose McClendon, Evelyn Ellis, Paul Robeson, Alain Locke, Robert Schlick, Heywood Broun, H. L. Mencken, Richard Reid, Aaron Douglas, Dorothy West, Waring Cuney, Helene Johnson, Augusta Savage, Richard Bruce, Arthur Fauset, and all of their numerous compatriots became movable fixtures in his bright and social art collection.

He was the Great God Gumby—God of his studio, God of all he surveyed. God could do no wrong. He allowed himself the luxury of temperament. It was temperament of the truest, most honest, most naïve, and highest sort. He was a true person, and in reality he was the God he called himself. He could go into fits of rage, of majestic and pompous ire, during which he would storm about, light flashing from his eyes, swear words spitting from his teeth, damnation laying low those whom a moment ago he had raised to such heights.

Gumby's salon continued to be popular until he was taken ill, and having spent all of his salaries in his studio and on his artists (for his artists were his protégés, with all the expenses thereby entailed), he found himself forced to accept the charity of the city. He went away to try to affect a cure for his tuberculosis. He spent five years taking the cure and finally left the hospital, a nearly-cured man, to return to Harlem, there trying to resume his activities in the arts and with the artists. His scrapbook collection, which had in the interim grown in importance, was sadly behind, and he immediately set about rebuilding it and recapturing the old urge to collect.

The Great God Gumby was still, and despite all, the Great God Gumby. His files of scrapbooks were and are still the source of last resort for the bibliophile and researcher. His newspaper clippings are still, despite the many hundreds which he lost during the five years internment in the tubercular hospital, more complete than even the Schomburg Collection at the 135th Street Public Library. He is an ardent anti-everything, and being biologically a complete revolutionary, he is fundamentally, essentially and totally correct in all of his judgments.

ON CARL VAN VECHTEN

One of the reasons [Langston] introduced me to Carl Van Vechten was that Carl Van Vechten could be helpful to me. I knew that when he introduced me. I knew it wasn't just that he [Langston] was interested and intrigued and amused that I thought Carl was a white monkey. Langston, as I have said before, was one of the most generous people in the world. He helped everybody [who] could be helped.

My mother would say, "You can't help Bruce. He doesn't let you help him. He does everything to keep you from helping him." . . . It's probably true. I've never been able to toady enough.

Years later . . . while he was taking pictures of me for his famous "black gallery," . . . (he was high and tight, and I was tight, and he was so tight that he was taking pictures of me looking at the [bust of] Antinous—Hadrian's favorite), and Carl said, "Look up more," and, standing behind me, put his hand on my shoulder [and] said, "If you had just patted me on the head and said, 'Carl, you're a nice boy,' you could have had anything you wanted. You could have gone to Paris." That's all that was ever said about it. But it was enough to let me know that I didn't toady successfully. I don't think it had a thing, really, to do with any sexual urge toward me.

I think it's just that . . . there's a certain kind of knee-bending that I don't do . . . Actually what Carl was saying . . . was that by my not doing it, he knew that I wasn't interested in him in a way that he wanted me to be interested in him. And telling me I was stupid not to have just said it—said, "You're a nice boy." I would never [have] had to have done anything but just pay that little obeisance to him. [But] it would never occur to me to do that. I liked Carl, you see. Why would it occur to me to create a lie for him, to him?

Years later, after the photograph episode, when Carl was about seventy-five or something . . . Dorothy Peterson and Grace and I used to eat at Carl's house with Carl and his wife . . . We were friendly, all through our contretemps, and

Nugent with a bust of Antinous (Emperor Hadrian's favorite).
Photograph by Carl Van Vechten (1936).

we had many of them, because I would always say and do whatever came into my mind. And it intrigued Carl . . . but it was annoying, frequently, sometimes so much so that he wouldn't speak . . . for months. But he was always amused and intrigued and thought I would be amusing and intriguing, and why can't he just . . .

You know, I never went to Carl's house again after I went there once and he [told me], "I am not receiving." Well, that was the last time he was going to have to tell me he wasn't receiving! I didn't know the amenities—you know, that you usually call an older person to warn him that you [are] coming. I was passing by, I wanted to see Carl, I knew where he lived, I went in, the doorman called me up, and that's the answer I got. And he'd never have the chance to give *me* that answer again! So in my way, you see, I was as adamant about my behavior as he was about his. The only difference being that his was more conventional than mine.

Eventually we compromised. And Grace was a conventional woman, and Dorothy was [too], so dinners with Carl followed the pattern that Carl liked. . . .

At his 75th birthday, which was celebrated in the library on 135th street, he did an amusing thing, but one that showed what our relationship was, to some extent. I had gone up to pay my respects to him, and he had put his hand in his coat Napoleon fashion and said, "I did that to turn the volume on so I could hear what you were saying. I get so bored with people, I just turn it off. And," he said, "you're not supposed to tell anybody this, but you better take advantage of it while it's on." [But] I had finished my amenities, and that was that.

After everyone had gone out there was another interesting thing. It was the first time that Zora and Langston [had been] together. And they weren't "together together," if you know what I mean. They had had their contretemps. And in my usual fashion, I paid no attention to that. Zora was my friend, Langston was my friend, and I don't take sides . . . I just made Langston and Zora speak with each other. I was talking to one of them, and the other was passing, and I grabbed [her] and pulled him and got us to talking, and then left them together. Carl was amused at that. He said, "I've been trying to do that, and I can't do it, and you just did it." . . .

In a peculiar kind of way, I was very fond of Carl. And in his usual fey way (because he certainly was one of the most fey people that I have ever known) . . . he was remarkable. He was one of the few people I know who could have his mind go in two directions at the same time—the manipulative part and the feeling part . . .

Sometimes at dinner, either at Dorothy's [Dorothy Peterson] . . . or at the

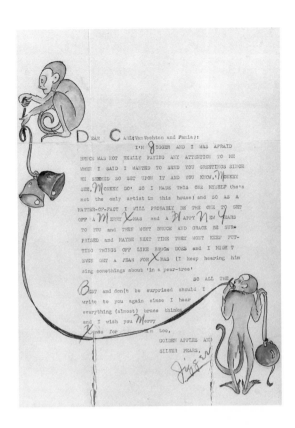

Letter from Nugent to Carl Van Vechten, 1961.

Van Vechtens', Carl would come out with one of those kind of things. He said, "Nine times out of ten, you know exactly what I'm doing, don't you?" And I said, "I think so." But Fania would say, "You know, Bruce, you're one of the only people Carl takes that from."

Carl would sit looking like a pontifical white monkey. Nod his head. I thought something about Carl that a number of people didn't think: I thought he was also a sweet person. He had an element of sweetness that—you know, I say Langston was a sweet person. That's the kind of "sweet" I mean. Carl really had this element. I think he . . . frequently thought it was a weakness, and so didn't permit it to get "out of hand." To which I would of course have said, "It's not out of hand, it's out of heart."

Carl is also one of the only people who's said to me something that—well, he said it, and other people have said it. Carl used to say, "You're the great innocent." And that used to always tickle me, because I'd always think of what I did with Mario and what I did with—see, because any time you say anything like that, it always gets back to *sex* with me, so how can [I] be innocent and do all these things I sexually do? But he meant—I kind of know what he meant, now. Wallie—he said it once in front of Wallie, or he said it and Wallie heard about it. And Wallie said, "He doesn't mean that you're innocent, he means you're vulnerable." Well, I think both of those are true, although I would be more inclined to believe the vulnerable than the innocent. But then, I'm more inclined to believe Wallie than Carl anyhow.

IMAGES

Plate 1. Untitled, Salome Series (1930). The Salome Series (Plates 1–7) includes some of Nugent's most extraordinary work. He referred to the series by this name in conversation; it may have been connected to a proposed theatrical production. All the drawings are dated 1930.

Plate 2. *Hagar*, Salome Series (1930).

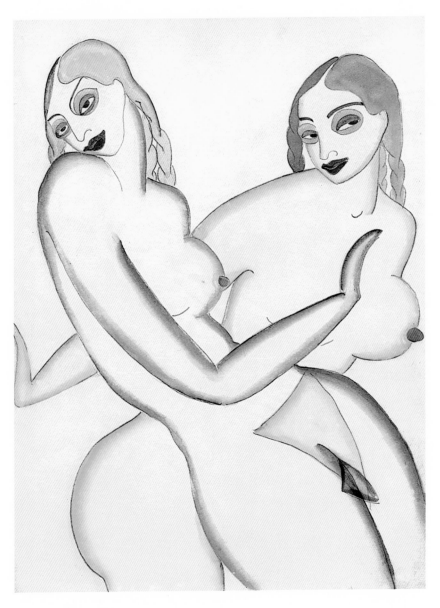

Plate 3. Drawing, Salome Series (1930).

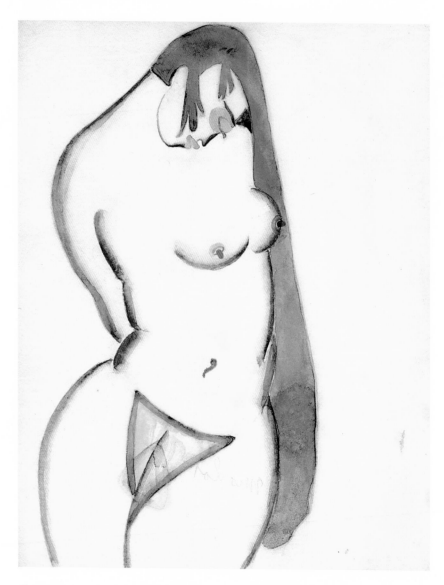

Plate 4. *Mrs. Lot*, Salome Series (1930).

Plate 5. *Lucifer,* Salome Series (1930).

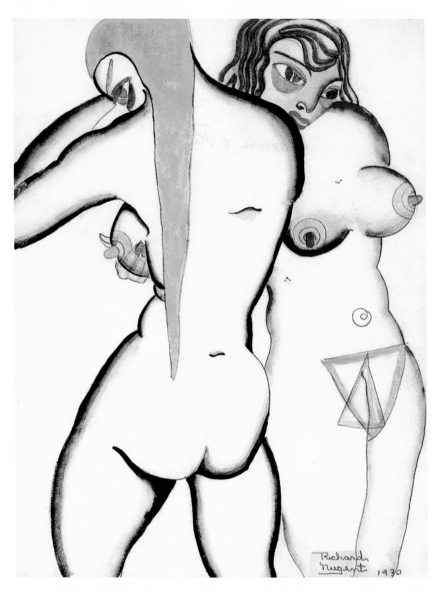

Plate 6. *Naomi and Ruth*, Salome Series (1930).

Plate 7. Drawing, Salome Series (1930).

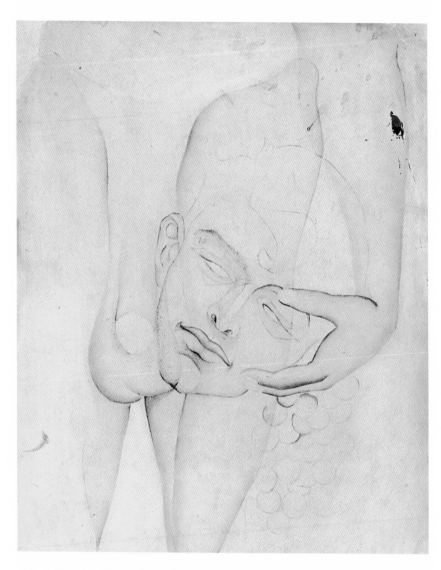

Plate 8. Drawing (date unknown).

Plate 9. *Judas and Jesus* (1947). Plates 9–11 show Nugent at his most polished and technically facile.

Plate 10. *David and Goliath* (1947).

Plate 11. *Don Juan and Carmen* (1947).

Plate 12. *Study in Black and White* (1965). *Study in Black and White* and *Angry Man* were included in a group show of several African American artists at Temple Emanuel-El in Yonkers in 1965.

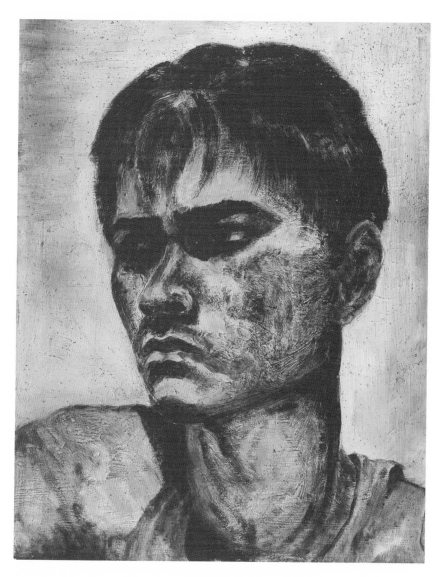

Plate 13. *Angry Man*, Cuban Prisoner (circa 1965).

Plate 14.
Portrait (1936).

Plate 15.
Tito (1980).

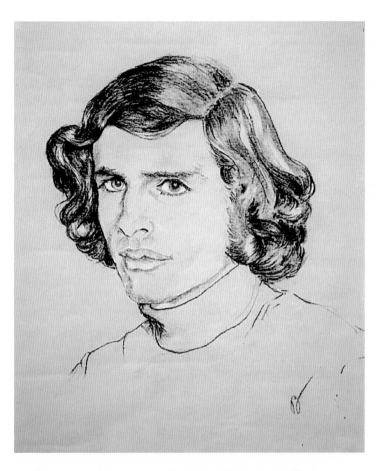

Plate 16. *Nelson Arnstein* (circa 1970). Nelson Arnstein is the son of the late Daphne Arnstein, who was a close friend of Nugent's and a fellow member of the Harlem Cultural Council board.

Plate 17. *A. D'A, Roma* (1975). This is a portrait of the young man with whom Nugent was deeply involved in Rome in the seventies.

Cano (1979).

Drawing (date unknown). This drawing is the cartoon for the central portion of an unfinished 48" by 9" oil painting. None of the drawings of monks (Figures 43–47) are dated, but they were likely done after World War II.

Drawing (date unknown).

Drawing (date unknown).

Drawing (date unknown).

Drawing (date unknown).

Drawing (date unknown).

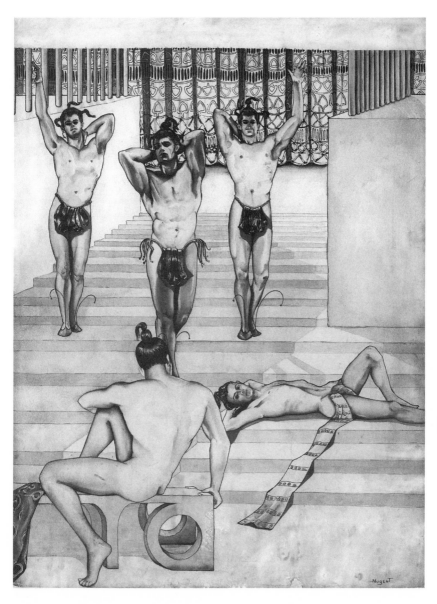

Drawing, Gilgamesh Series (date unknown). The works in the Gilgamesh Series are stage designs for a production of *Gilgamesh* that Nugent's friend Bernard Kay planned. The project apparently never came to fruition. Nugent's papers contain photostats of three additional *Gilgamesh* designs.

Drawing, Gilgamesh Series (date unknown).

AFTER THE HARLEM RENAISSANCE

Included in this section are works from the 1930s to the 1980s, covering a wide range of genre and style.

TRANSITION

Nugent probably wrote this apparently autobiographical piece when he was twenty-five, as he states—that is, in 1933–34. In the spring of 1933 he was dancing on Broadway in Run, Little Chillun'.

This I bother to call my life? I am twenty-five, but I am not even yet my quarter century. I have been other ages, and yet have not been them either. I am incomplete. Possessing more than most, I am incomplete.

There is no one to weep that I waste. I rue the fact that I was not born Jewish—or at least with Jewish instincts. Then would I help keep more perfect a body which, through being perfect, I neglect. It was a sad oversight on the part of my ancestors to neglect a fusion with Jewish blood.

Bodies. I worship bodies. I spend the morning lounging on the sand, watching supple bodies of Jews. And bother not to show that I also have a body.

My art is because it must be. It is merely an overflow. And I do nothing, not even thank God.

Would a song be like this?

> There is a sun—
> To hang (or maybe not)
> For clouds complete elusions—
> And a sea
> To which all colors come
> To bring with ceaseless
> Tireless motion suave
> And graceful—even more,
> The knowledge

I only accept
With lassitude and comfort.
Acknowledge
And note
And admire.
There is a sun—
(Or may be not)
And a sea (or may be not)
I am too with comfort
Bound.

No. One doesn't sing a song like that.

POPE PIUS THE ONLY

This is among Nugent's finest works, bringing as it does modernist technique to bear on the African American experience. It originally appeared in Dorothy West's little magazine, Challenge, *in 1937.*

It was decidedly uncomfortable. But then Rome had burned, so who was he? Algy sniffed his smoke and burned. The fire around his feet was beginning. Slowly and hotly they burned and then—poof—the acrid trail singed clean his legs, and—poof—his crotch—poof-poof—his eyebrows. So Algy just stood and burned, and the heat on his feet was so great as to seem cold, and he remembered how hot a tub of water could be before adequate testing. Like dry ice. He had seen dry ice smoke under water once. Algy floated along and turned over on his back, his little gills fanning. And knew he was no longer a cinder with black face and hands, because the noise of the waters had washed him clean, washed him in the blood of the lamb. So he'd have lamb with mint sauce for the asking. As long as he lived and burned like hell. Algy turned over and swam with flaccid strokes, for his gills were very, very weary.

It was then that he met the merman, a truly remarkable creature with his legs each going off into a tail. And Algy remembered mermaids and thought, "how comfortable, how cozy" and burrowed deep into the bowels of the earth. He had been smoking "reefers," known in better circles as marijuana. In yet other and different circles as weed, or griefer. But Algy had been smoking "reefers"— and he let his head drop forward, where it hung heavy and pleasant on his chest while he thought for hours about tossing it back to wobble pleasingly unstable atop his spine. For hours he thought, forcing his will to lift his head from his chest and juggle it precariously above his shoulders. And it was a full minute before he did. He knew that it was only a minute, that the hours of time had somehow been cramped into that one minute, only he knew that it was hours too. Time was very unimportant, or maybe he meant elastic. But it had been of greatest importance that he drop his head, first forward, then back, and let it loll. The simple combined movement would "set his gauge." Then space would converge, and thoughts and time; dimensions would become distorted and correct; he would become aware and super aware and aware of awareness and on and on in a chain of dovetailings and separate importances. Everything would have its correct perspectives—time, thought, deed and the physical surrounding him and surrounding that and—first first dimension, second dimension, third, fourth and fifth dimension—no need to stop there—the incredible dimension of the pin point, the worm, the man—at one and the same time blending yet separate. Not only did he have to imagine the fourth side of things now, he could see it. See all sides—top, bottom, four sides, outside *and* inside.

And when he arose his slow maneuverings would be swift as an arrow, while all the while they would be as slow as death and normal. Above all, normal, despite conflicting sensations which did not conflict. So he swiftly at a snail-like pace rose from his seat. And his eyes dilated contractedly and his vision was photographic, stereoscopic and omnipotent.

He went on down Seventh Avenue. Nineteen thirty-five, summer and fall. E.R.A., N.R.A., P.W.A., W.P.A. Almost like Russia for initials. Huey P. Long and General Hugh Johnson, only Long was dead and so was Pushkin. Long live Pushkin.

Algy stepped through an idea, and the glamour of a Russian court warmed him after the icy blasts outside. On all sides of him, and inside too, the white faces surrounding him were red or pink or other than white. They were the white man. White Russia, coursing about him and through him. His insides must be quite white by now because he was Pushkin, and somehow, somewhere there was a blending which made his yellow skin black. White Russia with red faces, or at least so he felt as he reached for a sable with which to soothe his hurt and waxed prophetic. Hannibal had crossed the Alps with elephants, so Pushkin smiled a grin across Mongolia and thought of Catherine the Great as an army whispered by. And he withdrew into his red boots lined with black and white and wrote a poem.

His elephant slipped and an avalanche cascaded down the Roman side. He only smiled and wept when his army thought, "Hannibal, be careful." Formerly he thought Rome warm, but that was near the sea, and it is cold on the heights. Oh, he was great with future, but he thought "Oh, Hannibal, I weep for an olive," and sighed as he bit into a Turkish delight. Alexander the Beautiful, the youthful soldier with Greek behavior.

The taste of Turkish delight was strange to Crispus Attucks. It filled his mouth with strangeness. Boston was a wheel within a wheel high up in the middle of the air. He bowed pleasantly to Phillis Wheatley as he passed, for she had passed on. And thought, "What a thing indeed is Sunday school, springing as it did with biblical flourish through Africa." And his black hands did not tremble as he laughed to see the dish run away with the spoon. But he stumbled and fell, his head was so high, his palms so pink. And as his blood foamed on his lips, he only wished he were in other circles, breathing in to dry his throat. "Reefers." He most decidedly wanted to be in the vernacular.

But he lit instead a star. There was a rite connected with this. He loosened first the end of Capricorn with his thumb and forefinger, caressing it gently into useful shape; then, stars converging, stars diminishing, he struck a match to his reefer. So he strolled on down Seventh Avenue, "trucked on down the midway," alive and atingle the whole dead length of him, aware and dreaming from his "stomps" to his "conk," and thought I could have meant "kicks" or even feet—and skull, or even head—but only in circles where words were English instead of "jive"—

> stomps—feet
> sky-piece—hat
> skull—head—

atingle and dead from toe to head. He must not make a poem on Seventh Avenue. Or be Ira Aldridge or Dumas *père*. Instead—instead—from toe to head —glide—slide—ride the crest—breast—best of Seventh Avenue. So he walked on down Seventh Avenue and then crossed One Hundred and Twenty-Fifth Street. And he stood in the crowd and was Georgia and Mississippi, a sort of walking delegate, and when they hanged John Brown he was a shadow, the sun full upon him. He sorrowed as he laughed and took off his head with a courtly bow and said, "Good evening white folks." Then he ran like hell. He had forgotten to say Mister White Folks. He giggled. It sounded so funny. "Mr. White Folks. Mr. White—*Monsieur Blanc*." He tittered as he ran and led an army to revolt in French. It was fine. A fine language being Toussaint or Christophe or Dessalines. It was too fine—with scarlet breeches, mulatto bitches, and high black places for whites to stumble from. And the fires of the burning sugar fields made a nice light to see him by and a pungent acrid caramel smell to

Illustration for "Black Gum," the story of a lynching by William V. Kelley, which appeared in the January 1928 issue of *Opportunity*.

carve words in the dark of a French dungeon. But they cut him to pieces, and that was confusing—cut him into one Herndon and nine Scottsboro pieces of eight. So he walked in glory and was Emperor Jones and sang whenever he was hailed the title the people called him.

Shim-sham-shimmy, and Charleston. He danced the gri-gri down Seventh Avenue and stopped for another gri-gri-griefer. Algy drew deep on the "reefer" and knew how good it was that he did not think. That no thought of Haile Selassie frowned on him. He couldn't think and that was well, for who wants time and space and physical fact—deed and thought contort distraught. Viva la Mussolini and cock-a-doodle-do—until time to sleep.

But water babies see many things, Algy knew, for as he swam beneath the carcass of a sea anemone, he thought, "how like Verlaine. How Gauguin the antennae." *Mouchoir* was the word—the strangely succinct word with which to wipe clean his muddied mood. So Algy blew his nose and slightly swam down the Nile, the Blue Nile, and the Nile, the White Nile, and joined the Italian army. But only to work black magic, for he conjured—

"Abrac-Adowa" and lo it fell, crashing mightily from 1896, and Algy entered Addis Ababa with forty thieves. They were looking for peace—pieces of eight—

which were Africa and others through Africa. So Algy thought, "how simple," and Adigrat fell regained.

And it burned—the chains at his wrist were white hot now and Algy thought, "how needlessly painful, how annoying," and turned over to sleep through the lynching. But his lips were parched. Not that he liked it, but there he was—he'd no idea that being the fly in the ointment could be so sticky.

LUNATIQUE

"Lunatique" is taken from one of Nugent's late novels, variously titled in manuscript either "Letters into Limbo" or "Uranus in Cancer." The dream sequence, however, was written much earlier; a handwritten version appears in one of Nugent's early notebooks from the twenties.

Angel lived in a small town on the New Jersey palisades. He was a strange boy. The older people in the town all treated him in that kindly manner reserved for harmless dreamers or mentally retarded persons. He was a slight, delicately built lad who had done well at school—until he was fourteen.

Then he had changed overnight. His slim lips perennially smiled mysteriously to unheard excitements, which were heard by his ears alone and caused his cheeks to blush faintly. His slim legs and waist had acquired an androgynous grace that garbed him as transparently as his smile did his face. His straight-lashed eyes became luminous with seeing things that others never see. One night shortly after he was fourteen, he had a dream.

He dreamed he was in a barn—an immense barn in one corner of which were four men, backs toward him. Four beautifully modeled men—headless. Headless and beautiful. One was red and one was yellow and one was black and one was white, and each body glistened like lacquer. Like satin with a light cast on it.

There was one window in the far wall. Outside the sky was an electric flame—a blue electric flame—but this he only *knew*, for it was immense. It was the sky. In another corner was a great cartwheel. And in another was a pitchfork.

These figures, these headless men, were searching blindly for him—searching beautifully, threateningly, blindly. Becoming frightened at their gestures, he made a dash for the doors. His haste was great, and the doors stuck. Then they suddenly opened, and there in the doorway was an enormous man. Blue. Lacquer-blue, and so large that he filled the doorway. Where his head should have been, his neck fit close against the lintel, and from it depended, like a scarf—a table scarf—a drape of silver cloth with crystal pendants.

As Angel started, the blue man made a threatening gesture, and the boy turned and ran—blindly. Red and yellow and black and white, the four men were still groping, searching. From where their lips should have been issued voices—beautiful, blasphemous voices. He cowered. He felt safer huddled still and silent *below* their groping arms, huddled among the hay and manure. Then an immense rat scurried from nowhere—a beautiful rat with variant, brilliantly-colored fur, like batik. Its head was hideous: an unpleasant skin was drawn too tightly over its naked protruding skull.

It attacked him viciously; his only weapon was a straw. With lightning-like movements it darted in and out, in and out. The beautiful blasphemous voices, the fear of the red and the black and the yellow and the white hands and of the glorious blue figure—all wove an accompaniment above him. The straw pierced the soft, brilliant fur at the rodent's neck, and its head rolled off and disappeared.

Then hundreds and thousands of rats—headless rats—poured out in a stream of vivid color. They nestled around him and made strange cooing sounds. They mounted high—so high they were smothering him. Pleasant, slumberous—smothering in color, soft, alive, and pulsing. Pleasant about his thighs and shoulders and cheeks.

Then a rat ran across his face, and its serpent-tail dragged nausea into his somnolence. So, remembering the magic straw, he shook himself free from his living blanket and abolished their tails with a touch, and soon was sinking again into a pleasant daze, content to be smothered, the accompaniment of the blasphemous voices sifting through the vibrant color like a lullaby. Then, groping blindly, the red man stepped on the mound of rats. Stepped on the mound of rats and him.

Immediately four pairs of hands grasped him. Tossed him from one to the other. Beat him. Grasped him by the heels and rammed him head foremost into the floor, and his head rolled off and over into a corner, where it was stopped by the pitchfork. And all this while color grew on the great cartwheel—grew in bright, enameled splashes. Then, groping, searching frantically for his head, he was assailed by many fears. How to see to keep out of the reach of the men— the red, the white, the yellow, the black—and the great blue man in the door- way. All this while his head was watching his mad and hazy search. And time was not. Still he searched in time and the barn . . . until he stumbled against the pitchfork. And there he found his head.

He placed it on his shoulders. It immediately betrayed his position by voicing all the fears his body had been knowing. He saw a loft above him. He climbed up into it. Ranged below him were the four—the red, the white, the yellow and the black. He stood at the edge, and from the wall of the loft, welling out like an immense breaker, was a wave of women, all entwined. All colors. Bodies in all positions and contortions. Abdomens, arms, necks, breasts, feet, heads, torsos, hair—an enormous wave of women surging toward him in an endlessness. He was fascinated, but he knew he would be submerged—drowned—if that wave reached him. Nearer and nearer and nearer and nearer until . . . Then he jumped. Back to the four pairs of waiting hands, and . . . he floated down. Black hands and yellow, red hands and white—they grasped him. Flung him into a far corner and followed him. And his body was much misused. And all this time the wheel grew colors—brilliant enamel-colors. Then he exploded and floated slowly up, like gas, around the four, held in by the four walls and the wheel. The enormous cartwheel started to spin. Faster, faster . . . many colors, gyrating colors . . . faster and faster, and he expanded more and floated higher . . . up like gas . . . and he could *feel* himself expand. He would pervade the *whole* barn, keeping a level just above the necks of the de-headed men. The cartwheel with its enamel colors spun and gave off an aura—a shimmering, vivid aura like a flame. And into this aura he projected himself. Pleasure, shock, tingle . . . and he withdrew. Into the aura again . . . again . . . exquisite electric pleasant pain. And after each shock made his surface quiver and ripple, Angel could see a beautiful head being formed on the beautiful blue man, and the head became matter. And with a gesture like a God's gesture of creation, Angel threw the pitchfork into the wheel . . .

It was shattered into myriads of bits of shining color. And the men—the red, the yellow, the black and the white—exploded into fragments of brilliant color. The barn and everything in it vanished . . . and there was Nothing. Only the Blue Man remained—the Blue Man and the blue flame that was the Sky. Angel was a step or so below the Blue Man. And he *must* reach the Blue Man's level . . . and merge . . . merge . . . . .

When he woke up, he was frightened. And ashamed. It wasn't the dream so much. He liked remembering that. But something strange had happened with him in the night. His mother's voice calling to him to get up had startled him and frightened him and made him more ashamed. He wished he could destroy the bed or hide it—hide from his mother the damp, faintly cream-colored evidence.

He kept his long, straight lashes lowered as he sat across the table from her at breakfast. When he left the house that morning, he was smiling. His long lashes hid his shining eyes and made tiny rainbows of light dance over the street before him. When he went to bed that night he saw that his mother had laid the bed afresh. And it was only in the middle of the week.

From that dream on, Angel lived in a sensuous and uncharted world, alone but not lonesome or unhappy. He no longer played with the other children. Day by day he lapsed deeper and deeper into the softly spoken Italian old-country idioms and adages of his mother. And into the remembered gentle memories of the equally softly-spoken Spanish aphorisms of his father. The unsaid sound of them all rang in his ears like a far-away melody. By the time he was sixteen, and the other boys were playing pool at the corner parlor, or learning loitering on the streets, he was living dreams.

He talked to *himself* and listened to the unhearable music. *They* would lounge, talking sexually and wise in conversations punctuated only by insolent silences whenever some girl passed, to be broken before she had walked out of these obvious silences by some remark about her possibilities. These remarks, crudely worded as they were, lent a more insolent and stiffly-proud lilt to the girls' walk.

Adorio was the most adept at this exciting baiting. No one called him Adorio — they all called him Cano because of his pale hair. His so innocently insolent eye and caressing voice lent subtleties to his words that kept the vision of him, crowned with platinum, before the girls' eyes long after they had run the exciting gauntlet of gazes and remarks. He was the one whom the girls instinctively saw and sized up even as they were pleasurably steeling themselves to pass the group. There was a curl to his silver-blonde hair that fell carelessly over his eye to contrast so provocatively with his Puerto-Rican being and complexion, a twist to his wistful and arrogant lips that lent further assurance to his slender body so animal in its appeal. He wore his clothes with that carelessly sure instinct for adornment that made Indians' bodies so vibrantly nude within clothes. It was Cano who was the acknowledged leader of the group of adolescents. Cano read (privately) many books and had (even more privately) written some poems. But that was his private life. With the others he was just stronger, faster, more worldly and cleverer. Inevitably and unquestioningly, he was their leader.

One day Angel was passing them. There was the usual idle chatter, and they baited him a little, as they usually did, almost by a reflex that dictated their expressions when some outsider appeared. But Angel lived outside himself and never heard them. He could not know that the sight and sound of them caused *his* walk to lilt a little and invested *it* with a touch of the same coquetry that painted the girls.

Angel was a mildly interesting topic for the boys, like a dog to tease (and pet) but never harm. They had known him all his life, but he was different and not important. Their conversation spattered around—wondering what he did all day, or what he thought about—into tepid curiosity as to his sex life. There was nothing he could do in that line . . . no girl would want to try . . . he was too pretty . . . he probably just masturbated. Perhaps that was the way he was . . . they say too much of it will make you crazy. If he were a girl, they could all have a good time . . . too bad there wasn't a nutty *girl* in town. One of them said maybe he *was* a girl. Maybe he was a *pato* like they had met down at the ferry terminal, who had been in the toilet looking at everybody when they took a leak, and whom they had chased after they had used him. Scared the hell out of him. But that was all just idle talk, because if Angel was like that, someone would have found out, and they would all know. But maybe . . . he was so nuts, maybe they could, anyhow . . . for an apple-on-a-stick or a dime. That would be fun. And convenient too, if it worked. That was how it all began.

But Angel walked on magic. People were only names or facts or voices to be seen with a pleasant smile to carry on his lips long after he had forgotten them. Angel lived completely alone in his vague, crowded thoughts of nothing. But the boys all knew he almost always went at dusk to sit on the edge of the palisade, and one night a giggling group of them went to bait him and have some fun. The rest watched while one went over and talked to him. Watched while he tried all the obvious tricks unsuccessfully, watched him cradle his crotch with an overtness too blatant to be sensual, watched him walk a few steps away from Angel and take a curving leak into the river far below and turn back to him as he slowly and with a little difficulty put his semi-hard self away again and ostentatiously zipped his fly.

In the summer heat erections were almost always growing, so night after night they tried to lead him into their unsubtle traps, and it was all fun. They had a new game. Then Cano said he bet *he* could get him, and they all knew by now it couldn't be done, because Angel was too vague to even know what they were trying to do—too soft-headed to get frightened or mad even. Nothing held his attention. In the middle of whatever they might be saying, Angel's gaze would wander and his conversation would be of other things entirely. So they bet Cano he couldn't.

Angel was lying on his back with his head on his arms looking up when Cano came and sat beside him. Angel looked at him and smiled his smile and said, "Hello, Adorio. I'll bet I could reach right up there and take a star if I wanted to."

And Cano said, "I'll bet I could easier than you." Angel looked at him and smiled more. He was quite used to having people talk to him as though he was crazy and having them say crazy things to him. So he just smiled and asked, "How, Adorio? Nobody but I can *really* do that."

Cano looked at him lying there. It was the first time he had ever really looked at Angel—the first time he had talked or tried to talk to him since they had been in the same class at school. That is what Angel is like—a kid, a very small and beautiful kid. And Cano remembered something his mother had said to him when *he* was a kid, so he said it to Angel. He said, "Don't look at me, Angel." He pronounced Angel's name with the same beautiful aspirated "gee" like an "aitch" as did Angel's mother. "Look at the sky," he continued, "and then the stars will be in your eyes, and I can have one for the asking. And if you look closely enough, you'll see them in *my* eyes, taken from yours."

Cano was surprised at the effect achieved by that almost-forgotten bit of mother's love, for Angel's eyes filled with tears and he looked happier than anyone should. "That's right, Adorio, that's right," Angel said. And he talked then—talked on and on with an intimacy that held Cano. And Cano became embarrassed at being the cause of such happiness and said he guessed he'd better be going now.

So Cano was unsuccessful too. But when the fellows teased him, he still insisted that he could and went back on other nights. It became quite a game, because the others were always watching. Even after the others lost interest and stopped watching, he continued—it was a habit, like praying. Besides, Angel was such a strange one. Cano could talk to him—could tell him things that burn to have an ear to hold them, but that a man smothers inside himself and has lonesome feelings about. Angel would listen and hear, and his vague irrelevant remarks seemed almost to be answers, and they helped relieve Cano. He grew almost to understand Angel's speech—to know what he meant when he said, "Blue piled on blue piled on blue." Nor did it any longer seem strange, but like poetry.

And Angel also had no secrets now. With Cano he too was alone, only with someone, and Angel liked that. Cano became a part of the vagueness that was Angel's only reality. And blue piled on blue, mounting high—kingdoms crashing noiselessly above. Pale pink and gold and white turrets silently sinking in the blue piling on blue piling on blue. Angel walked on soft green, cool and damp, shedding tiny tears on the brown of his feet. Fallen stars folded their petals one by one and closed on slender stems. He walked through blue piled on blue piled on blue, and it was soft and scented. Above, the wind flung a silver disk high above the tumbling towers. He walked on and on, and then he stopped. He was standing on the edge of nowhere, and below him blue piled on blue until it seemed black. Before and below him the sea sent beautiful green sirens up the river. In they came, beautiful green sirens with long silver hair. In they came, beckoning, singing, retreating—again and again. Their beautiful green-brown thighs beckoned. Their heaving pear-encrusted breasts called. One of his feet caressed nothingness . . . their voices sounded so soft . . . his one foot caressed nothingness over blue piled on blue so deep it seemed black . . .

Then it seemed that over their shining bodies there came a silver being. Green-brown arms raised to caress him, silver hair to enmesh him. Passionate breasts soothed the soles of his feet. Still the silver one came. At last, Angel drew back his foot from over space. He knew he would wait for this shining creature who walked through blue piled on blue . . . who walked up, shedding a glow. Up, until he was standing beside Angel.

Angel could say nothing. The silver one had eyes like opals. He stood beside the boy and surveyed him from toe to hair, and Angel was ashamed of a mole on his left side over his heart.

The silver one smiled. Suddenly, Angel was warmed and at ease. The silver one's feet rested so lightly on the green beside his own. He smiled and said, "You are very young, Chicito, to witness the death of day . . ." And he sat down, and Angel sat beside him. "Very young, and pretty, too, to see the destruction of day." Angel wanted to look at him, but Adorio's eyes were upon him.

"Why does blue pile on blue?" Angel looked at him as he asked, but saw that the silver one's eyes were seeing visions, other worlds.

"You know I am the moon," the silver one answered. It was not a question. "And you are Angel." He looked at Angel and smiled. "For you have sung me often. You have often sung moon-songs." Angel was embarrassed and pleased.

"But how could you trample the soft, green-brown breasts and thighs of the sirens with their silver hair, Moon?"

The moon shook his bright head impatiently. "Women . . . women . . . I've been here since Eve, Angel."

Angel gazed out over the blue. "And Adam," he added.

"Adam? Adam? Who is Adam?"

Angel plucked a folded star from its slender green stem. He was pleased. There was something for him to tell the moon. "But tell me of women, Moon."

And the silver moon told him of women—of women in the Land of Red Snows who danced nude in the cool warmth of his smile . . . beautiful and nude. The spot where his arm touched Angel was pleasant and electric to the boy. And the moon told Angel of women who lived in pond lilies and were so shy he barely could brush their lips with his kisses.

"Where your arm touches mine gives a pleasant feeling, Chicito," he said, and smiled and talked more of women . . . and Angel flushed. The moon talked long, but all the boy knew was that their shoulders touched and that the moon's shoulders were broad and his voice was melodious. The silver one talked long, and Angel was carried almost into dreams, and after a time his voice came fainter and fainter and Angel looked in dismay. It was as though the moon was fading . . . fading . . . white winds were pushing aside the blue piled on blue, and soon . . . there was no moon. Day came, flushing pink as though ashamed at having chased the moon . . .

That night, Angel went again to the edge of the palisade. Moon was waiting for him. Angel sat down nearby. "Tell me more, Moon." And the moon told of women whose lips he had kissed.

"Ah yes, Chicito. I am an adulterer . . . I've fondled Eve's breasts, kissed Pompadour's thighs, caressed Anne Boleyn's eyelids, nestled in the hollow of Sheba's throat . . ." And so he talked. But Angel knew only that their thighs touched, and he thrilled. Knew that the moon's lips were light and wistful.

"I've known Jeanne d'Arc and Du Barry . . ." He lay his hand on Angel's for an instant. "The feel of your thigh is soft, Chicito, and pleases me." He smiled his disturbing smile, opal eyes glowing, and talked on. "And know there never was a virgin, Chicito. I've loved them all . . . and touched them each." He glanced at Angel impressively. But Angel's thoughts were sad and must have tinted his face, for with the most profound concern, the moon leaned closer and asked, "What now, Chicito? Boys should be gay when they are young. What thoughts have you to cause such an unhappy expression?"

Angel looked at him, then spoke. "Day is almost here," he answered and bowed his head forward. His long straight lashes traced lacy shadows under his eyes.

"Does it matter so much, Chicito?" the moon asked. His voice was very soft now, almost as if he were not there. Angel had not the courage to answer or to look . . . and the morning winds piled high the white billows in the sky and red clouds raised the sun slowly up. The pale moon had gone. But day—*this* day— would not be as other days had been.

This day he took a ring from his mother's little trinket box. It was a small ring that held two fiery opals captive on a woven, white-gold thread—two opals just like the moon's eyes.

That night the moon and he sat at the edge of nothingness—sat and dangled their feet down over blue piled on blue 'till it seemed black. And the moon was talking.

"Yes, they all love me." He paused naively. "I remember the time Melissande first noticed me . . ." On and on he talked, but all the boy could know was that their legs caressed from ankle to hip, so close were they.

"And she, who made and ruined Caesars, left her perfumed divans, the handsome guards, and her many strong street-men to woo me . . ." He stood and looked down on Angel. "But then, I am beautiful, am I not, Chicito?" He stood there pleased and shy for Angel to survey his beauty.

"Yes you are, Moon," Angel answered, and he lowered his long, straight lashes over his eyes again, so that he might always have before his eyes the beauty that was the moon's. The moon smiled and dropped impulsively beside him.

"And they would finger my hair." He looked at Angel and smiled a gentle, mysterious smile. "Would you, Chicito?" And the moon put his head in the boy's lap, and as he talked, Angel ran his fingers through the silver silk of his hair again and again. The moon talked on and on. Then he noticed the ring on Angel's finger. He sat up, and Angel felt the moon's leg against his again. Taking the boy's hand on his palm, the silver one looked at the ring closely.

"The stones are beautiful, Angel. Like my eyes."

"Yes," Angel answered softly, and the moon lay his head again in the boy's lap and talked . . . then paused and gazed off into dreams.

"Your hands have a gentle touch, Chicito." He settled himself more comfortably and, looking up at Angel, talked more of love. He talked for a long, long time, but all Angel knew was that the moon's head was in his lap. That his hair was soft and silver. That was all Angel knew as he sat weaving unformed dreams. All he knew, until suddenly he saw that it was day, and . . . his hands were empty in his lap.

That day passed swiftly, and soon it was again night. The moon had been talking long and softly. He looked at Angel. "You have the feel of love in you *muchacho*," he said. "Don't you know love?" And Angel was confused, and he blushed.

"I don't know how to love, Moon."

"Don't know *how*?" The moon seemed incredulous. "But come Chicito, I'll remedy that. First I'll teach you to kiss." He stood and drew Angel to stand with him. Angel trembled so his knees were weak, for he could see the slim denim hips, the bare torso, the silver hair, the opal eyes and every smoothness and bulge of contour. The moon took Angel's face between his lean, hard, soft-palmed hands and, pressing close, held Angel captive for a moment. The muscles of his forearm felt hot against Angel's shoulders, and his torso felt hot through Angel's shirt. Then, drawing the boy's face forward, the moon kissed him almost painfully on the lips. His opal eyes were open and inquired into Angel's and Angel could feel the fair, silky hair brush his forehead—could feel his breath being drawn from his throat in a long, trembling, sob-like gasp. His knees weakened even more, and he could not stand. The moon held him, hot body against hot body, heart beating rapidly against rapidly beating heart. He drew away from the boy, and Angel sank to the earth to hide his trembling. The moon sat beside him, curious-seeming.

"You seemed—"

Quickly Angel interrupted him and talked . . . talked about anything . . . talked about nothing . . .

"But I couldn't love you, could I, Chicito?" The moon seemed disturbed, but not unhappy. Angel continued talking . . . about anything . . . about nothing . . .

Angel talked about popes and their minions, and the moon listened so intently that the boy became embarrassed anew and said kiss me again, Moon—but he only thought it and was silent and still and halted . . . and when the moon kissed him sudden-and-long, the boy was astonished and happy and unbelieving. The moon spoke on in tentative tones, softly and tremblingly, half frightened and half calculating, half conqueror and half conquered.

"I was thinking of those to whom I've never made love—" he said in a trembling voice. And he began to loosen Angel's shirt. And Angel thought, "What we partake of, we become," and remembered it as a thought he had had at his first communion.

That night the moon made a god of him—made love to him. The boy heard the moon moan beautifully as, almost roughly, he pressed Angel's head close against his short hairs, and his warm, pearly flood jetted hot and magic between Angel's lips, and the moon gave a final life-giving death-spasm, and his hands became soft and tender on the back of the boy's neck as he relaxed. And Angel slept there where he was, his cheek on the moon's crotch. When he awoke, the moon was gone.

Angel walked slowly home through the velvety black. He heard two men talking somewhere . . . "Look at that red moon. Tomorrow is gonna be hot as hell . . ." Angel went on through the black, and suddenly he burst out laughing. He tried to stop, but he laughed and laughed and laughed, and there in the doorway was his mother.

She looked funny in her long white nightgown there in the open. Almost as funny as what those men had said . . . and he laughed, and his laughter was nearly tears. "But the moon was only blushing, mother," he gasped to her.

It was daylight, and he was in bed. His mother had just left the room, and he could hear her talking with the doctor in the other room. "And I found him out there on the porch. It was three o'clock in the morning, and—" His mother's voice dropped to breathe the scandalous truth. "And naked. He was naked!"

Angel turned toward the window. The moon would never talk with him again. He would never feel the moon's silky hair . . . never see his opal eyes. He had embarrassed the moon, and the moon had run from Angel blushing. Angel's mother came into the room and sat beside him. She tentatively and in a rather foreign manner touched his hand.

"It's all right, *povero figlio mio.* Everything is all right. Don't weep, *bambino carissimo. Non piangia, prego.*" She wiped away his tears with her gentle fingers and sat there a long time looking at him through her tears and love. Then she spoke again, softly, as though she were saying a prayer or a lullaby. "*Il dottore* says that in a day or two, you'll be well again."

But Angel hardly heard her words. He let her voice soothe him as she tried to say the big words the doctor had used. She had never learned well to speak either the Spanish her husband had always used or her son's American. But she tried to say the words the doctor had said—the words that her Angel could understand because he had been to school in this language.

"Delirious. Fantasies. Nervous breakdown if he is not careful." Angel hardly heard, for he was waiting for the night. He *had* to see the moon.

That night, as soon as his mother had left him for the last time, he crept from the bed and made his way to the edge of nothingness and waited. But the moon was behind a cloud. Angel waited and waited, and when he finally tipped home he was cold and trembling with chill and unhappiness. The next night he went again. And the next, and the next.

On the fifth night, when he went, he could hardly sit up. He sank back on the grass, crushing the tiny folded stars on their delicate stems. He waited with eyes hard with dryness, for he no longer had tears to soften them. And he waited. He waited so long that his head became light, and his tongue became thick. His eyes blurred, and he sank into a bottomless pit of blackness.

It was there that they found him in the morning—the curious crowd of giggling boys—giggling because he was naked, and he had *never* been *that* crazy before, and there was an excitement they could all feel, because they knew him. Adorio was not with them. But Angel was in a bottomless blackness that warmed him more than does sleep.

It was twilight when he awoke that day. He watched the blue pile on blue pile on blue and press against the squares of his closed window. He watched it pile so deep it seemed black. The doctor had told his mother not to be frightened. He would have to be watched. It was not dangerous. It would all pass, and he would be the same as before, but that he might continue for a while to have these hallucinations . . .

Angel laughed a little, silently. One half of his heart was tender, for he could feel his mother's bewildered fear and love. His silent laugh tickled in the back of his brain; no one could hear but himself. Hallucination! He tossed his head from side to side. That word beat like an unpleasant and persistent rhythm in his head . . . Hallucinations? Never to see the moon again? Tears came to his eyes. His head turned back to the window. Hallucinations? Black . . . blue piled on blue until it seemed black against the closed window. Hallucinations . . . ? He turned his head away again. He tried to hold back his tears. He did not want to worry his mother. Hallucinations . . . ? He turned to the window and tossed back, and . . .

There, standing beside the bed, was the moon. The moon was silent and just smiled a sad little smile, and Angel was happy—so happy he felt his insides explode, like in the dream. Then he was happy and well, because he could feel Moon's hair brush his forehead as Moon leaned over and kissed him. He nearly slept, and when his mother came, he heard her say, "He'd better sleep now, Adorio. It made good for him to see you. I thank you, *amico bello di mi figlio.*" She led him away. And Angel smiled and slept and grew well, because he knew the moon was Adorio.

When Angel was well, he went with Adorio to the block and the guys soon accepted him, because he was Cano's friend. They grew to know him some and to like him—even to like some of the things he said sometimes that were so different from anything others said. Even when he knew the answer to things they didn't know. There was nothing crazy about him like they had thought. He just saw things they didn't see until he showed them and said things they never said until they heard them from him. And besides, he could do everything they could do, almost as good as Cano could. They all laughed and liked him and called him Chico like Cano did. Only when they were alone did Cano call him, "Angel," or did Angel call him, "Adorio."

And Chico went with the guys wherever they went, and when they stood and watched the girls, Chico watched and said things, too. Now the girls responded most to Cano *and* Chico and it was mostly for *both of them* that their walk become bolder and their eyes more sparkling. Cano taught Chico to know what it was that a woman wanted a man to be and how to be it—how to make love to women and how to be as loving when he did so as Cano was with him.

Cano shared these things with Chico because he wanted everything for Chico that he wanted for himself. For Adorio loved Angel—loved him more completely than he had ever loved anyone before. Loved him the same way he wanted to love a woman, but at the same time differently, too, for he loved Angel as he loved *himself,* and there was manhood to share and have with him. Adorio loved Angel more deeply than he loved any of the girls, and was tender with him when they were alone, and loved love with him as with no one else. And he could talk with Angel as he never could with women. Or men either. And Angel—Angel lived only for Adorio. He was one with Adorio.

When Chico made love to girls as Cano taught him, it was Adorio having made love to him that made him so adept, for he knew how it was to want to be loved, and he wanted them to love him as he loved and wanted Adorio. So he was Cano's other self who loved the girls.

Then the war came. They joined the army together when Cano wanted to, and they trained together. All the men knew that they were buddies. Later they were sent to Italy together. Once, when they were in Anzio and were tired and dirty, and their squad had returned from a decimating encounter and they had been relieved, they were sitting, huddled, all of them too tired to do more than merely breathe. The others were thinking what buddies Cano and Chico were and how always when any of them needed help, one of the two would appear as if by magic, and then the other would be there, too . . .

Cano and Chico drew apart from the rest of them, as usual, and went to the top of a small knoll. They sat there beside each other, facing away from the others and looking back to where they had come from—just happy in each other's presence and closeness. They each could smell the other's sweat and dirt and knew it to be the smell of the other. The others watched them go, and it was right, because they were buddies and loved each other and were friends.

For a while they sat there in the evening gloom on the far side of the little hillock—just sat there and were tired and happy in the presence and closeness of each other. And Angel could feel the length of Adorio's leg close and loving against his, like a whispered word or lover's kiss. As they sat, the moon, round and full and as big as all Italy, came suddenly into an opening in the clouds, and they were bathed in an eerie and beautiful kind of almost-daylight. Angel looked at Adorio's silver hair and to the hand on his lap, open to let the cap fall out. And Angel looked into the opal eyes Adorio turned to him above his weary and yet happy mouth.

With an almost-sad smile, in answer to what Angel was thinking, he said, "There I am, Chicito . . . I am the moon." He reached for Angel's hand. And Angel took the tiny gold circlet—his mother's opal ring—from his finger and gave it to Adorio, who put it on his smallest finger and made his kind of love to Angel after he had kissed him. And when Angel's head lay in his lap and they were relaxed, Adorio sighed wearily and whispered, "They are beautiful Chicito, like my eyes . . ." Adorio leaned forward and kissed him.

Suddenly they heard the call and had to rejoin their comrades. In that engagement Adorio was killed. Afterwards, Angel carried the body in his arms from the combat, and the others let him sit apart and cradle his friend, dry-eyed and with a faint smile, until the medics reached them. All Angel said was, ". . . The moon is behind a cloud . . ."

The next week their contingent was shipped to England, and when Angel was rotated to New York and separated from the service, he was alone. He was twenty years old, and he was alone.

He went back to the little town on the palisades, where he was honored as a hero, and Cano was honored posthumously. And Angel was alone. The other guys all looked at the alone Chico. They had read about that battle and about Cano and Chico. They were all proud and sad; they all knew that Angel was alone . . .

YOU THINK TO SHAME ME

You think to shame me, and use to flay me
Disgust for the life I've lived.
I tell you I love you, and you taunt me
With the fact of my promiscuity.
I tell you I love you, and you say to me,
"As you have so many men? Can you love?
Is it not perhaps a habit of speech
Grown glib with frequent using?"

Those are the words you speak to me
When I tell you I love you;

Yet *you* love *me*.
You must, you shall
You must and shall or I die—
For truly I say that I love you.
Think but an hour, one little count;
And read these poor words I ineptly write.
That at least you owe me,
If only for moments of physical bliss—
A gift I know I've given,
And a gift that you have accepted.

You say my body is my vice
And the vice of better men.
Perhaps. My body has been misused;
Misused a thousand times or more:
"Misused," I say in deference,
Politeness to your phrasing.
I call it not misuse. But let's not quibble.

My body has been misused.
Misused a thousand times or more;
Misused by many men and lads and you.
True—many is the body I have explored
Feverishly with my lips and tongue
And many are the lips I've kissed.
Many the boy who, fever-fired, searched
With blind weapon to pierce me through.
And did—with my assistance,
And breathed into my ear
The burnt breath of satiation.
Many the man before whom I have bowed
And whose eyes I have only known cast down
To view me from above lips that twist
In the smile that passion brings
To quiver beneath flaring nostrils.

Oh many and many the man
Who, with some wife grown big with child
And with no whore free or handy
Has bawded with me in bouts of love

And learned satiation through relief in bawding.
In fields and in alleys, in cities and in towns,
On docks and on ships and in bushes and in beds,
On rooftops and in hallways, in corners and in cars;
With young men and not, with boys and with lads
I've lain and I've tossed and I've kissed,
And because of these happenings—incidents small,
Though large at the time that I knew them—
You say I do not love you.
I say I do love you, *because* of these things.
I say I love you—
For such happenings are a search for a real thing,
And each is the real thing until done and proved not.

How did I come to know you?
You remember and use it against me.
I remember and say that I love you.
How did you come to know me?

As others had—as all others had—
Half through libidinous curiosity,
Half through accident.
You entered and were bewildered as you tended
Nature's demands and all the while
Could read the explicit graffiti before you
Over the urinal,
On the public wall.
Your face became flushed, your eyes embarrassed.
Although you thought yourself alone,
And disgust tightened a frown upon you,
Pity, vague and weighted down,
Settled on your shoulders. Then you turned,
Perhaps feeling my gaze upon you, and saw me
While adjusting your clothes and blushed again
To think someone had seen you blush before.

"What kind of men write things like these,
Where anyone can stand and see them?" you asked
And blushed again as you looked at me,
And found me quite unblushing.

I was amused and answered then,
"Men like me, I guess—or frantic men—
Afraid with age—or maybe just men
A little mad, at the moment, with lust—
Or maybe just weak and frightened lonesome
Or perhaps just some normal man with pornographic urge
Who knows it pays to advertise, but never knew
Just how he could unveil his thought
In idiom fit for more conventional space."

And you were embarrassed again and looked at me
Perhaps in hope I jested,
As indeed I did,
But with great truth and, I think,
Quite some perspicacity.
But I kept a straight face
And met you eye to eye to eye, and you were made
More embarrassed still
And blushed yet more becomingly.

Oh, I noticed all about you then—
I had noticed some before—
Your sweet-drawn legs
Imagined in line
Through your trousers, warm-brown,
Alive and draped with rare unconcern
To fall sharp-creased-though-careless to your instep—
Your stance, broadly strong,
As slightly straddled you'd spread your legs to stand
Unconscious of suave line of calf, of thigh, of groin.
I saw your hands, familiar with your person
In complete and unaware and normal function
Instinctive—but beautiful!
I saw you exposed—and the promise of you
Before I had followed the line of your drawing
To round your hips—indent your waist
And hollow your buttocks above muscled thighs,
Or to sculpt complete your torso—all,
All but your eyes above your nose

And shadowed by your hair that fell,
So naively disarranged,
And sculpted your temples, cheeks and stare—
I noticed all about you then,
Except your eyes below their brows
That somehow pointed out your lips,
So thin, so full, so gently straight.
Then it was that you turned and saw me
And blushed and asked aloud,
"What kind of men are men like these
Who write such thoughts abroad
For all the world to see and scorn
And ridicule with glee?
What kind of men think thoughts like these
For everyone to know—?"
Your embarrassed smile was lame
While I sat and watched it slowly find
Its place upon your lips, and answered softly,
"Me."

"But how—?" you asked, "But why—?
Or if you do—but you can't—"
You did not say that last to me,
But spoke it in your gaze instead,
And I could read your thoughts and knew
What fears and disbeliefs
And (perhaps) shameful hopes you had,
For I saw your eyes—slow-slanting out—
And found the pupils strangely hued as,
Tangled with your lashes, they peered
Faint blue and gray and green and chrome
And flecked with silver-gold,
Holding embraced a midnight iris
That also fragmented light,
And there I read your thought and answered,
"Why?"

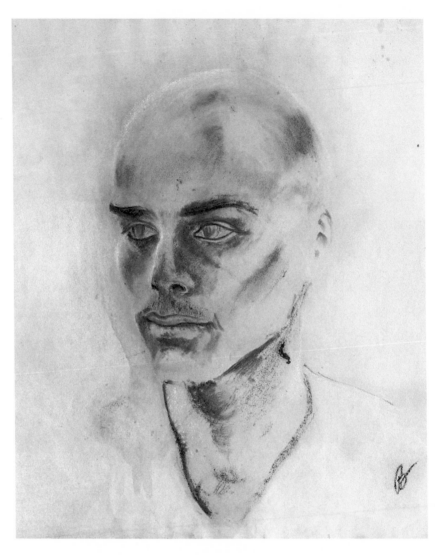

Portrait (date unknown).

Portrait (1970).

YOU SEE, I AM A HOMOSEXUAL[1]

This piece is transcribed from one of my taped 1983 interviews with Nugent. It expresses his essential character astonishingly well. The poem he discusses here, "Shadow," was published in Opportunity *in 1925 at about the same time as "Sahdji." These were his first published appearances.*

The Harlem Renaissance had been happening all this while. And I was a part of that. I mean, I was part of a little group in it called "the Niggeratti." And so, while I hadn't published things like Langston [Hughes] or Countee [Cullen] or even Wallie [Thurman], I had written one poem that Langston had retrieved from a wastebasket and given to Charles S. Johnson the year before, or two years before. . . .

It was a poem called "Shadow." . . . It created kind of a sensation at the time. It was considered to be a race poem, although I hadn't meant it to be . . . and it was considered to be *quite* something. I mean, here was a poem that the newspapers picked up and would . . . print when it was necessary to say something about blacks—something good about blacks—and art and et cetera. And it got quite a bit of unwarranted acclaim. It appeared in almost every anthology of Negro poetry at the time. . . . Considering that I didn't have any others, it's not surprising. Or considering that nobody *knew* whether I had any others or not, and that I didn't think that any of my poetry was good enough anyhow.

THW: You said you didn't intend it to be a race poem. What did you intend it to be?

I intended it to be a soul-searching poem of another kind of lonesomeness, not the lonesomeness of being racially stigmatized, but otherwise stigmatized.

You see, I am a homosexual.

I have never been in what they call "the closet." It has *never* occurred to me that it was anything to be ashamed of, and it never occurred to me that it was anybody's business but mine. You know that good old Negro song: "Ain't Nobody's Business What I Do?" And the times were very different then. Everybody did whatever they wanted to do. And who cared?

There was a great admixture—the mixture of blacks and whites during that particular two or three years. Whites making p-i-l-g-r-i-m-a-g-e-s to black Harlem, *doing* the cabarets or Clinton Moore's private parties. Whites being able to mingle freely in every way, including sexual, with blacks. Blacks suddenly having the freedom to have white sex partners. . . . Blacks very sought-after for

SHADOW

Silhouette

On the face of the moon

Am I.

A dark shadow in the light.

A silhouette am I

On the face of the moon

Lacking color

Or vivid brightness

But defined all the clearer

Because

I am dark,

Black on the face of the moon.

A shadow am I

Growing in the light,

Not understood as is the day,

But more easily seen

Because

I am a shadow in the light.

—Richard Bruce Nugent, 1925

everything, from cabarets, to *everything*. And my particular schtick was that I liked men.

A difficulty for me was that I certainly didn't know how to *ask* anybody. It always seemed to me to be kind of silly to have to ask somebody, "Would you please go to bed with me? I do this, and I do that, but I don't do *that*." It just seemed silly to me. I suppose I have a form of stage fright. I suppose I was afraid of rejection. Because I'd been rejected when I *had* made it clear to certain Negroes in Washington, D.C. that I found them sexually attractive. I hadn't been put down; I'd just been rejected. Well, how much rejection can you take? I finally decided that . . . I wasn't what they *liked,* even if they did fool around. . . . So I . . . stopped making myself available to blacks. . . .

I don't quite know how I discovered that *Latins* were more open to such, I can't say "advances," but "opportunities" such as I presented. But I *had,* by the time that the Negro Renaissance was fading away *as* the Renaissance, but Harlem was still in vogue, acquired, I suppose the only word for it right now would be a "stable" of Latins who would come across the bridge from the Bronx into Harlem, and yell up to my window "Bruce! Bruce!" And I would be so titillated and excited and go down and let Paul or Georgolio in.

Of course I was going to all the parties and everything at the time. . . . Almost all of life that wasn't in cabarets was in either barrooms . . . [or] rent parties. . . . If you were "nice people," you didn't go to rent parties, but I wasn't ever "nice." If you told me that isn't where you should go, that was, of course, where I went. So I would go to all the bars; they were all owned by Italians. And they were very simpatico. They just *liked* me, and I liked them. Of course they liked me, because I liked them so damned much. And friends of mine, like Wallie, loved to go to bars with me, because if we didn't have any money, I could always get drinks on the house. Not on the house, but on a tab. I had always run up a tab, and Wallie would say, "How do you pay 'em?" And then some snide person like Clinton would say, "How does he *pay* 'em? Look at how they look at him."

But that isn't how I paid them. I don't think I ever had a bartender, sexually. But I had *eyes* for them, and I really liked them. And Italians, who were the first Latins I knew—*nobody* appreciates being liked and wanted and being desired as much as Italians do. Nobody. Or nobody *shows* it as much. I don't know . . . how other people feel. I am particularly immune to the sting of the WASP, so I *don't* know if other people did [appreciate it].

I knew that sometimes the British did, because all British visitors, of course, went right to Harlem to find themselves a black bedmate for at least one night, and I was fairly visible, and so I was invited to many of their rooms, *bathed thor-*

oughly, so I wouldn't really contaminate their sheets, and had my sex, or their sex, and there would always be a pittance left on the mantel for me, because they always went out and left me there, which was a sign, of course, that I was absolutely trustworthy. I remember being *very* insulted when I found money left for me, because I hadn't considered myself quite the whore that I now know I was. . . .

Latins—they were really quite something. A very interesting kind of rapport grew up for me, and *any* Italian that I happened to even meet to buy things from or anything, I always *knew.* Even if they were blond and blue-eyed, I knew that they were Italian. And they turned me on. When I turn on, I guess I light up, because they knew it immediately, and they *liked* it, and they would be *nice* to me. . . . They were so nice to me. . . . They were as accepting of me as the others were rejecting of me. So it's not strange that even to this day . . . my favorite people are Italians, or other Latins, but mostly Italians, because I knew them first. I've known them longest, and, I think, known them best.

I can understand their racial prejudices. The American Italians have strong racial prejudices. But you know . . . to them, I was like that sign so prevalent now: "You Don't Have to Be Jewish to Like It." Or, like it was down South, you know: "He's an exceptional Negro." I was always the exception to them—those who were prejudiced—so I never *experienced* their prejudice. But I knew it was there. And I knew it didn't include me at all. There were many ways in which I knew that. I mean . . . these hot-natured lads . . . would introduce me to their families . . . their mothers and fathers . . . something they wouldn't do with other people . . . with whom they had these "extracurricular affairs." And in many ways I was made to know that I wasn't accepted *just* because of my sex, but *despite* it, and *despite* my color. In other words, I was *accepted,* period.

They would fight for me. No one during those first years, and I guess now, even—no one [could] say anything that they thought was insulting about me or to me without them springing to my defense.

Enough raving about my predilection for and fondness for Italians. God knows, they're good sex. Italians, it seems to me, and other Latins to a lesser degree, consider and regard and accept sex as an appetite, and if their appetite is—to carry the analogy further—if the appetite is meat and potatoes, they pick . . . meat and potatoes. If the appetite is a dessert, they pick a dessert. And sometimes they'd pick very lah-de-dahs. . . . They were, and are, kind of wonderful that way, as I found out years later when I went to Rome . . . where the American prejudice against blacks doesn't exist. It was like a veil had been lifted, and I could suddenly see what it was about the Italians that I had liked so *much,* because that veil had existed for me only in my head. I *knew* it was there, but I'd never *felt* it. But to know that there's a barrier, you don't have to bump into it to always be aware of it, whether it bothers you or not. I mean, whether it is intrusive or not. It was there. Still is. But as I say, I was an exception to them, and probably still am. And I suppose with cause . . . with justification . . . I so sincerely liked *them.* It's a little difficult not to like somebody a *little* bit that so *sincerely* likes you and shows it. And some of my friends, even now—well, I guess I've passed beyond the stage where some of my friends were embarrassed by this overt liking I have for several things: Italians, Latins, and menials.

I have a *real* empathetic *love* for Italians, Latins, and menials. And the only way I can ever show love is to *show* it. And so I do. I *never* want anyone to feel any of the rejection that I have felt frequently. I have been a busboy; I've been a waiter; I've been a porter; I've been a menial. And I know how *excluded* menials are from the lives or the concern or the regard of the people they serve. And, you know, it's not enough to say "Well, what d'ya expect. After all, you're gettin' paid for it." That's not enough. You just are not *human,* really. . . . Nobody who ever serves me . . . I hope, is *ever* going to feel that from me. Never. You know, I'd rather love a . . . *shit* than hurt, accidentally, a person by that kind of regard. And believe me, some of the people that I've loved have been shits, too. Some of the Italians. Some of the Latins. But again, I've been an exception. They haven't shit on my parade.

NOTES

INTRODUCTION

1 Richard Bruce Nugent, interview by Thomas H. Wirth [hereafter THW], tape recording, 27 June 1983, collections of THW and Schomburg Center.

2 Richard Bruce Nugent, "Lighting FIRE!!" insert to the reprint of FIRE!! (Metuchen, N.J.: FIRE!! Press, 1982).

3 Wallace Thurman, Infants of the Spring (New York: Macaulay Company, 1932), 21, 44.

4 Nugent, interview by THW, tape recording, 19 June 1983.

5 Ibid.

6 Langston Hughes to Carl Van Vechten, 24 June 1925, Remember Me to Harlem: The Letters of Langston Hughes and Carl Van Vechten, 1925–1964, ed. Emily Bernard (New York: Alfred A. Knopf, 2001), 22.

7 I have adopted the spelling of "Niggeratti" used by Nugent (and by Thurman in Infants of the Spring). That spelling self-consciously emphasizes the "ratty" aspects of the group and is consistent with Nugent's pronunciation. Langston Hughes, however, spelled the word "Niggerati" in his autobiography, The Big Sea. Hughes's version renders the irony more genteel.

8 Langston Hughes, "The Negro Artist and the Racial Mountain," Nation 122 (23 June 1926): 694.

9 Langston Hughes and Milton Meltzer, Black Magic: A Pictorial History of the Negro in Entertainment (Englewood Cliffs, N.J.: Prentice-Hall, 1967), 113.

10 Alain Locke to friend, undated, Alain Locke Papers, box 164-12, Moorland-Spingarn Collection, Howard University, Washington, D.C.

11 My use of the term gay with respect to men in the Harlem Renaissance period follows the lead of George Chauncey: "Gay" refers to men who perceive themselves as different from "normal" men because of their self-acknowledged sexual interest in other males; it does not include men who respond to sexual advances from other males, but who nonetheless consider themselves "normal." See George Chauncey, Gay New York: Gender, Urban Culture, and the Making of the Gay Male World, 1890–1940 (New York: Basic Books/HarperCollins, 1994), 24–25.

12 Ibid., 264.

13 The connections between the European avant-garde and the Harlem Renaissance should be explored further. Nancy Cunard's anthology, Negro (London: Wishart and Company, 1934), for example, is as massive and significant a collection of material on the Black experience as any that had been produced up to that time. Yet, American scholars of the Harlem Renaissance scarcely mention it. Nugent was one of her acquaintances.

14 Richard Bruce Nugent, private conversation with THW, 1984. Nugent's chance reunion with Roditi one Sunday in 1984 at the Hatch-Billops Collection in New York was among the most memorable occasions of my friendship with Nugent.

15 Anthony Tommasini, *Virgil Thomson: Composer on the Aisle* (New York: W. W. Norton, 1997), 225.

16 There is no evidence that Van Vechten was sexually involved with any of his intellectual or literary friends in Harlem. However, he left among his archives photographs, mostly taken by himself, that document his sexual interest in young black men. See Jonathan Weinberg, "'Boy Crazy': Carl Van Vechten's Queer Collection," *Yale Journal of Criticism* 7, no.2 (fall 1994): 25–49; and James Smalls, "Public Face, Private Thoughts: Fetish, Interracialism, and the Homoerotic in Carl Van Vechten's Photographs," in *The Passionate Camera: Photography and the Bodies of Desire*, ed. Deborah Bright (New York: Routledge, 1998), 78–102. This sexual interest was surely a factor in stimulating his enthusiasm for Harlem.

17 1929 Daybook of Carl Van Vechten, Carl Van Vechten Papers, box III, Manuscript Division, New York Public Library. Salon hostesses Ettie and Carrie Stettheimer were sisters of artist Florine Stettheimer, who later designed the sets for *Four Saints in Three Acts*. Mabel Dodge Luhan and Muriel Draper were also salon hostesses—trendsetters in New York's "high bohemia." Maurice Wertheim and his wife Alma were patrons of the arts. Max Ewing was a spectacularly handsome young writer. Larry Block was Langston Hughes's editor at Knopf. Witter (Hal) Bynner was a well-known poet. Emily Clark was the founder and editor of the literary magazine *Reviewer* and the second wife of the important '20s novelist James Branch Cabell. Louis Cole was a nightclub dancer and entertainer, who later enjoyed considerable success in Paris. The "drag" was one of the spectacular annual drag balls sponsored in Harlem by Hamilton Lodge No. 710 of the Grand United Order of Odd Fellows. Pod's and Jerry's was a cabaret. This was a remarkable evening in that it introduced Gertrude Stein's *Four Saints in Three Acts* to some of the movers and shakers of the American cultural avant-garde. Five years later, the opera was produced at the Hartford Atheneum with an all-black cast, followed by an extended run on Broadway. As it turned out, Edward Perry was instrumental in helping Virgil Thompson (the composer), John Houseman (the director), and Frederick Ashton (the choreographer) recruit the singers and dancers. See Tommasini, *Virgil Thompson*, 243–50, and Steven Watson, *Prepare for Saints* (New York: Random House, 1998), 66–69, 74–75, 179–86, 240–42. Regarding Emily Clark, see *Letters of Carl Van Vechten*, ed. Bruce Kellner (New Haven, Conn.: Yale University Press, 1987), 40 (footnote re. Emily Clark). Regarding Louis Cole and Pod's and Jerry's, see *The Harlem Renaissance: A Historical Dictionary for the Era*, ed. Bruce Kellner (New York: Methuen, 1984), 76, 285 respectively.

18 Richard Bruce Nugent, interview by Jeff Kisseloff, n. d. in Jeff Kisselhoff, *You Must Remember This: An Oral History of Manhattan from the 1890s to World War II* (New York: Harcourt Brace Jovanovich, 1989), 289–90. The historian George Chauncey confirms that the term "closet" was not used in gay circles before the 1960s. See Chauncey, *Gay New York*, 6–8.

19 Richard Bruce Nugent, transcript of an interview by Jewelle L. Gomez for the film *Before Stonewall*, 17 April 1983, photocopy, collection of THW, 4. I am indebted to Rodney Evans for providing me with the copy of the transcript.

20 From "Harlem Nite Life" by Frank Byrd in the *Inter-State Tattler*, 18 July 1930, from the Gumby Scrapbook 139, Rare Book and Manuscript Library, Columbia University. The ellipses are in the original. Richard Bruce was Nugent's nom de plume during this period. Mary Fair (Horwood) was a well-known young lady of Greenwich Village, immortalized by Maxwell Boden-

heim in his poem "Greenwich Village Jazz II," in *Bringing Jazz* (New York: Horace Liveright, 1930), 52–54. When Nugent and Horwood met, they were intrigued to learn that they had both, at different times, been lovers of the same man. Countee Cullen married Yolande Du Bois in the "Harlem social event of the decade" in April 1928; by the end of the year, the marriage had disintegrated on account of the groom's lack of sexual interest in the bride (David Levering Lewis, *W. E. B. Du Bois: The Fight for Equality and the American Century, 1919–1963* [New York: Henry Holt, 2000], 220–28). Robert Schlick was a gay poet who had recently married Pamela Bianco, a painter who later became a noted writer/illustrator of children's books.

21 Chauncey, *Gay New York,* 253–56.

22 Lewis, *W. E. B. Du Bois,* 205.

23 Sterling Brown, interview by Genevieve Ekaete, "Sterling Brown: A Living Legend," *New Directions: The Howard University Magazine* 1 (winter 1974): 9.

24 David Levering Lewis, *When Harlem Was in Vogue* (New York: Knopf, 1981), 120–21, 149–55.

25 See, for example, Locke's undated letter to "Jenkins" in the Glenn Carrington Papers at Howard University. (Carrington was a member of Locke's circle of protégés—a Howard student who went to Harlem after graduation, met Nugent and other Renaissance luminaries, and became an inveterate collector in the Van Vechten mode.) Locke wrote:

> Of course my main desire is to be helpful and bring a good mind out of the fog of nervous uncertainty. Your religious background has particularly made it difficult for you to face yourself except in terms of a split-personality—aspiring repentant idealist and sinful victim of the flesh.
>
> I believe repressed homosexualist emotions and fixations are primarily responsible for your condition—and that the attempt to sublimate has broken down your social adjustments both with whites and Negroes, but more so with the impending practical entry into the Negro world, which of course you know is hopelessly conventional on this point and offers no ready choice between practical intercourse on a vulgar background and plane and complete hypocritical suppression.
>
> Of course, my own homosexual experiences and temperament may be the intuitive basis of this diagnosis, but I do believe I have reached this conclusion independently of such an intuition. (Glenn Carrington Papers, box 145–25, folder 34, Moorland-Spingarn Research Center, Howard University, Washington, D.C.)

26 See also Locke's undated letter, also in the Glenn Carrington Papers, addressed to "Dear Lad."

> Dear Lad,
>
> . . . I was too glad to see you after so long an interval.
>
> I said with affected indifference "Hello." You answered with intimate assurance "How art?"—And I nearly fainted.
>
> You see—all week I have been debating in my mind whether or not my intuitive intimations about our friendship were well-founded; whether I should and could receive you into the very inner chamber of my life.—It is a fraternity of friends—and only [on] all Hallow's Eve and St. Agnes Eve can we receive new friends into the circle.—I had planned several talks during the week—both to be sure of you and of myself. Imagine my consternation when you greeted me as one already initiated.—We use "thee" and "thou" in addressing

each other. It is just too uncanny for words!! Where on earth did you pick that up? — Surely you could not possibly have met one of us before. Well, — it seems destined to be. (Glenn Carrington Papers, box 145–25, folder 34.)

27 Arnold Rampersad, *The Life of Langston Hughes*, vol. 1, *1902–1941: I, Too, Sing America* (New York: Oxford University Press, 1986), 66–71, 83, 90–94.

28 For a fuller description and analysis of the Locke-Cullen correspondence, which extended over many years and definitively establishes Cullen's homosexuality, see Alden Reimonenq, "Countee Cullen's Uranian 'Soul Windows,'" *Journal of Homosexuality* 26 (1993): 143–65.

29 1925 Daybook of Carl Van Vechten, Carl Van Vechten Papers, box III.

30 Nugent, interview by THW, tape recording, 27 June 1983, collections of THW and Schomburg Center.

31 Nugent to Locke, 28 November 1928, Alain Locke Papers, box 164–75, folder 18, Moorland-Spingarn Research Center.

32 Locke to Nugent, 2 February 1929, Glenn Carrington Papers, box 145–25, folder 33. I am indebted to Barbara Smith for bringing the Locke-Nugent correspondence in the Carrington Papers to my attention.

33 Locke to Nugent, 25 April 1929, Glenn Carrington Papers.

34 Richmond Barthé to Richard Bruce Nugent, 20 December 1977, collection of THW. Barthé was mistaken about the date; *Porgy*'s Chicago run was in November–December 1928. "David" and "Jonathan" are references to the biblical narrative of the love between David and Jonathan —a love which David describes after Jonathan's death as "surpassing the love of women" (1 Sam. 18–20; 2 Sam. 1:26).

35 Nugent, private conversations with THW.

36 "Trade" or "rough trade" were terms used in gay circles to refer to men of masculine demeanor—ideally sailors, soldiers, or some other embodiment of the aggressive masculine ideal—who do not pursue other men but do accept their sexual advances. See Chauncey, *Gay New York*, 16, 20–21.

37 Eleonore van Notten, *Wallace Thurman's Harlem Renaissance* (Amsterdam: Editions Rodopi, 1994), 96–97, 209–10.

38 Nugent, from notes of conversations with THW, especially 8 January 1983, 15 January 1983, and 29 December 1983, collection of THW.

39 L. S. Alexander Gumby, untitled autobiographical essay, *Columbia Library World* (January 1951): 2–8. The particular intimacy of the Gumby-Newman relationship is established by a 1917 letter from Newman to Gumby, which reads in part: "When I say you're a bitch it's only half what you are, if white people were half as good as you they would be able to shit on the front porches and get away with it. . . . Your room and you are a god-send to me. . . . I certainly will never forget you to my dying day." Charles W. Newman to L. S. Alexander Gumby, 15 June 15 1917, Gumby Scrapbook, "Letters," vol. 1 of 2 (n.p., n.d.), collection of THW. The existence of such interracial homosexual relationships so early in the century is not widely known.

40 "Book Studio Group Honors Cullen, Poet," *Amsterdam News*, 17 September 1930, Gumby Scrapbook 36, Rare Book and Manuscript Library, Columbia University, New York.

41 Gumby to Nugent, 30 May 1951, collection of THW.

42 Reimonenq, "Countee Cullen's Uranian 'Soul Windows,'" 156. The letters are deposited in the Countee Cullen Papers, Amistad Research Center, Tulane University, New Orleans.

43 Henry Louis Gates Jr., "The Black Man's Burden," in *Fear of a Queer Planet: Queer Politics and Social Theory*, ed. Michael Warner (Minneapolis: University of Minnesota Press, 1993), 233.

44 Survey of the Month, *Opportunity* 5 (May 1927): 154.

45 Camara Dia Holloway, *Portraiture and the Harlem Renaissance: The Photographs of James L. Allen* (New Haven, Conn.: Yale University Art Gallery, 1999), 5, 22.

46 "Why 'Run, Little Chillun' Runs," *Literary Digest* (15 April 1933): 13.

47 Lewis, *When Harlem Was in Vogue*, xii.

48 Henry Blake Fuller, *Bertram Cope's Year* (Chicago: Alderbrink Press, 1919; Chappaqua, N.Y.: Turtle Point Press, 1998).

49 Robert McAlmon, *Distinguished Air* (Paris: Contact Editions Press, 1925).

50 E. M. Forster, *Maurice* (New York: W. W. Norton, 1971).

51 Blair Niles, *Strange Brother* (New York: Liveright, 1931).

52 Nugent to Van Vechten, 19 December 1925, Nugent Correspondence, Van Vechten Papers, James Weldon Johnson Memorial Collection, Beinecke Rare Book and Manuscript Library, Yale University.

53 Thurman, *Infants*, 283–84.

54 Joris-Karl Huysmans, *Against Nature (A rebours)*, trans. Margaret Mauldon (Oxford: Oxford University Press, 1998), 90.

55 Carl Van Vechten, *Peter Whiffle: His Life and Works* (New York: Alfred A. Knopf, 1922), 170–71.

56 Ibid., 147–48.

57 Carl Van Vechten, *The Blind Bow-Boy* (New York: Alfred A. Knopf, 1923), 56–57.

58 Ibid., 117.

59 Van Vechten to Mabel Dodge Luhan, 8 October 1924, *Letters of Carl Van Vechten*, ed. Bruce Kellner.

60 Van Vechten, *Blind Bow-Boy*, 160.

61 Byrne R. S. Fone, *A Road to Stonewall* (New York: Twayne, 1995), 223.

62 Steven Watson, introduction to Charles Henri Ford and Parker Tyler, *The Young and Evil* (New York: Gay Presses of New York, 1988), vii.

63 Robert Scully, *A Scarlet Pansy* (New York: William Faro, 1933). For a discussion of when *A Scarlet Pansy* was written, see Fone, *Road to Stonewall*, 227.

64 Published while she was still a slave, Wheatley's *Poems on Various Subjects, Religious and Moral* (1773) challenged the then-current presumption that persons of African descent were congenitally lacking in higher cognitive faculties. The high quality of Wheatley's poetry, written when she had spoken English for only ten years and in an era when few white women could even begin to equal her facility, was a powerful blow to those who would deny the full humanity of people of African descent.

65 Fone, *Road to Stonewall*, 109–10.

66 Van Notten, *Wallace Thurman's Harlem Renaissance*, 109–18.

67 See, for example, Benjamin Brawley, "The Negro Literary Renaissance," *Southern Workman* 56 (March 1927): 177–84.

68 Ibid.

69 See W. E. B. Du Bois, "Opinion," *Crisis* 22 (June 1921): 55. See also Du Bois to Mrs. E. A. Duffield, 1 August 1923, *The Correspondence of W. E. B. Du Bois*, ed. Herbert Aptheker (Amherst: University of Massachusetts Press, 1973), 1:276.

70 W. E. B. Du Bois, "The Criteria of Negro Art," *Crisis* 32 (October 1926): 290–97.

71 W. E. B. Du Bois, "Two Novels," *Crisis* 35 (June 1928): 202.

72 W. E. B. Du Bois, "Opinion," *Crisis* 31 (January 1926): 115.

73 Alain Locke, "Beauty Instead of Ashes," *Nation* 126 (18 April 1928): 432–34.

74 Ibid.

75 Alain Locke, "Fire: A Negro Magazine," *Survey* 58 (15 August–15 September 1927): 563.

76 Chauncey, *Gay New York*, 103–4.

77 Alain Locke, "Art or Propaganda?" *Harlem* 1 (November 1928): 12.

78 Alain Locke, "Spiritual Truancy," *New Challenge* 2 (fall 1937): 81–85.

79 It has been plausibly argued that both Emma Lou and Alva are autobiographical figures representing different aspects of Thurman's personality. See Van Notten, *Wallace Thurman's Harlem Renaissance*, 223–37. In this interpretation Alva embodies Thurman's conflicted feelings toward his own homosexual impulses. Such an interpretation is unlikely, however, to have occurred to Thurman's contemporary readership.

80 Thurman, *Infants of the Spring*, 169. See also David Blackmore, "'Something . . . Too Preposterous and Complex to Be Recognized or Considered': Same-Sex Desire and Race in *Infants of the Spring*," *Soundings* 80 (winter 1997): 519–29.

81 Suzette A. Spencer, "Serving at a Different Angle and Flying in the Face of Tradition: Excavating the Homoerotic Subtext in *Home to Harlem*," *CLA Journal* 42 (December 1998): 164–93.

82 Claude McKay, *Banjo* (New York: Harper and Brothers, 1929), 324.

83 Claude McKay, *Home to Harlem* (New York: Harper and Brothers, 1928), 272.

84 Ibid., 157–58.

85 Ibid., 196–97.

86 Ibid., 200.

87 Gregory Woods, *A History of Gay Literature: The Male Tradition* (New Haven, Conn.: Yale University Press, 1998), 210.

88 Chauncey, *Gay New York*, 78.

89 McKay, *Banjo*, 22.

90 Ibid., 260.

91 Ibid., 326.

92 Chauncey, *Gay New York*, 113–14; Anthony Rotundo, *American Manhood: Transformations in Masculinity from the Revolution to the Modern Era* (New York: Basic Books, 1993).

93 Claude McKay, *Constab Ballads* (London: Watts and Company, 1912). Reprinted in *Claude McKay: Selected Poems*, ed. Joan R. Sherman (Mineola, N.Y.: Dover Publications, 1999), 11–15.

94 Wayne F. Cooper, *Claude McKay: Rebel Sojourner in the Harlem Renaissance* (Baton Rouge: Louisiana State University Press, 1987), 46.

95 Reimonenq, "Countee Cullen's Uranian 'Soul Windows'" 147–55.

96 Countee Cullen, "Timid Lover," *Copper Sun* (New York: Harper and Brothers, 1927), 20. The word *acolyte* is redolent of same-sex desire and may be a reference to Bloxam's notorious story "The Priest and the Acolyte," which appeared in *Chameleon* (Oxford, 1894).

97 Countee Cullen, *The Black Christ* (New York: Harper and Brothers, 1929), 105.

98 Countee Cullen, *Color* (New York: Harper and Brothers, 1925), 92, 94. The reader of Cullen's lines is reminded of Oscar Wilde's well-known line, "And all men kill the thing they love," from "The Ballad of Reading Gaol." Nugent's story "Tree with Kerioth Fruit" similarly depicts Judas's betrayal of Jesus as an act of love, motivated by the need to bring Jesus's prophecy to pass.

99 Reimonenq, "Countee Cullen's Uranian 'Soul Windows,'" 157.

100 Cullen, *Copper Sun*, 67.

101 On Cullen's relationship with Duff, see Reimonenq, "Countee Cullen's Uranian 'Soul Windows,'" 147.

102 Cullen, *Color*, 12.

103 Cullen, *Copper Sun*, 9.

104 Peter Powers, "'The Singing Man Who Must be Reckoned With': Private Desire and Public Responsibility in the Poetry of Countee Cullen," *African American Review* 34 (winter 2000): 661–78.

105 Rampersad, *The Life of Langston Hughes*, 133; Nugent, from notes of a private conversation with THW, 4 December 1983, collection of THW.

106 Langston Hughes, "Poem[2]" (1925), *The Collected Poems of Langston Hughes*, ed. Arnold Rampersad and David Roessel (New York: Alfred A. Knopf, 1994), 52.

107 Langston Hughes, "Boy," *Carolina Magazine* (May 1928): 38.

108 Woods, *A History of Gay Literature*, 210.

109 Hughes, *Collected Poems*, 97.

110 Alain Locke, "The Art of the Ancestors," *Survey Graphic* 6 (March 1925): 673.

111 I am indebted to Ellen McBreen for this insight.

112 Ann Douglas, *Terrible Honesty: Mongrel Manhattan in the 1920s* (New York: Farrar, Strauss, and Giroux, 1995), 55–59.

113 Walker, a free black man who settled in Boston, published his *Appeal to the Coloured Citizens of the World* (Boston: David Walker, 3d ed., 1830) in 1829–30. In ringing terms, he denounced the institution of slavery as a patent violation of Christian precepts. He attacked with particular effectiveness Christian clergy who were apologists for slavery and Americans who professed to be Christians but who profited from or cooperated in the enslavement of their fellow men. His argument for immediate emancipation was radical and uncompromising—a shock even to the abolitionists of his time.

HARLEM

1 Wallace Thurman, "Harlem's Place in the Sun," *Dance Magazine* 10 (May 1928): 23, 54.

2 Richard Bruce Nugent, "The Dark Tower," *Opportunity* 5 (October 1927): 305–6.

GENTLEMAN JIGGER

1 Details of Thurman's ancestry are from Eleonore van Notten, *Wallace Thurman's Harlem Renaissance*.

2 Thurman, *Infants*, 46–47.

HARLEM RENAISSANCE PERSONALITIES

1 Nugent, interview by THW, tape recording, 27 June 1983, collections of THW and Schomburg Center.

AFTER THE HARLEM RENAISSANCE

1 Nugent, interview by THW, tape recording, 19 June 1983, collections of THW and Schomburg Center.

BIBLIOGRAPHY

RICHARD BRUCE NUGENT: PUBLISHED WORKS AND INTERVIEWS

"'. . . and More Gently Still': A Myth." *Trend: A Quarterly of the Seven Arts* 1 (June–July–August 1932): 53–54.

Beyond Where the Stars Stood Still. New York: Warren Marr II, n.d. [1945]. Illustrated with drawings by Richard Bruce Nugent. Reprinted, with the corrected title "Beyond Where the Star Stood Still," in *Crisis* 77 (December 1970): 405–8. One of the illustrations, "Carus," is reproduced in Kalaidjian, *American Culture between the Wars,* 93.

"Cavalier" [Richard Bruce, pseud.]. In *Caroling Dusk,* edited by Countee Cullen, 205–6. New York: Harper and Brothers, 1927.

"The Dark Tower" [by Richard Bruce, pseud.]. *Opportunity* 5 (October 1927): 305–6.

"An Interview with Bruce Nugent: Actor, Artist, Writer, Dancer." By James V. Hatch. In *Artists and Influences,* edited by Camille Billops and James V. Hatch, 81–104. New York: Hatch-Billops Collection, 1982.

Interview by Jean Blackwell Hutson. Videotape, 14 April 1982. Schomburg Center for Research in Black Culture, New York City.

Interview by Jeff Kisseloff. In *You Must Remember This: An Oral History of Manhattan from the 1890s to World War II,* edited by Jeff Kisseloff, 282–300. New York: Harcourt Brace Jovanovich, 1989.

Interview by Jewelle L. Gomez. For *Before Stonewall,* produced by John Scagliotti, directed by Greta Schiller and Robert Rosenberg. Cinema Guild CG 102, 1986. 87 min. Videocassette. Interview transcript, 17 April 1983. Photocopy. Collection of Thomas H. Wirth.

Interviews by Thomas H. Wirth. Tape recordings, 19 June 1983–5 September 1983. Collections of Thomas H. Wirth and Schomburg Center.

"Lighting *FIRE!!*" Insert in a facsimile edition of *FIRE!!* Metuchen, N.J.: FIRE!! Press, 1982.

"Marshall's: A Portrait." *Phylon* 5 (Fourth Quarter 1944): 316–18.

"My Love." *Palms* 4 (October 1926): 20.

"Narcissus." *Trend: A Quarterly of the Seven Arts* 1 (January–February–March, 1933): 127.

"The Now Discordant Song of Bells." *Wooster Review* 9 (spring 1989): 34–42.

"Pope Pius the Only." *Challenge* 2 (spring 1937): 15–18.

"Richard Bruce." In *Caroling Dusk,* edited by Countee Cullen, 205–6. New York: Harper and Brothers, 1927.

"Sahdji." In *The New Negro,* edited by Alain Locke, 113–14. New York: Albert and Charles Boni, 1925. Reprinted in Peplow and Davis, *The New Negro Renaissance,* 209–11.

"Sahdji: An African Ballet" [Richard Bruce, pseud.]. In *Plays of Negro Life: A Sourcebook of Native American Drama,* edited by Alain Locke and Montgomery Gregory, 387–400. New York: Harper and Brothers, 1927.

"Scheme." [Gary George, pseud.]. *Challenge* 1 (January 1936): 30–31.

"Shadow" [Richard Bruce, pseud.]. In *Opportunity* 3 (October 1925): 296. Reprinted in Cullen, *Caroling Dusk,* 206–7, and in Pool and Bremen, *Ik Zag Hoe Zwart Ik Was,* 122–23.

"Smoke, Lilies and Jade" [Richard Bruce, pseud.]. *FIRE!!* 1 (November 1926): 33–39. Reprinted in Huggins, *Voices from the Harlem Renaissance,* 99–110; Smith, *Black Men, White Men,* 17–30; Lewis, *The Portable Harlem Renaissance Reader,* 569–83; Ruff, *Go the Way Your Blood Beats,* 205–221; and, with an introduction by Samuel R. Delany, in *James White Review* 16 (winter 1999): 21–26.

"What Price Glory in Uncle Tom's Cabin" [Richard Bruce, pseud.]. *Harlem* 1 (November 1928): 25–26.

RICHARD BRUCE NUGENT: IMAGES

Drawing of male head. *Opportunity* 4 (March 1926): cover. Reproduced in *Print* 52 (May/June 1998): 61.

Two drawings. *FIRE!!* 1 (November 1926): 4, 24. The drawing on p. 4 is reproduced in *Print* 52 (May/June 1998): 58. The drawing on p. 24 is reproduced in Kaladjian, *American Culture Between the Wars,* 96, and on the endpapers of Watson, *The Harlem Renaissance.*

Illustrations, "Jazz—A Stepping Stone," by Frederick Millar. *American Monthly* (April 1927): 35–36.

Drawing. *Opportunity* 5 (August 1927): 227.

Illustrations, "Lawrence Avenue," by James T. Logan. *Opportunity* 5 (August 1927): 232–35.

Illustrations, "Game," by Eugene Gordon. *Opportunity* 5 (September 1927): 264.

Drawing (Male Head). *Opportunity* 5 (October 1927): 289.

Drawings (Male Heads). *Ebony and Topaz: A Collectanea,* edited by Charles S. Johnson, [7], [8], 46, 114, 166. New York: Opportunity/National Urban League, 1927.

Drawings for Mulattoes. Ebony and Topaz: A Collectanea, edited by Charles S. Johnson, 103–6. New York: Opportunity/National Urban League, 1927. Reproduced in Gubar, *Racechanges,* 108–11, dustjacket. Numbers 2 and 3 of this series are reproduced in Kaladjian, *American Culture between the Wars,* 71, 72. Number 3 appears in Watson, *The Harlem Renaissance,* free front endpaper; in Kaladjian, *American Culture between the Wars;* cover in McClendon, *The Politics of Color,* dustjacket; and in *Print* 52 (May/June 1998): 61.

Illustration (Lynching Victim), "Black Gum," by William V. Kelley. *Opportunity* 6 (January 1928): 13.

Illustrations, "Harlem's Place in the Sun," by Wallace Thurman. *Dance Magazine* 10 (May 1928): 23, 54. Three of the illustrations are reproduced in Watson, *The Harlem Renaissance,* 59.

Salome. Harlem 1 (November 1928): 28.

Illustration, "Cease Nudging Nevermore," by Octave Lilly, Jr. *Crisis* 77 (February 1970): 48.

Frankincense. Crisis 78 (December 1971): cover.

Drawing (Women Dancing). *Black American Literature Forum* 19 (spring 1985): 17. Also in *Print* 52 (May/June 1998): 61.

Drawing (Two Women Dancing). Steven Watson. *The Harlem Renaissance: Hub of African-American Culture, 1920–1930,* 153. New York: Pantheon Books, 1995.

Drawing (Woman with Green Hair, Salome Series). On the cover of *Pagan Operetta,* by Carl Hancock Rux. New York: Fly by Night Press, 1998. Also in *Print* 52 (May/June 1998): 57.

Two drawings from the Salome Series. *Art Journal* 57 (fall 1998): 22, 26.

David and Goliath. Art Journal 57 (fall 1998): 28.

Smoke, Lilies and Jade. In *To Conserve a Legacy: American Art from Historically Black Colleges and Universities,* edited by Richard J. Powell and Jock Reynolds, 217. Andover/New York/Cambridge: Phillips Academy/Studio Museum in Harlem/MIT Press, 1999.

Untitled twelve images. *Transition* 11 (2001): 89–106.

ARTICLES ABOUT NUGENT

Boone, Joseph Allen. "Bruce Nugent, 'Smoke, Lilies, and Jade': Harlem as a Homo State of Mind." In *Libidinal Currents: Sexuality and the Shaping of Modernism,* 220–32. Chicago: University of Chicago Press, 1998.

"*FIRE!!* Burns Anew." *Bywords* 3 (December 1983): 1. Washington, D.C.: Institute for the Preservation and Study of African American Writing.

Garber, Eric. "Richard Bruce Nugent." In *Dictionary of Literary Biography.* Vol. 51, *Afro-American Writers from the Harlem Renaissance to 1940,* edited by Trudier Harris and Thadious M. Davis, 213–21. Detroit: Gale Research Company, 1987.

Harris, E. Lynn. "Renaissance Men." *Advocate* (March 2, 1999): 49.

McBreen, Ellen. "Biblical Gender Bending in Harlem: The Queer Performance of Nugent's *Salome.*" *Art Journal* 57 (fall 1998): 22–28.

McGruder, Kevin. "Richard Bruce Nugent: Black, Gay, Rebellious." *Brooklyn Pride* 4 (February 2001): 1.

Penn, Carol A. L. "An interview with Mr. Bruce Nugent." *Harlem Cultural Review* 5 (September 1983): 2.

Sample, Maxine J. "Richard Bruce Nugent (1906–1987)." In *African American Authors, 1745–1945: A Bio-Bibliographical Critical Sourcebook,* edited by Emmanuel S. Nelson, 349–52. Westport, Conn.: Greenwood, 2000.

Schwartz, A. B. Christa. "Chapter 6. Richard Bruce Nugent: The Quest for Beauty." In *Gay Voices of the Harlem Renaissance,* 214–52. Ph.D. diss., University of Sussex, 1999.

Silberman, Seth Clark. "Lighting the Harlem Renaissance AFire!!: Embodying Richard Bruce Nugent's Bohemian Politic." In *The Greatest Taboo: Homosexuality in Black Communities,* edited by Delroy Constantine Simms, 254–73. Los Angeles: Alyson Books, 2001.

———. "Looking for Richard Bruce Nugent and Wallace Henry Thurman: Reclaiming Black Male Same-Sexualities in the New Negro Movement." In *In Process* 1 (1996): 53–73.

Smith, Charles Michael. "Bruce Nugent: Bohemian of the Harlem Renaissance." In *In the Life: A Black Gay Anthology,* edited by Joseph Beam, 209–20. Boston: Alyson Publications, 1986.

Washington, Michelle Y. "Souls on Fire." *Print* 52 (May–June, 1998): 56–65.

Wirth, Thomas H. "Richard Bruce Nugent." *Black American Literature Forum* 19 (spring 1985): 16.

SECONDARY RESOURCES

Baldwin, James. *Giovanni's Room.* New York: Dial Press, 1956.

Before Stonewall. Produced by John Scagliotti. Directed by Greta Schiller and Robert Rosenberg. 87 min. Cinema Guild CG 102, 1986. Videocassette.

Billops, Camille, and James V. Hatch, eds. *Artists and Influences.* New York: Hatch-Billops Collection, 1982.

Blackmore, David. "'Something . . . Too Preposterous and Complex to Be Recognized or Considered': Same-Sex Desire and Race in *Infants of the Spring.*" *Soundings* 80 (winter 1997): 519–29.

Bloxam, John Francis. "The Priest and the Acolyte." *Chameleon.* Oxford, 1894.

Bodenheim, Maxwell. *Bringing Jazz.* New York: Horace Liveright, 1930.

Brawley, Benjamin. "The Negro Literary Renaissance." *Southern Workman* 56 (March 1927): 177–84.

Bright, Deborah, ed. *The Passionate Camera: Photography and the Bodies of Desire.* New York: Routledge, 1998.

Chauncey, George. *Gay New York: Gender, Urban Culture, and the Making of the Gay Male World, 1890–1940.* New York: Basic Books/HarperCollins, 1994.

Cooper, Wayne F. *Claude McKay: Rebel Sojourner in the Harlem Renaissance.* Baton Rouge: Louisiana State University Press, 1987.

Cunard, Nancy, ed. *Negro.* London: Wishart and Company, 1934.

Cullen, Countee. *Color.* New York: Harper and Brothers, 1925.

———. *Copper Sun.* New York: Harper and Brothers, 1927.

———. *The Black Christ.* New York: Harper and Brothers, 1929.

———, ed. *Caroling Dusk.* New York: Harper and Brothers, 1927.

Douglas, Ann. *Terrible Honesty: Mongrel Manhattan in the 1920s.* New York: Farrar, Strauss, and Giroux, 1995.

Du Bois, W. E. B. *The Souls of Black Folk.* Chicago: A. C. McClurg, 1903.

———. "Opinion." *Crisis* 22 (June 1921): 55.

———. "Opinion." *Crisis* 31 (January 1926): 115.

———. "The Criteria of Negro Art." *Crisis* 32 (October 1926): 290–97.

———. "Two Novels." *Crisis* 35 (June 1928): 202.

———. *The Correspondence of W. E. B. Du Bois.* Edited by Herbert Aptheker. Amherst: University of Massachusetts Press, 1973.

Ekaete, Genevieve. "Sterling Brown: A Living Legend." *New Directions: The Howard University Magazine* 1 (winter 1974): 5–11.

Fone, Byrne R. S. *A Road to Stonewall.* New York: Twayne, 1995.

Ford, Charles Henri, and Parker Tyler. *The Young and Evil.* New York: Gay Presses of New York, 1988.

Forster, E. M. *Maurice.* New York: W. W. Norton, 1971.

Fuller, Henry Blake. *Bertram Cope's Year.* Chicago: Alderbrink Press, 1919; Chappaqua, N.Y.: Turtle Point Press, 1998.

Gates, Henry Louis, Jr. "The Black Man's Burden." In *Fear of a Queer Planet: Queer Politics and Social Theory,* edited by Michael Warner, 230–38. Minneapolis: University of Minnesota Press, 1993.

Gubar, Susan. *Racechanges: White Skin, Black Face in American Culture.* New York: Oxford University Press, 1997.

Gumby, L. S. Alexander. Autobiographical essay. *Columbia Library World* (January 1951): 2–8.

Holloway, Camara Dia. *Portraiture and the Harlem Renaissance: The Photographs of James L. Allen.* New Haven, Conn.: Yale University Art Gallery, 1999.

Huggins, Nathan Irvin, ed. *Voices from the Harlem Renaissance*. New York: Oxford University Press, 1976, 1995.

Hughes, Langston. "Cabaret," "To Midnight Nan at Leroy's," "Fantasy in Purple," and "Suicide's Note." *Vanity Fair* 25 (September 1925): 62.

———. *The Weary Blues*. New York: Alfred A. Knopf, 1926.

———. "Boy." *Carolina Magazine* (May 1928): 38.

———. *The Big Sea*. New York: Alfred A Knopf, 1940.

———. *The Collected Poems of Langston Hughes*, edited by Arnold Rampersad and David Roessel. New York: Alfred A. Knopf, 1994.

Hughes, Langston, and Carl Van Vechten. *Remember Me to Harlem: The Letters of Langston Hughes and Carl Van Vechten, 1925–1964*, edited by Emily Bernhard. New York: Alfred A. Knopf, 2001.

Hughes, Langston, and Milton Metzer, *Black Magic: A Pictorial History of the Negro in Entertainment*. Englewood Cliffs, N.J.: Prentice-Hall, 1967.

Huysmans, Joris-Karl. *Against Nature (A rebours)*. Translated by Margaret Mauldon. Oxford: Oxford University Press, 1998.

Johnson, Charles S., ed. *Ebony and Topaz: A Collectanea*. New York: Opportunity/National Urban League, 1927.

Johnson, Georgia Douglas, and Richard Bruce Nugent. "Paupaulekejo." n.d. Playscript. Collection of Thomas H. Wirth.

Johnson, James Weldon, ed. *The Book of American Negro Poetry*. New York: Harcourt Brace, 1922.

Kaladjian, Walter. *American Culture between the Wars*. New York: Columbia University Press, 1993.

Kelley, James Bernard. *Male Texts, Male Lines: Legitimizing Gay Narratives, 1919–1933*. Ph.D. diss., University of Tulsa, 1999. UMI Digital Dissertations AAT 9943760 Abstract in Dissertation Abstracts International 60 (2000): 2917A.

Kellner, Bruce, ed. *The Harlem Renaissance: A Historical Dictionary for the Era*. New York: Methuen, 1984.

Kisseloff, Jeff. *You Must Remember This: An Oral History of Manhattan from the 1890s to World War II*. New York: Harcourt Brace Jovanovich, 1989.

Lewis, David Levering. *When Harlem Was in Vogue*. New York: Alfred A. Knopf, 1981.

———. *W. E. B. Du Bois: The Fight for Equality and the American Century, 1919–1963*. New York: Henry Holt, 2000.

———, ed. *The Portable Harlem Renaissance Reader*. New York: Penguin Books, 1995.

Locke, Alain. "The Art of the Ancestors." *Survey Graphic* 6 (March 1925): 673.

———. "Fire: A Negro Magazine." *Survey* 58 (15 August–15 September 1927): 563.

———. "Beauty Instead of Ashes." *Nation* 126 (18 April 1928): 432–34.

———. "Art or Propaganda?" *Harlem* 1 (November 1928): 12.

———. "Spiritual Truancy." *New Challenge* 2 (fall 1937): 81–85.

———, ed. *The Negro in Art*. Washington, D.C.: Associates in Negro Folk Education, 1940.

———, ed. *The New Negro*. New York: Albert and Charles Boni, 1925.

Locke, Alain, and Montgomery Gregory, eds. *Plays of Negro Life: A Sourcebook of Native American Drama*. New York: Harper and Brothers, 1927.

Looking for Langston. Directed by Isaac Julien. 45 min. Water Bearer Films WBF8030, 1989. Video-cassette.

McAlmon, Robert. *Distinguished Air*. Paris: Contact Editions Press, 1925.

McClendon, Jacquelyn Y. *The Politics of Color in the Fiction of Jessie Fauset and Nella Larsen*. Charlottesville: University Press of Virginia, 1995

McKay, Claude. *Constab Ballads*. London: Watts and Company, 1912.

———. *Harlem Shadows*. New York: Harcourt Brace, 1922.

———. *Home to Harlem*. New York: Harper and Brothers, 1928.

———. *Banjo*. New York: Harper and Brothers, 1929.

———. *A Long Way from Home*. New York: Lee Furman, 1937.

———. *Claude McKay: Selected Poems*, edited by Joan R. Sherman. Mineola, N.Y.: Dover Publications, 1999.

Niles, Blair. *Strange Brother*. New York: Liveright, 1931.

Peplow, Michael W., and Arthur P. Davis, eds. *The New Negro Renaissance: An Anthology*. New York: Holt, Rinehart, and Winston, 1975.

Pool, Rosey E., and Paul Bremen, eds. *Ik Zag Hoe Zwart Ik Was*. The Hague: Bert Baaker/Daamen N.V., 1958.

Powell, Richard J., and Jock Reynolds. *To Conserve a Legacy: American Art from Historically Black Colleges and Universities*. Andover/New York/ Cambridge: Phillips Academy/Studio Museum in Harlem/MIT Press, 1999.

Powers, Peter. "'The Singing Man Who Must be Reckoned With': Private Desire and Public Responsibility in the Poetry of Countee Cullen." *African American Review* 34 (winter 2000): 661–78.

Rampersad, Arnold. *The Life of Langston Hughes*. Vol. 1, *1902–1941: I, Too, Sing America*. New York: Oxford University Press, 1986.

Reimonenq, Alden. "Countee Cullen's Uranian 'Soul Windows.'" *Journal of Homosexuality* 26 (1993): 143–65.

Rotundo, Anthony. *American Manhood: Transformations in Masculinity from the Revolution to the Modern Era*. New York: Basic Books, 1993.

Ruff, Shawn Stewart, ed. *Go the Way Your Blood Beats: An Anthology of Lesbian and Gay Fiction by African-American Writers*. New York: Henry Holt, 1996.

Rux, Carl Hancock. *Pagan Operetta*. New York: Fly by Night Press, 1998.

Scully, Robert. *A Scarlet Pansy*. New York: William Faro, 1933.

Smalls, James. "Public Face, Private Thoughts: Fetish, Interracialism, and the Homoerotic in Carl Van Vechten's Photographs." In *The Passionate Camera: Photography and the Bodies of Desire*, edited by Deborah Bright, 78–102. New York: Routledge, 1998.

Smith, Michael J., ed. *Black Men, White Men: A Gay Anthology*. San Francisco: Gay Sunshine Press, 1983.

Spencer, Suzette A. "Serving at a Different Angle and Flying in the Face of Tradition: Excavating the Homoerotic Subtext in *Home to Harlem*." *CLA Journal* 42 (December 1998): 164–93.

Stein, Gertrude. *Four Saints in Three Acts: An Opera to Be Sung*. New York: Random House, 1934.

Survey of the Month. *Opportunity* 5 (May 1927): 154.

Thurman, Wallace. *The Blacker the Berry*. New York: Macaulay Company, 1929.

———. *Infants of the Spring*. New York: Macaulay Company, 1932.

Tommasini, Anthony. *Virgil Thompson: Composer on the Aisle*. New York: W. W. Norton, 1997.

Toomer, Jean. *Cane*. New York: Boni and Liveright, 1923.

Van Notten, Eleonore. *Wallace Thurman's Harlem Renaissance*. Amsterdam: Editions Rodopi, 1994.

Van Vechten, Carl. *Peter Whiffle: His Life and Works*. New York: Alfred A. Knopf, 1922.

———. *The Blind Bow-Boy*. New York: Alfred A. Knopf, 1923.

———. *Firecrackers*. New York: Alfred A. Knopf, 1925.

———. *Nigger Heaven*. New York: Alfred A. Knopf, 1926.

———. *Letters of Carl Van Vechten*, edited by Bruce Kellner. New Haven, Conn.: Yale University Press, 1987.

Walker, David. *Walker's Appeal . . . to the Coloured Citizens of the World. . . . Third and Last Edition*. Boston: David Walker, 1830.

Watson, Steven. *The Harlem Renaissance: Hub of African-American Culture, 1920–1930*. New York: Pantheon Books, 1995.

———. *Prepare for Saints*. New York: Random House, 1998.

Weinberg, Jonathan. "'Boy Crazy': Carl Van Vechten's Queer Collection." *Yale Journal of Criticism* 7, no. 2 (fall 1994): 25–49.

West, Dorothy. *The Living is Easy*. Boston: Houghton Mifflin, 1948.

———. *The Wedding*. New York: Doubleday, 1995.

Wheatley, Phillis. *Poems on Various Subjects, Religious and Moral*. London: A. Bell, 1773.

"Why 'Run, Little Chillun' Runs." *Literary Digest* (15 April 1933): 13.

Wilde, Oscar. *Le Morte Darthur*. London: J. M. Dent, 1893–94.

———. *Salome*. London: Elkin Matthews and John Lane, 1894.

Woods, Gregory. *A History of Gay Literature: The Male Tradition*. New Haven, Conn.: Yale University Press, 1998.

ARCHIVES

Carrington, Glenn. Papers. Moorland-Springarn Research Center. Howard University, Washington D.C.

Cullen, Countee. Papers. Amistad Research Center. Tulane University, New Orleans, Louisiana.

Gumby, L. S. Alexander. Scrapbooks. Rare Book and Manuscript Library. Columbia University, New York.

Locke, Alain. Papers. Moorland-Spingarn Research Center. Howard University, Washington, D.C.

Schomburg Center for Research in Black Culture, New York.

Van Vechten, Carl. Papers. Manuscript Division, New York Public Library.

Van Vechten, Carl. Papers. Nugent Correspondence. James Weldon Johnson Memorial Collection. Beinecke Rare Book and Manuscript Library, Yale University, New Haven, Connecticut.

Wirth, Thomas H. Private Collection. Elizabeth, New Jersey.

INDEX

Patton, Sari Price, 219
Paupaulekejo, 3
Perry, Edward, 18–19, 21, 30, 54, 87, 274 n.17
Peter Whiffle, 42–43
Peterson, Dorothy, 226–28
Petit, Leland, 178
Plantation (nightclub), 152
Porgy, 8, 15–19, 25, 30, 32, 161, 214, 216
Powell, Adam Clayton Sr., 22

Reiss, Winold, 57, 178; *Interpretation of Harlem Jazz*, 58
Robeson, Paul, 16, 28, 148–49, 225
Roditi, Edouard, 18, 32, 273 n.14
Run, Little Chillun, 31–32, 243

Sacco, Nicola and Bartolomeo Vanzetti: execution of, 149, 158–59
"Sahdji," 3, 19, 63–64, 268
St. Claire, Stephanie, 155–56
Salome series, 59–60, plates 1–7
Schlick, Robert, 21, 225, 275 n.20
"Shadow," 268–69
Small's Paradise, 150, 154
"Smoke, Lilies and Jade," 11, 14, 19, 38–40, 41–42, 44–45, 47, 49, 61, 63, 75–87
Smoke, Lilies and Jade (image), 74
Stefansson, Harold, 15, 50–51, 184
Still, William Grant, 3
Strange Brother, 41, 178
Sufi Abdul Hamid, 156
Swanson, Gloria. *See* Winston, Mr.
Sydney, Iolanthe, 15

Thomas, Philander, 18; photo of, 16
Thompson, James W. (Abba Elethea), 37
Thompson, Louise, 26, 32
Thompson, Virgil, 20, 274 n.17
Thorne, Elder, 155
Thurman, Wallace, 1, 2, 5–6, 13–15, 18–19, 30, 32, 45–46, 49, 75, 147, 163–72, 230, 268–70; homosexuality of, 18, 22, 26, 28, 278n. 79; photo of, 27; same-sex desire in the work of, 50–51
Toomer, Jean, 2, 6
Transvestite of Harlem, 221–23
Tyler, Parker, 32, 44–45

Vanity Fair, 4
Van Vechten, Carl, 4, 6, 12, 20, 22, 30, 32, 41–44, 46, 148, 151, 168; and Alain Locke, 24; and Nugent, 226–330; self-portrait, 19; sexual interest in men, 18, 274 n.16
Vanzetti, Bartolomeo. *See* Sacco, Nicola
Viana, Juan Jose, 11

Walker, A'Lelia, 18, 217–20
Walker, David, 60, 279 n.113
West, Dorothy, 15, 32, 225, 244
Wheatley, Phillis, 45, 148, 277 n.64
White, Walter, 2, 4, 28
Wilde, Oscar: influence on Nugent, 41–42, 45
Williams, Wilson, 33
Wilson, Frank, 15; photo of, 16
Winfield, Hemsley, 31
Winston, Mr. (Gloria Swanson), 221–23
Wirth, Thomas H.: Nugent and, 1, 40
Wright, Richard, 32

CREDITS AND COPYRIGHT ACKNOWLEDGMENTS

Illustrations

Illustrations not otherwise credited are reproduced from original artworks or publications in the collection of Thomas H. Wirth (THW).

page ii   L. S. Alexander Gumby Collection, Rare Book and Manuscript Library, Columbia University. Courtesy of Columbia University.

   4   Remenyi Papers. Courtesy of the Western Reserve Historical Society, Cleveland, Ohio.

   16   L. S. Alexander Gumby Collection, Rare Book and Manuscript Library, Columbia University. Courtesy of Columbia University.

   20   Photograph by Carl Van Vechten. Copyright © 2002 Van Vechten Trust. Collection of THW. Used by permission of the Van Vechten Trust, Bruce Kellner, Successor Trustee.

   27   Portrait of Wallace Thurman. Estate of Louise Thompson Patterson. Courtesy of Mary Louise Patterson.

   60   "Illustration," by Aaron Douglas. Copyright 1929, renewed © 1957 by Viking Press Inc., from *Black Magic* by Paul Morand, translated by Hamish Miles. Used by permission of Viking Penguin, a division of Penguin Putnam, Inc.

   66   James Weldon Johnson Memorial Collection, Beinecke Rare Book and Manuscript Library, Yale University. Courtesy of the Beinecke Library.

   74   Collection of the Howard University Gallery of Art. Courtesy of the Howard University Gallery of Art.

   157   L. S. Alexander Gumby Collection, Rare Book and Manuscript Library, Columbia University. Courtesy of Columbia University.

   215   Photograph by THW. The bust of McClendon by Barthé, from the estate of Richard Bruce Nugent, is now in the Art and Artifacts Division, Schomburg Center for Research in Black Culture, The New York Public Library, The Astor, Lenox, and Tilden Foundations.

   227   Photograph by Carl Van Vechten. Copyright © 2002 by Van Vechten Trust. Collection of THW. Used by permission of the Van Vechten Trust, Bruce Kellner, Successor Trustee.

   229   James Weldon Johnson Memorial Collection, Beinecke Rare Book and Manuscript Library, Yale University. Courtesy of the Beinecke Library.

Plate 12   Collection of the late Daphne Arnstein. Courtesy of Daphne Arnstein.

Plate 14   L. S. Alexander Gumby Collection, Rare Book and Manuscript Library, Columbia University. Courtesy of Columbia University.

Plate 16   Collection of the late Daphne Arnstein. Courtesy of Daphne Arnstein.

Text

page 12   "I've met a couple of interesting fellows . . ." Langston Hughes to Carl Van Vechten. From *Remember Me to Harlem,* edited by Emily Bernard. Copyright © by Emily Bernard and the Estate of Langston Hughes. Used by permission of Alfred A. Knopf, a division of Random House, Inc.

   17   "*Porgy* will be with you soon . . ." Alain Locke to an unknown correspondent. Moorland-

Credits and Copyright Acknowledgments   293

Thomas Wirth is an independent scholar, publisher, and bibliophile.

Library of Congress Cataloging-in-Publication Data
Nugent, Richard Bruce, 1906–1987.
Gay rebel of the Harlem renaissance : selections from the work of
Richard Bruce Nugent/ edited and with an introduction by
Thomas H. Wirth ; foreword by Henry Louis Gates Jr.
Includes bibliographical references and index.
ISBN 0-8223-2886-0 (cloth : alk. paper)
ISBN 0-8223-2913-1 (pbk.: alk. paper)
1. African American Literary collections.   2. Gay men—Literary collections.
3. African American arts.   4. Harlem Renaissance.   I. Wirth, Thomas H.,
1938-   II. Title.
PS3527.U34 G39   2002   818'.5209—dc21   2001008587